WATERFALLS
OF THE WHITE
MOUNTAINS

◆

Avalanche Falls in winter

WATERFALLS
OF THE WHITE
MOUNTAINS

————◆————

30 TRIPS TO 100 WATERFALLS

Bruce, Doreen, and Daniel Bolnick
Photographs by the authors and Robert Kozlow
Illustrations by Doreen Bolnick

Second Edition

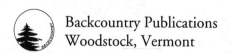
Backcountry Publications
Woodstock, Vermont

An Invitation to the Reader

Over time, trails can be rerouted and signs and landmarks altered. If you find that changes have occurred on the routes described in this book, please let us know so that corrections may be made in future editions. The author and publisher also welcome other comments and suggestions. Address all correspondence to:

Editor, Waterfalls of the White Mountains
The Countryman Press
P.O. Box 748
Woodstock, Vermont 05091

Cover photographs by Robert Kozlow
Illustrations © 1990 by Doreen Bolnick
Maps by Doreen Bolnick and Jacques Chazaud, © 1990, 1999 Backcountry Publications
Text and cover design by Ann Aspell

Library of Congress Cataloging-in-Publication Data
Bolnick, Bruce R.
         Waterfalls of the White Mountains: 30 trips to 100 waterfalls /
     Bruce, Doreen and Daniel Bolnick ; photographs by Robert Kozlow ; illustrated
     by Doreen Bolnick.
             p.   cm.
     Includes bibliographical references (p. 296) and index
     ISBN 0-88150-464-5 (alk. paper)
1. Hiking—White Mountains (N.H. and Me.)—Guidebooks. 2. Waterfalls—New Hampshire. 3. Waterfalls—Maine. 4. White Mountains (N.H. and Me.)—Guidebooks. I. Bolnick, Doreen. II. Bolnick, Daniel. III. Title.
GV199.42.W47B65 1999
917.4204'43—dc21   99-1110
                                                                        CIP

Published by Backcountry Publications, a division of The Countryman Press
PO Box 748, Woodstock, VT 05091
Distributed by W.W. Norton & Company, Inc.
500 Fifth Avenue, New York, NY 10110

Printed in the United States of America
10

*Dedicated to the early explorers of New England,
the trail builders, and today's trail maintainers
who have led us to the White Mountains' treasures.*

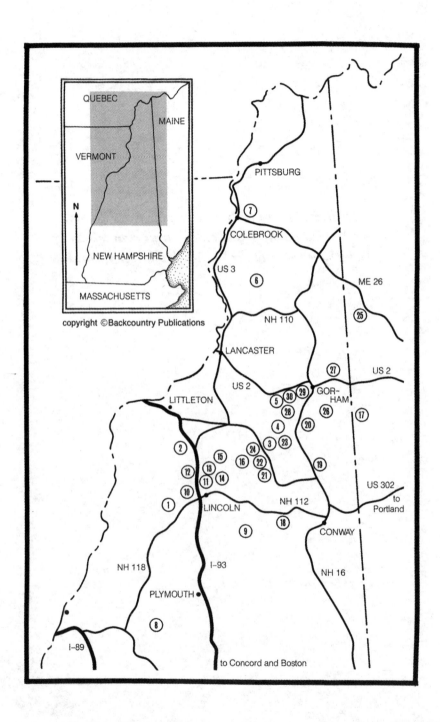

QUEBEC

MAINE

VERMONT

N

NEW HAMPSHIRE

MASSACHUSETTS

copyright ©Backcountry Publications

PITTSBURG

⑦

COLEBROOK

US 3

⑥

NH 110

LANCASTER

ME 26

㉕

㉗   US 2

US 2

⑤ ㉚ ㉙ GOR-
    ㉘   HAM

LITTLETON   ㉖

④   ㉖   ⑰

②   ㉔ ③ ㉓   ⑳

      ⑮   ⑯ ㉒

   ⑫ ⑱   ㉑   ⑲

      ⑪ ⑭

   ⑩   US 302
                              to
①   Portland

LINCOLN   NH 112

        ⑱

   ⑨   CONWAY

NH 118   I-93   NH 16

PLYMOUTH •

   ⑧

I-89

to Concord and Boston

CONTENTS

---◆---

THE SACO WATERSHED

THE ANDROSCOGGIN WATERSHED

APPENDIXES

FOREWORD

Of the ancients' four primal elements—fire, earth, air, and water—the first is perpetually in motion and the second is almost universally stable. (The exceptional rarity of moving earth—avalanches, mud slides, earthquakes, volcanoes—is what makes such events so terrifying.) But the other two can offer us serenity or thrilling motion. The stillness of a misty lake at dawn contrasts radically with stormy winds or turbulent waters. This range of experience with air and water brings us some of nature's grandest moments.

The White Mountains, and those who roam them, know better than most the exhilaration of air and water in fluctuation. The notorious winds of the Presidential Range have received ample attention. Less celebrated are the White Mountains' cascading streams—or less celebrated until Bruce and Doreen Bolnick documented the splendor, beauty, and unique personalities of more than 100 waterfalls. That was in 1990, when the first edition of their guide began appearing in bookshops and outfitter stores all over New England and beyond. The instant success of their book reflected both the eloquence of their writing and the elemental appeal of wild falling waters to lovers of the outdoor world.

A quiet companion on the Bolnicks' researches for that first edition was their then teenaged son, Daniel, who had been hauled along on family outings since "he was young enough to fit into a parka pocket," as his parents recalled. Now, less than a decade later, with the elder Bolnicks off exploring waterfalls, wildflowers, and other exotica of Africa, the son has picked up the challenge of revising and strengthening this guide. His lifelong love affair with waterfalls has ensured a brilliant result.

Here are all the cascading torrents, the forest-bound rills, the well-known tourist attractions, and the often overlooked gems. The perceptive prose of both the original edition and the new passages added herein gives us practical advice for finding each waterfall, vivid rendering of the particular attractions of each, and a larger perspective on the sensitive environment wherein the tumbling waters live and the responsibility we all share for safeguarding the future of this precious resource.

Here is a book to treasure, as we all prize those moments of quiet contemplation or breathless awe in the presence of the waterfalls of the White Mountains.

Laura and Guy Waterman
East Corinth, Vermont

ACKNOWLEDGMENTS

This book could not have been written without a great deal of help. Without a doubt the most critical assistance came from the organizations that have established and maintained the superb network of White Mountain hiking trails. Our project would have been virtually unthinkable without the accumulated efforts of both paid staff and volunteers who have worked with the Appalachian Mountain Club (AMC), the United States Forest Service, the Randolph Mountain Club, the Chatham Trail Association, the Waterville Valley Athletic and Improvement Association, and the Dartmouth Outing Club. The AMC and the Forest Service also made vital contributions through their publications, particularly the *AMC White Mountain Guide* and a large stack of Forest Service public-information materials.

Another major debt is owed to the staff of the Reading (Massachusetts) Public Library, the source of most of the research material for the book, either directly or through interlibrary loan.

One other organization that deserves heartfelt thanks is Boy Scout Troop 702, formerly led by Mr. George Taylor. It was on Scout trips to the White Mountains that the seed for this book germinated and took root. The critical catalyst was seeing how much the Scouts enjoyed visiting waterfalls.

Many other individuals made important contributions to the project. The order of citation here bears no implications about the importance of the contributions. The following people provided valuable information, suggestions, and encouragement at an early stage of the project: the late Malcolm Choate, one of the original conspirators behind the formation of the AMC's 4000-Footers Club; John Derby, retired public information officer for the Forest Service, whose own love of the waterfalls was highly contagious; the late Daniel Doan, author of *Fifty Hikes in the White Mountains* and *Fifty More Hikes in New Hampshire* (both from Backcountry Publications); our old friend Dr. Pancras van der Laan of Lancaster, a storehouse of north-country hiking knowledge; and Sharon van der Laan, who sheltered our son on occasions when he wanted to be with his friends rather than hike.

Robert Donovan kindly and generously served as technical adviser on photography and provided a tremendous amount of help with printing the photographs. The late Ed Lee also helped with prints before he passed away. Robert Lautzenheiser, retired New England climatologist for the US Weather Bureau, was our resource for weather statistics. Professor Wallace

A. Bothner of the Department of Earth Sciences at the University of New Hampshire provided invaluable comments on the geology of the White Mountain waterfalls. Professor Malcolm Hill of the Geology Department at Northeastern University also answered numerous geological questions. Captain Henry P. Mock, Chief of Law Enforcement, New Hampshire Fish and Game Department, let us spend a day looking through the state's search-and-rescue files for information on accidents. Robert Trevor provided technical advice on mapping. Douglas Philbrook of Gorham and Ned Therrien, public-information officer for the US Forest Service, went out of their way to track down information. To all of these people we offer special thanks.

We also want to express our gratitude to others who provided useful information, including: Gary W. Carr, District Manager, White Mountain National Forest Androscoggin District; Roger Collins, Ammonoosuc District Ranger; Eugene S. Daniel III, editor, *AMC White Mountain Guide;* Barbara Eastman, Librarian, Chatham; Francis N. Haynes, Librarian, Colebrook; Earl Jette, Director, Outdoor Programs, Dartmouth College; Barry Kelley, White Mountain Lumber Company; Kenneth Kimball, Director of Research, AMC; Arlene Lewis, Librarian, Lunenburg, Vermont; Henry Murphy; Frank Rymes, of Scout Troop 119, Lexington, Massachusetts; Robert Walker, Saco District Ranger; Laura and Guy Waterman; Ken Wiley, Regional Park Supervisor, Maine Department of Conservation; and Eileen Woodland, US Forest Service.

It seems to be a tradition to thank one's editors near the end of the list of acknowledgments. This custom certainly does not reflect their role in putting the book together. We owe a great deal to many people at The Countryman Press, including editor in chief Helen Whybrow; managing editor Ann Kraybill; Cristen Brooks, Hugh Coyle, and Fred Lee in the production department; and Emily Webb, our publicist.

INTRODUCTION

◆

They left their home of summer ease
Beneath the lowland's sheltering trees,
To seek, by ways unknown to all,
The promise of the waterfall.

Some vague, faint rumor to the vale
Had crept—perchance a hunter's tale—
Of its wild mirth of waters lost
On the dark woods through which it tossed.

Somewhere it laughed and sang; somewhere
Whirled in mad dance its misty hair; . . .

—*The Seeking of the Waterfall,*
John Greenleaf Whittier, 1878

This book is the first guide dedicated to the waterfalls of the White Mountains, which rank among the finest of New England's outstanding scenic attractions. The book is meant also as an invitation to seek out the waterfalls. We invite you to linger at the falls, to explore the ledges and ravines, to watch the sunlight flicker on ripples in the clear mountain pools, to lose your thoughts in the swirling currents, and to mingle in the company of the streams and forests.

The waterfalls are gifts from the clouds to hikers and tourists, youngsters and oldsters, artists and photographers, and all who take pleasure in the song of a tumbling brook. Some falls are miniature treasures hidden in deep forest, while others strike boldly down high mountain walls. Some are itinerant fountains that vanish and reappear with the rains. Others surge with vitality throughout the summer. Each has a personality of its own, and each waterfall changes, in ways subtle or profound, with the passage of the seasons and vagaries of the weather.

How many waterfalls, cascades, and cataracts can be found in the

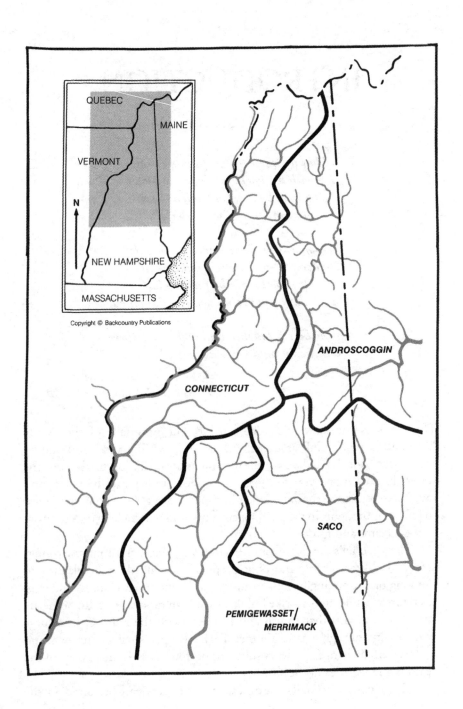

QUEBEC

MAINE

VERMONT

N

NEW HAMPSHIRE

MASSACHUSETTS

Copyright © Backcountry Publications

ANDROSCOGGIN

CONNECTICUT

SACO

PEMIGEWASSET/
MERRIMACK

White Mountains? There is no single answer. Counting every spot where the descent of a rushing stream is beautiful enough to attract admirers, the total would be many thousands. Would you choose to count the hundreds of seasonal waterfalls, which in spring dwarf and shame their perennial peers but that vanish come drier conditions? Well over a hundred are notable enough to have been named or specially identified. Many more cascades, some as pretty as any in the White Mountain region, remain unnamed, inaccessible, and their praises unsung.

This book describes thirty waterfall trips, each covering from one to as many as a dozen waterfalls that can be visited in a single outing. Each chapter includes information on how to reach the falls, trail conditions, and highlights along the way, as well as descriptions of the falls themselves. Do you want to know which cascades have wonderful swimming holes with good sunlight? Which waterfalls are great for exploring? Which are well suited for children? Which are easy to reach and which require strenuous hikes? Which are crowded and which are isolated? Which are tallest? Which lose their flair during dry spells? Which have etched deep gorges or fascinating contours in the bedrock? You will find the answers here.

In all, sixty-five waterfalls and cascades are described thoroughly. Excursions to another thirty-five falls are discussed more briefly. (This tabulation is problematic, however, since it is not always clear what to count. For example you can get a higher total by counting individually each of the lovely cascades on Cascade Brook in Franconia Notch.) An alphabetical master list of White Mountain waterfalls is also included, with all the landmarks mentioned in the text, as well as those falls that did not make the cut to be included in trip chapters.

Every chapter also includes a "historical detour," which relates some of the rich history of the White Mountain region: the Indian wars, the heroic explorers, the indomitable settlers, the elegant Victorian inns, the coming of the railroads, the devastation of vast forests by logging and fire, the birth of environmental awareness, the blossoming of winter sports, the once-flourishing towns that have disappeared. When visiting the waterfalls you can often sense ghosts of the past if you know to watch for them.

In geographic scope the book is restricted to waterfalls of the White Mountain region, but the region is defined generously. As shown on the map opposite the contents page, the waterfall trips range from Mount Cardigan in the southeast to Colebrook in the north and to Grafton Notch, Maine, in the east. The trip chapters have been grouped in four sections, reflecting nature's division of watersheds. The rains, snows, and mists that water the region all flow to the sea by one of four major rivers: the Connecticut, the Pemigewasset/Merrimack, the Saco, and the Androscoggin. Within each watershed section, trips appear roughly in upstream order—as if to lead you on an adventure up the waterways that drew early settlers into the heart of the White Mountain wilderness.

WATERFALL NOMENCLATURE

Many of us have probably wondered at one time or another about how to distinguish between a small mountain and a large hill. Or where to draw the line between a large pond and a small lake, or a drizzle and a light rain. In the present context the compelling question is: What's the difference between a *waterfall*, a *cascade*, and a *cataract?* From the high priests of the English language, the editors of the *Oxford English Dictionary*, one learns that the term "waterfall" generally describes a single landscape feature with a fairly vertical drop. But this term also encompasses the other two categories. "Cascades" are smaller waterfalls, often in a series, and need not have steep drops or strong currents. In contrast, a proper "cataract" is a larger waterfall, more precipitous, and more powerful. Like all good oracles, the *OED* editors are vague about how big a drop is required for a tumbling current to fall into any one of these categories. They simply note that a waterfall issues "from a height" and leave it to others to argue their precise meaning.

Moving from theory to reality, the three terms are often used quite properly. But often, too, the labels are muddled. For example Crystal Cascade (chapter 20) is bigger, steeper, and stronger than Hitchcock Falls (chapter 29). The First Ammonoosuc Cataract at Gem Pool (chapter 4) is neither big nor steep, while Thompson Falls (chapter 20) includes a series of long slides that look a lot like cascades. Happily, waterfalls were often christened by people who were more concerned with poetry than pedantry.

WATERFALL ORIGINS

Even on the vast scale of geologic time, the White Mountains are very old. Yet the region's many waterfalls and cascades, its steep ravines, and its towering cliffs are hallmarks of recent geologic events. They are youthful features on an ancient brow.

The oldest exposed bedrock formations originated from sandy sediments deposited on the floor of the Iapetus Ocean, an ancestor of the modern Atlantic Ocean that covered the region 600 million years ago. A period of volcanic activity ensued, burying the sands under a sheet of ash perhaps a mile thick. Later, more sediments of silt, sand, and impure limestone were added to the pile.

The mountain-building activity began about 470 million years ago. Fueled by enormous convection energies within the earth, Africa and Europe crept toward North America, slowly and intermittently closing the Iapetus Ocean over a period of nearly 100 million years. Under titanic pressures the accumulated bedrock strata were crushed, uplifted, folded, tilted, and stacked by the continental collision. Compression also recrystallized the original minerals to form new metamorphic rocks from the ancient sediments. Bedrock clues today reveal a "tectonic hinge" running laterally through the White Mountains toward the northeast. This hinge formed a buttress against which the encroaching land mass from the east collided, about 410 million years ago. Geologists speculate that land east of the hinge today might be a fused remnant of Africa.

After a long period of stability and erosion, the tectonic forces shifted into reverse about 190 million years ago. The continents began to pull apart to create the modern Atlantic Ocean, a process that continues today. During this period of extension, large volumes of pressurized magma welled up through fractures deep in the earth's crust and gradually cooled to form bodies of granite that are seen today at many waterfalls. (Similar "plutonic events" had taken place earlier.)

The magma intrusion ended more than 100 million years ago. With it ended the buildup of the White Mountains. Subsequent erosion has stripped off miles of overlying rock, exposing a quiltwork of ancient metamorphic formations and newer granite bodies that were tempered far beneath the earth's surface.

During the ensuing 100 million years of geologic stability, erosion and sedimentation produced a mature White Mountain landscape, with rolling hills, well-graded valleys, rounded ridges, and deep soils. Through the eons the mountain streams gradually eliminated virtually all the discontinuities in their line of descent. As one geologist visualized the conditions, "Very probably there were no falls or rapids and certainly none in any of the major valleys." (Chapman, 1974)

Then came the Great Ice Age. As the earth's climate began to cool about two million years ago, accumulating snows formed Alpine glaciers on the flanks of the higher White Mountain summits. These local glaciers carved out great basins, or *cirques,* like Tuckerman's Ravine and the Great Gulf.

The continental ice sheet arrived in the area around 50,000 years ago.

More than a mile thick, the vast river of ice covered the entire landscape, including the Presidential summits. With its great weight and the abrasive power of grit and stones caught in its grip, the creeping ice mass scoured the region clean of soil, and then carved its signature in the bedrock. Moving across the mountains, it plucked off huge blocks of stone, leaving precipitous cliffs. Passing through the valleys, it sheared off side walls, creating the deep U-shaped notches that now characterize the region.

A mere 15,000 years ago the ice sheet began to recede, taking perhaps 3000 years to melt away. It left behind a rejuvenated landscape, dotted with young waterfalls and cascades. Some, called "hanging waterfalls," were produced because the glaciers obliterated their formerly mature streambeds. Instead of descending gradually to the valley floor, the waters now plunged over sheer notch walls. Exemplifying this category are the high waterfalls of Crawford Notch (chapters 3, 21, 22, and 24).

Other displaced streambeds were rerouted over smaller cliffs where they cut new gorges, as at Glen Ellis Falls (chapter 20). In places displaced streams crossed narrow bands (called dikes) of soft basalt, where magma had once spurted through fissures in ancient rock beds. These dikes eroded quickly, creating flumes, such as the famous Flume gorge in Franconia Notch (chapter 11) and the gorge at Sabbaday Falls (chapter 18).

Some small but very beautiful waterfalls were formed when gritty outwash from receding ice surged across bared ledges of granite. In spots, abrasive turbulence produced fascinating potholes and gorges, such as those seen at the Basin (chapter 12) and Screw Auger Falls (chapter 25).

Waterfalls usually developed at a contact between tough and less resistant rock. Moriah Gorge (chapter 26), and Cold Brook Fall (chapter 30) are clear examples. In some cases glaciers displaced a stream over a boundary contact that had not previously been eroded. Elsewhere the ice carried away sediments that had filled in ancient waterfalls. In the millions of years to come the sediments will be replaced, and the stubborn rock walls will erode away. Most of the waterfalls will again disappear. Look closely, and you can see that the work is under way.

In appendix A you will find a table of technical information on the bedrock geology at many of the waterfalls. If you are interested in learning more about the region's geologic history, refer to the relevant sources cited in the bibliography.

WATERFALLS IN THE BOOK

For every major waterfall covered in the text there is a summary of Hiking Data showing:

- *Distance, parking area to falls:* The number given is the approximate one-way hiking distance in miles. A familiar rule for calculating hiking time—including brief rest stops—allows one hour for every 2 miles, plus thirty minutes per 1000 feet of ascent. A hiker in good condition carrying a light pack can move faster. Then again, a hiker who wants to enjoy the excursion can move slower! We recommend taking time to explore the woods and streams and to linger at the waterfalls.
- *Altitude gain:* The figure given is the approximate net altitude difference (in feet) from trailhead to waterfall, based on contour counts from topographic maps. The figure excludes ups and downs along the trail, and is generally rounded to the nearest 50 feet.
- *Difficulty:* This subjective hike rating factors in distance, vertical climb, steepness, and quality of the walking surface. You may interpret the ratings by the following criteria: *Easy* means that a septuagenarian in reasonable health can make the trip (we've confirmed this!). So can a cooperative four-year-old child. *Strenuous* means that even experienced hikers in fit condition will find the trip quite fatiguing—although their efforts will be amply rewarded. *Moderate* means neither easy nor strenuous.

The waterfalls themselves are described in the text. One key characteristic of each waterfall and cascade is its height. The height figures provided in the text are based on reports found in other documents. Only in a handful of cases did we find any indication that a waterfall actually had been measured. Typically, the source documents state the height without explanation. Such figures were accepted and used here if they were confirmed by a visual check in the field.

For some falls different sources report different heights. For others the reported figures appeared implausible in the field. And in many instances no height reports were found at all. In all such cases we report best guesses based on visual comparisons with two familiar standards: a basketball hoop and our 35-foot chimney at home. One attempt was made to be scientific. We invested in an expensive altimeter that claimed accuracy to 10 feet. For practice we calibrated the instrument to the altitude of our living room. That night a low-pressure system passed through town, and in the morning the altimeter showed the living room 110 feet higher than it had been the evening before. End of experiment.

Our field work took us to far more waterfalls and cascades than could fit in the book, so selectivity was required. A few cuts were easy because some falls were not worth the hike. Other cuts were matters of judgment. Generally, the final selection was based on both intrinsic value and variety. Those falls that did not make it into the text are mentioned in the master list. By design, the trips selected include convenient roadside falls as well as back-country beauties for marathon hikers. They cover popular tourist haunts and isolated cascades that you might well have all to yourself. The tallest falls are here, together with many small charmers.

Regrettably, the mightiest cataracts on the main rivers of the White Mountains could not be included in the book because years ago they were tamed by dams. Of Berlin Falls on the Androscoggin River, Thomas Starr King (1868) wrote: "We do not think that in New England there is any passage of river passion that will compare. . . ." Fifteen Mile Falls below Dalton, according to Robert Pike (1967), contained the most treacherous drop on the Connecticut River log drives. To see these powerful waterfalls today, however, you will have to visit the library, not the mountains.

VISITING THE FALLS

The vast majority of White Mountain waterfalls and cascades are easily accessible to casual hikers, tourists, and families as well as seasoned trail veterans and energetic mountaineers. Even for dedicated peak baggers, the waterfalls are refreshing excursions on sweltering summer days and days when the summits are locked in clouds or gripped by ice and snow. This section provides information that may be helpful for anyone setting out on a waterfall trip.

TRAIL MAPS

The maps and trail descriptions in part two of the book provide all the information you will need to reach the waterfalls. But a good topographic map should be consulted for a complete picture of the local geography and the web of connecting trails, especially when hiking alternate routes or hiking beyond the falls. There are three popular topographic map resources for the region:

- *Appalachian Mountain Club (AMC) Trail Maps:* Long the standard for White Mountain hikers, these maps come packaged with the invaluable *White Mountain Guide* published by the Appalachian Mountain Club. The maps are also sold separately at some outlets. They are compact, lightweight, durable, and easy to read. We carry the pertinent AMC map on virtually every hike.

- *DeLorme's Trail Map and Guide to the White Mountain National Forest:* This handy publication has a regional topographic map on the front and thumbnail trail descriptions on the back. It is like a compact, one-sheet version of the AMC trail-guide package, but the map cuts off some outlying areas, its contour lines are hard to read, and hiking routes are drawn less precisely in areas with dense trail systems.

- *US Geological Survey quadrangle maps:* The USGS maps, which are available for every part of the region, use fine contour intervals that reveal more detail than the AMC and DeLorme maps. But each quadrangle covers a limited area, so many hikes sprawl over more than one map. Also, the USGS maps are less durable, bulkier, often less up-to-date, and less readily available than the others. (To order USGS maps, call 1-800-USA-MAPS.)

Each chapter heading includes a map note showing the trip's location on the appropriate AMC map and on the DeLorme map. For trips not covered by the AMC and DeLorme maps, USGS map information is provided instead.

Map Legend

▬▬▬ Main road
▬▬▬ Side road
— — — Jeep track, logging road, or Forest Service road
▰▬▬ Main waterfall trail
········· Other trail
⚐ Appalachian Trail
AMC Appalachian Mountain Club
✳ Waterfall, cascade
▲ Mountain summit
△ Cliff, ledge

WATERFALL MOODS

*But what folly to attempt to draw in words
the curves and colors, the coyness . . ., the flashes
and the moodiness, the laughter and the plaints
of these daughters of the clouds!*

—Thomas Starr King, 1868

At best, descriptions and photos on the flat pages of a book only hint at the spirit of a waterfall. Moreover, each waterfall's demeanor varies from year to year, even from day to day, depending on the weather. Over the course of a year, however, the mountain streams exhibit a regular cycle of moods.

Spring, the time of rebirth of the forests, is the season for mesmerizing, torrential currents. Streams and rivers swell with melting snows and seasonal rains, briefly transforming waterfall lambs into wolves. The mountains throw an aqueous extravaganza, sprouting waterfalls in gullies where one finds nothing but damp rock two months later.

Spring in the north country does not adhere to the calendar. At the equinox the mountain streams are often still tight in the grip of winter. Beginning in early April spring unfolds northward, climbing gradually to higher elevations. Once the mountains are in full thaw, the period of high water can last one to two months, depending on the rains. When the radio brings news of spring floods in the north country, then the show is at its climax!

Spring is a season of colorful wildflowers, opening buds, migrating warblers, and cool, invigorating air. It is also a season of mud-wallow trails that are highly vulnerable to erosion, of pools too icy for most mortals to swim, of clouds of spray that bar photography at the largest waterfalls, of wet or icy rocks too treacherous for exploring. And beginning in late May, it is the season of blackflies (see "Other Hazards" below).

In summer the waterfalls put on a gentler face, and their mood grows playful. This is the season when the roar of the current is muted, the pools are deliciously clear and refreshing, the sun is high and bright, the rocks are dry and warm, and the days are long and lazy. Though more spectacular in the spring, the waterfalls are more fun in the summer. And more crowded, too.

Summer visitors do have opportunities to see the mountain streams in full surge. Two or three days of rain or evening thunderstorms are enough to restore spring conditions, temporarily. The amount of runoff at any particular waterfall depends on the pattern of precipitation (thunderstorms can be highly localized), the soil moisture conditions, the local bedrock structure, and the shape of the watershed. Chart 1 shows how the volume of water in the Ellis River swelled and ebbed following some summer rains.

If you want to time a summer trip to catch the waterfalls after a rain, be sure not to confuse the weather in the mountains with the weather at home. Coastal storms, for example, can soak the Boston area without touching the White Mountains. And vice versa. During August 1988, while southern New England suffered through a serious drought, Mount Washington had over 11 inches of rain (4 inches above normal). The waterfalls were in splendid form!

In early autumn the mood of the waterfalls reflects the luxuriant hues of the foliage. Northernmost sections of the region begin donning fall outfits in early September and reach a brief peak of vivid color shortly after the equinox. The color burst moves gradually southward, like the ebbing tide of forest life that rolled north in the previous spring. This is the time of year when the waterfall scenery is most dazzling in the hardwood forests at lower elevations, and at higher points with panoramic views.

By mid-October the vivid display has usually ended. The brightest leaves have dropped to the forest floor, where they form a crisp, thick carpet underfoot. More subdued tones of birch and oak leaves linger a few more weeks on the bough. Then the trees grow bare, the days grow short, the sun hangs lower in the sky (when it shines at all), and the nights are visited with hard frost. As autumn turns to winter, the waterfalls become cold, gray, and rimmed with veils of ice. Their mood is more somber, yet still beautiful.

Like the black bear, the waterfalls are usually hibernating by the winter solstice. If winter's cold arrives before deep snows, as often is the case, the waterfalls are transformed into fascinating blue-ice sculptures. Frigid currents can be heard under the winter crust or seen through windows in the ice. Huge icicles dangle from ravine walls. Gradually, snows blanket the forest and hide all but the highest and steepest waterfalls from view—while storing up the moisture to replenish the mountain streams come spring.

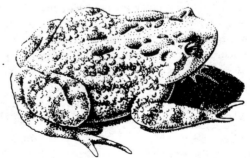

American Toad

Chart 1

HYDROGRAPH FOR THE ELLIS RIVER
Near Jackson, New Hampshire

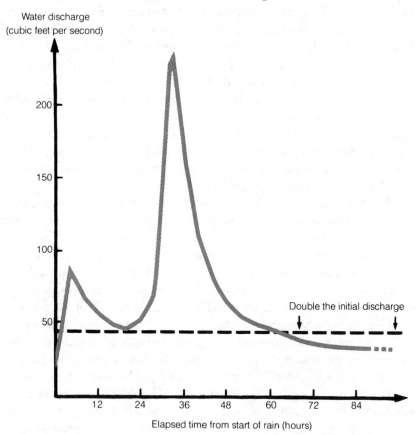

This hydrograph shows the volume of the water flow in the Ellis River at Jackson during and after a period of summer rain. Time zero marks the onset of a moderate rainfall that caused the river to rise for 4 hours, beginning at 1800 hours on August 28, 1998. Then, beginning at 1700 hours on August 29, the river volume rose sharply for more than twelve hours. Over the 2-day period, precipitation at Pinkham Notch totaled just over 2 inches of rain, while 1.4 inches fell at North Conway. After peaking, the river took 29 hours to drop back to *double* its initial water volume. After 96 hours (4 days) the river was back down to its initial level. We are grateful to Frank Blackey of the US Geological Survey office in Bow, New Hampshire, for providing data for this graph.

WHITE MOUNTAIN WEATHER

With confidence we can predict that New England weather will amaze onlookers and confound forecasters. As Mark Twain put it, "There is a sumptuous variety about the New England weather that compels the stranger's admiration—and regret." All this variety has considerable significance for your waterfall trips. Afternoon weather may be completely different from morning weather. Three-day forecasts may be wrong as often as right. The weather in the mountains may be entirely unlike the weather three hours away. And in general, weather statistics are nearly useless for trip planning. In the White Mountains in July you can encounter anything from subzero windchills (on summit ridges) to torrid heat, and in January anything from -30°F (before windchill) to 60°F. For more timely information on conditions before you set out, call the Concord office of the National Weather Service at 1-603-225-5191. Or call the Appalachian Mountain Club information service in Pinkham Notch at 1-603-466-2725.

Beyond this basic weather briefing, a few points should be noted relating to waterfall trips in particular.

- Other things being equal, the daytime temperature drops as you gain elevation. Sunlight heats the earth's surface, which in turn warms the air. As the warm air rises, it cools by roughly 5 degrees Fahrenheit per 1000 feet of altitude.
- Waterfalls often have their own microclimates created by evaporating mists, shady forest cover, damp mosses and rocks, and cool breezes fueled by temperature differentials along the streambeds. Even on the hottest days some waterfall ravines are too chilly to encourage swimming.
- The microclimate is also affected by the exposure to the sun and the amount of adjacent open ledge. Southern slopes tend to be considerably warmer than northern slopes, and wide beds of rock can absorb enough heat to be wilting on a cool autumn day.
- Wind is often more important to your comfort than temperature. A stiff breeze on an exposed outcrop may refresh you on a hot day or chill you to the bone on a cool day. It is always a good idea to bring along a windbreaker.
- Finally, for those who enjoy quantifying conditions, tiny zipper-pull thermometers are not very accurate, but most camping-goods stores sell full-size thermometers in protective pocket-clip tubes that can be taken along on any excursion.

Paper Birch (left), Yellow Birch,
Heart-leaved White Birch

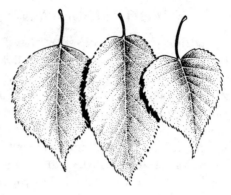

WEATHER AND TRAIL CONDITIONS

Hiking guide authors tend to prefer some consistency in trail routes over time. The weather, with its associated blown-down trees, landslides, erosion, and washed-out bridges, is their nemesis. In January 1998, much of New England was subjected to a now infamous ice storm. Residents dealt with power cuts, downed trees on their roads, and dangerous travel conditions. The weight of ice bent trees to their breaking point, leaving vast areas of forest as a tangled web of bent and broken trees to block any hiker's progress. The AMC, Forest Service, and volunteer trail crews put in many long hours clearing blocked trails, and a few trails were closed or rerouted. A more devastating storm, the hurricane of 1938, closed over 700 miles of trail. In wet years the saturated soils of the mountain slopes become more prone to landslides, occasionally wiping out a section of trail. Hawthorne Falls, in the northern Pemigewasset region, once lay along a major trail, but after a landslide in 1954, the trail was rerouted. For the past forty-five years, Hawthorne Falls has been the exclusive domain of bushwhackers and other creatures of the mountain forests.

Beyond changes in trail routing, weather can affect the day-to-day trail conditions you encounter on your hikes. Heavy rains will obviously make trails muddy and vulnerable to erosion when you hike. Please avoid hiking in the muddiest conditions, or at least try to hop on rocks or roots. Detouring around muddy spots may keep your feet clean, but this will lead to a web of side trails. Rain also raises river levels. If you are planning a hike after long or heavy rains, expect high water. This is ideal if you want to see the waterfalls at their most powerful, but you should consider whether your planned route will involve fording any rivers. People have been swept away and drowned in White Mountain rivers. As of 1998, six out of a total of 126 recorded fatalities in the Presidential Range were due to river drownings. Other fatalities may be chalked up to slipping on icy trails. As a waterfall hiker, you might be on wet, steep rock at times, so be sure to take care in slippery conditions.

HIKING TIPS

The most important rule of hiking is the familiar refrain: Pack out what you pack in. Keeping the waterfalls and trails litter free is everybody's business. An updated version of the old rule is to pack out *more* than you pack in. Rather than gripe about litter, why not pack some out and leave the forest cleaner than you found it?

On a related theme, hikers should be aware that tramping feet contribute to erosion and destruction of plant life on the forest floor. We all share a responsibility to minimize the adverse effects of our presence in the forest by staying on trails wherever possible and by being sensitive to the erosion problem when we do venture off trail. Sometimes "leaving nothing but footprints" is leaving too much. Similarly, hikers must exercise extreme caution with fire. If you expect to use open fires, find out the fire danger for that day (it is generally posted along major roads), and use established fire rings. The ashy scars left from building fires on the ground detract from other hikers' experience of the wilderness.

Another basic precept is the old Boy Scout oath: *Be prepared.* For anything more than a very short hike it is important to have:

- comfortable, appropriate footwear that has been broken in
- clothing suitable for weather conditions and activities (remember that weather conditions may change for the worse, and that cotton does not provide insulation when wet)
- rain and wind gear
- a first-aid kit
- a map and compass
- more than enough water or other nonalcoholic liquids (our most common regret on hikes is having along too little to drink)
- snacks
- insect repellent and sunscreen
- an agreed-upon route and clear plans on where to meet if the party gets separated

- plenty of time to finish the hike and return before dark and/or a flashlight

That may sound like a lot of preparation, but the essential items fit easily into a small day pack or a large fanny pack, and the precautions are simple enough. The effort to gather gear together will be repaid many times over if it proves to be needed just once. Also, before going on a long hike into an area that is not heavily traveled, you are wise to let someone know your plans. Then assistance can be mobilized in the unlikely event of an accident.

It should be noted that winter waterfall hikes require special equipment. At a minimum you should have layered clothing that will keep you dry and comfortable, boots with liners, snowshoes with crampon bindings, and some means to keep your drinking water from freezing.

The final fundamental rule of hiking is: Enjoy yourself! Allow time for resting, communing with the waterfall, studying the flora, examining the rocks, stalking the songbirds, sleuthing animal signs, and simply watching the clouds drift by. It would be a shame to miss the proverbial forest for the trees; likewise, it would be a shame to miss them both for want of time. To enhance your enjoyment you may wish to consult some of the nature guides listed in the bibliography.

DRINKING WATER

Unhappily, even the purest-looking running water in White Mountain streams is *not* guaranteed safe to drink without being treated, filtered, or boiled. The problem is microscopic organisms, and the villain is human and animal waste. One organism in particular, *Giardia lamblia,* has become a significant health hazard. When ingested it causes an extremely unpleasant intestinal disorder called giardiasis.

Despite a major public education campaign that has been continuing for years, people still frequently drink from White Mountain streams—especially at waterfalls where the running currents and clear pools give a false appearance that the water is spring pure. We once approached the leader of a party of young campers at Franconia Falls to suggest that because of *Giardia* it was not safe for the kids to be filling canteens from the stream. He replied that *Giardia* "can't be a problem here" because there were no beaver ponds on the stream. He was wrong on two counts. First, there were large beaver ponds farther upstream that he did not know about. And second, the spread of *Giardia* does not require beavers. We hope the youngsters were lucky enough to avoid the disease, but it would have been better not to have relied on luck.

If you do drink untreated water and come down with serious intestinal problems a week or two later, make sure your doctor tests for giardiasis. Otherwise you may suffer up to six weeks of distress.

Giardia is easy to avoid. First, carry enough liquids so you will not be tempted to drink from the streams. Second, be careful not to ingest stream water if you go for a swim or dunk your head. Third, use treatment tablets (Potable Aqua is a widely available brand) or a filter system (such as Pur) if you must drink stream water, as on overnight trips. But be certain to use a brand that is labeled as effective against *Giardia* and other waterborne bacteria.

Finally, avoid contributing to the spread of *Giardia*. Be absolutely certain when hiking or camping not to deposit human or pet wastes within 100 feet of open water (preferably 200 feet). Wastes should be buried 6 to 8 inches deep, where soil organisms for decomposition are most effective. Keep a lighter in your backpack to burn your toilet paper when you are done (or better yet, carry it out). Animals sometimes try to dig up your wastes, leaving the paper scattered around, which nobody likes to see.

OTHER HAZARDS

Apart from possibly contaminated drinking water, what sorts of hazards does one face on a waterfall hike? Do people fall off cliffs? Are people mauled by bears? Poisoned by snakes? There are indeed hazards, and being aware of them can help keep your waterfall trip trouble free.

The northern mountain forests are basically benign. They harbor no poisonous snakes (any more), and virtually no poison ivy (or poison oak, or poison sumac). Some wild animals—such as black bear, wildcat, eastern coyote, porcupine, and even the gentle moose—are potentially dangerous at times, but they are rarely seen. No instances have been recorded in many years of unprovoked wild-animal attacks on hikers. If you chance to see wildlife, just leave it alone. Above all, don't go out of your way to bother the animals. If you do encounter an animal acting aggressively or strangely, get away as quickly as possible: Rabies is spreading into northern New England. Lyme disease also appears to be spreading north, so after a hike you should check yourself carefully for any ticks and remove them in an appropriate way (consult a first aid book). Simply pulling off a tick once it has attached itself to you may increase the risk of disease transmission.

Insect pests can be extremely troublesome. The most hated is the blackfly, which generally prowls for warm flesh from late May until early July. (We have run into them in isolated locations, especially at higher elevations, into August.) When at their worst, blackflies are a swarming "malediction," to use Samuel Drake's apt description (1881). An early White Mountain explorer, John Josselyn, found in 1672 that "Black flies were so numerous in the country that a man cannot draw his breath but he will suck them in" (quoted in King, 1868). Most years, however, the blackflies are no more than a nuisance that can be controlled by wearing a long-sleeved shirt, long pants tucked into socks, and bug dope. For good measure you can also carry along a net helmet and cotton gloves. Reportedly blackflies don't bite through clothing, but they do have diabolical ways of sneaking in for a meal.

A much less common insect hazard is bee sting. Hives are not often found by trails, but we have experienced or seen enough stings to urge caution, especially when hiking off trail. Bee hives may be located in holes in the ground, rock crevices, old stumps, or fallen tree trunks. Being reasonably watchful will prevent most painful encounters. Individuals who experience severe bee-sting reactions must carry medication on hikes.

Judging from rescue records compiled by the New Hampshire Fish and Game Department as well as news reports over the years, the most prevalent cause of serious injury on waterfall trips is slipping and falling. This happens most often on the trail, but serious falls also occur when individuals recklessly climb steep, dangerous ledges at the waterfalls themselves. Rescue records attribute these accidents to factors such as fatigue, intoxication, carelessness, and preexisting medical problems.

Injuries from falling often result in broken bones. We know of only two instances of a fatality from falling during a visit to a waterfall. In October 1986, a party returning by way of Frankenstein Cliff from Arethusa Falls (see chapter 22) was overcome by darkness on a wet, cloudy evening. One member hiked out to fetch a flashlight. On returning he fell off Frankenstein Cliff to his death. In July 1995, a visitor from Massachusetts died when he fell off the top of Arethusa Falls, the tallest single-drop waterfall in the region.

Drownings have been more numerous. At high water, currents can be overpowering and life threatening. A whirlpool undertow at Upper Falls of the Ammonoosuc claimed a number of victims before swimming and trespassing were prohibited by the landowners. This area is now public land once more, and swimming is allowed, but the death toll there should discourage any would-be swimmers. Other drownings have occurred at swim-

Common Garter Snake

ming holes along the Pemigewasset River. Even river crossings can be dangerous in high water. Hikers have slipped and drowned while fording the notorious and misnomered Dry River (chapter 23). Some waterfalls have deep pools surrounded by tall cliffs that invite the adventurous to jump off into the pool. This is, simply, a bad idea. Many injuries and some deaths occur in this manner, as it is difficult to judge the depth of the pool and hard to see boulders or ledges lurking under the water's surface.

One other fatality in conjunction with a waterfall trip occurred when a youth was separated from his party and lost his way returning from No. 13 Falls (chapter 15). He died of exposure before rescue teams could find him. We have not seen any record of other fatalities from exposure on waterfall hikes, but exposure (hypothermia) is certainly a serious hazard, particularly above tree line. Most fatalities on Mount Washington have resulted from hypothermia, typically caused when hikers were caught unprepared by violent storms. Getting wet in a cold wind is a perfect recipe for rapid loss of body heat—and disaster.

To avert nearly all the major hazards, all one needs is common sense. Remember that carelessness or horseplay can spoil an otherwise wonderful outing. So if currents look at all dangerous, stay out of the water. If ledges look steep and dangerous, avoid them. If the weather is threatening, stay away from exposed ridges and have proper gear for unexpected storms. Avoid hikes that exceed your physical condition. Keep an eye on your children. Plan your trip so you have ample time for rests to avoid fatigue, without getting caught by darkness. Don't let your party get separated deep in the backcountry.

Notably, the New Hampshire Fish and Game Department has recently begun to bring criminal charges of reckless conduct against individuals whose thoughtless behavior or intoxication necessitated rescue operations that endangered others.

Regrettably, a final hiking hazard is the risk of having valuables stolen from automobiles, particularly at isolated trailheads out of view from the road. This is not a common occurrence, but it happens enough to warrant caution against leaving valuables in your car.

SWIMMING TIPS

It is hard for us to imagine anything more exhilarating than a dip in a crystal-clear mountain pool below a beautiful cascade on a hot summer day. Over half the waterfall trips in the book reach swimmable holes of one sort or another. But there are a few quirks about mountain pools that are worth mentioning before readers rush off into the woods with their beach towels and swimsuits.

The single most important quirk is that the water may be *cold!* Even in midsummer we have measured the water temperature in some pools in the upper forties. Fahrenheit. Though the water may appear exquisitely inviting, it is a major shock to jump in. A toe-dip test can help you distinguish between water that is deliciously cold, bitingly cold, and painfully cold. In fact, many people don't actually swim in most of the White Mountain pools. More often they jump in, take a few desperate strokes, and climb out before their skin gets bruised by goose bumps. How wonderful!

One does see swimmers, though. Many youngsters, for example, seem to be too hotblooded or too numb to be discouraged by cold water. Besides, at some pools on open ledges with a southerly exposure, the water can be in the balmy mid-70-degree range, varying with the sun and recent rains. A few well-bleached waterfalls, like Lower Falls (chapter 18) and Jackson Falls (chapter 19), seem designed for water sport. Others, such as Bridal Veil Falls (chapter 2) and No. 13 Falls (chapter 15), have superb pools but very cold water. There are waterfalls in shady ravines on northern slopes that never feel the full warmth of the sun, and still others on streams that feed public water supplies, where even wading is prohibited. The trip descriptions will help you sort out all the variations.

More seriously, there are dangers to swimming at waterfall pools. As pointed out in the "Other Hazards" section, strong currents during periods of high water are life threatening, and people have been injured climbing the steep and often slippery ledges that abut many pools. Diving, too, can be dangerous because refraction and shadows make it difficult to see underwater boulders or to judge their depth. Furthermore, it is obviously foolish to play in the currents above the lip of a waterfall or to get one's clothes soaking wet on a cold day miles up a mountain trail. As it says on a sign at Franconia Falls (chapter 14): SWIM AT YOUR OWN RISK.

None of this, however, detracts from the tremendous thrill of a brisk, refreshing—and safe—jump into a shimmering mountain pool. Even people too sensible to try swimming should at least practice a few head dunks on a hot day.

PHOTOGRAPHY TIPS

In his splendid book of White Mountain photography, *The White Mountains of New Hampshire,* Alan Nyiri confesses to spending nearly all his time visiting waterfalls during his first two weeks in the mountains. *Homo photographicus* is certainly a common breed at the waterfalls. Every shutterbug dreams of capturing the dynamics of the tumbling stream, the contours of the granite ledge, and the soft texture of the mosses and ferns. Waterfall photography can be tricky business, however. We are in no position to offer professional wisdom, but we do want to share a few easy-to-use tips accumulated from conversations with professional photographers in the course of working on this book. The following comments deal only with color photography, since this is by far the most popular, judging from the film inventories at White Mountain tourist shops.

Our first and best photography lesson was to bracket exposures. Light meters can be misled by glare and strong reflections off the water and wet rocks, especially when the glare is juxtaposed with dark forests and patches of deep shade. If the light meter reads bright spots, the dark zones will be underexposed. If the light meter reads dark zones, bright spots are washed out. Bracketing simply involves taking a number of frames at different exposures. You might shoot one frame at the light-meter reading, and then one or two letting in more light (slower shutter speed or larger aperture opening) or less light, as conditions warrant. This requires manual adjustments to the camera settings. Fully automatic point-and-shoot cameras cannot be manipulated this way. Bracketing greatly improves the odds of capturing your favorite shot at the proper exposure.

Regardless of the camera being used, being aware of the glare and contrast problems can come in handy. If direct sunlight makes it difficult to get a proper exposure, then you can get better shots when the problem is less severe. A light overcast is easier to work with than bright sun. On sunny days you can

Black-capped Chickadee

improve your odds by using an inexpensive polarizing filter. You can also wait for a passing cloud to cut the glare. Using a lens shade helps, too. Finally, the time of day makes a big difference in the quality of sunlight. At midday the lighting is intense and flat. Early morning or late afternoon sunlight produces far more interesting shadow patterns and colors.

A second invaluable lesson was learning to bring along a tripod (or a monopod, which is more convenient but less stable). This is worth the extra effort. At fast shutter speeds you will get sharper images using a tripod, while at slow shutter speeds a tripod makes all the difference between blur and success. It is difficult to get a crisp exposure with handheld shots at under ⅟₆₀ second. Moreover, slow shutter speeds (that is, relatively long exposures) often turn out to be what you end up using for waterfall photos. Many waterfalls are located in glens or ravines that are shaded most of the day. Lighting may be so dim that you either use a slow shutter speed or you don't take a picture. It may seem logical to use a fast film (like ASA 400) to overcome this problem, but a number of professional photographers insisted that a slower film (like ASA 64) produces better shots. Only after many disappointing rolls of slides did we follow their advice. It worked, but the slow film made long exposures—and therefore a tripod—indispensable.

A slow shutter speed is also useful for visual effect. Nearly every art photo of waterfalls that we see is shot at a very slow speed to make the currents appear streaked, thereby capturing a flavor of motion. We have read recommendations for shutter speeds of one second or more. From our own experience fairly natural effects are often achieved with a shutter speed of ⅟₁₅ to ⅟₃₀. A faster shutter freezes falling water, which in many cases ruins the effect. Furthermore, setting a slow shutter speed permits you to use a smaller aperture opening (higher f-stop), which improves your depth of field. In short, attractive shots often require slow exposures. And again, this necessitates using a tripod.

A slow shutter speed does complicate matters in certain respects. For example, it is nice having people in the picture, but they usually come out blurred when photographed at ⅟₁₅-second. Similarly you will often find a breeze wafting along a cascade, setting the foliage asway. If so, the flora around the waterfalls will be blurred at slow shutter speeds.

Composition, of course, is essentially a matter of taste. At some water-falls, however, a full view is difficult to achieve because it is not possible to back off to a proper angle without encountering obstructions in the line of vision. Another problem is that shots taken at the foot of a waterfall will foreshorten its height. This is an effective way to make a 60-foot waterfall appear insignificant.

Finally, all but the geniuses among us have to accept the fact that snapping two-dimensional, point-in-time photos will not capture the spirit of a mountain cataract. No photo album or slide show will convey the soft touch of the breeze, the faint rustle of hemlock boughs, or the pulsing rhythm of the cascade. The best way to share the experience of a waterfall trip with friends is to invite them along.

CAMPING INFORMATION

Appendix B presents a table listing all the roadside campgrounds in the White Mountain region that operate under the auspices of the United States Forest Service or the State of New Hampshire. The table also matches campgrounds to nearby waterfall trips by chapter number. During the summer and on fall foliage weekends, these campgrounds are often full by midafternoon. If you intend to camp, it is a good idea to reach the campground around midday. A few campgrounds (as noted in appendix B) permit advanced reservations, which can be made by phoning 1-800-283-2267.

One can also stay overnight in the backcountry. The most comfortable facilities by far are the Appalachian Mountain Club huts (also listed in appendix B). Each hut offers exhilarating mountain views, air so fresh that you want to bottle it and take it home, hearty meals, and warm comradeship. In addition, by providing meals, a bed and blanket, and a roof over your head, the huts make it possible to penetrate the mountain wilderness without having to lug a full pack. You need to carry only day-hike supplies, warm clothing for the cool mountain evenings, and a sleeping bag or sheet. The huts are usually booked up well in advance. For information and reservations call the AMC at 1-603-466-2727, or write Reservations, AMC Pinkham Notch Camp, Box 298, Gorham, NH 03581.

Less luxurious are the dozens of backcountry campsites and shelters along various trails in the White Mountain National Forest. These facilities are for self-contained backpackers. If that's your style, consult the *AMC White Mountain Guide* for details about site locations. Bear in mind, too, that these facilities are available on the basis of first come, first served. There is a good chance that after slogging with a full pack all the way in to a campsite, you will find it full. If so, you have to seek a suitable and permissible tent site off in the woods.

Camping is permitted anywhere in the White Mountain National Forest outside designated "Restricted Use Areas," or RUAs. The RUA regulations are designed to prevent degradation of the forests along popular trails and to help restore areas that have been damaged by overuse. Consequently, camping tends to be prohibited in precisely the places you would find most convenient for pitching a tent. Generally, RUA rules prohibit camping within a quarter mile of designated roads, trailheads, and backcountry facilities, or within 200 feet of designated trails, except at designated camping sites, marked with small brown tent signs. At certain locations, such as Sabbaday Falls (chapter 18) or anywhere above treeline, camping is prohibited altogether.

These regulations are in effect from May 1 to November 1, although a few restrictions apply year-round. You can obtain detailed information on prevailing RUA regulations from the US Forest Service (see appendix B). Pertinent restrictions are also posted at all trailheads. If you will be backpacking, check out the RUA restrictions and plan ahead accordingly. Incidentally, be prepared for difficulty in finding a suitable tent site because many locations have thick underbrush, tangled timber blowdowns, unsleepable slopes, or marshy soils.

Keep in mind that important conservation motives underlie the RUA rules. The same concerns imply that backpackers should be familiar with low-impact camping methods. The ideal today is to camp in a manner that leaves the forest looking as if no one had camped there. Formerly routine practices are now frowned upon, like creating fire circles of blackened rock, digging trenches around tents, and cutting wood for campfires. In addition, it is every camper's responsibility to deal properly with human wastes (see "Drinking Water," above), to exercise extreme vigilance with fire, and to carry out what you carry in.

PARKING FEES

The US Department of Agriculture has introduced a trial parking fee program in eighty national forests nationwide to raise money for maintenance of trails and facilities within the forests. Current policy states that each car parked in posted Forest Service parking areas must have a valid parking pass. A one-week pass costs $5; an annual pass, $20; or a pair of annual passes for a two-car family, $25. These may be purchased at most outdoor gear stores, AMC facilities, and other stores in the region. Because this policy is in its trial period, details may change when the period ends in September 2000. Call a local Forest Service office, or look for signs at the trailheads for updated information.

Paradise Falls

THE CONNECTICUT WATERSHED

◆

A segment of the Beaver Brook Cascades

CHAPTER 1

BEAVER BROOK
CASCADES

◆

Location: Kinsman Notch, on NH 112, west of North Woodstock
Maps: AMC #4 Moosilauke-Kinsman Map (I-3); DeLorme Trail Map (J-2)

Hiking Facts
Distance: Parking area to bottom of the cascades, 0.3 mile; to top of the cascades, 1.1 miles.
Altitude gain: 1300 feet (to altitude 3200 feet)
Difficulty: Moderate; short but very steep

◆

Just after the turn of the century, loggers had reduced the vicinity of Kinsman Notch to "a wilderness of devastation," in the words of Karl Harrington (1926). Yet today the Beaver Brook Trail from the Notch to the summit of Mount Moosilauke is a virtual stairway to heaven. In less than a mile the trail climbs the equivalent of 130 stories of rock stairs, with each landing graced by lovely cascades.

The trail does have a few unheavenly features, though. First, there are some very steep stretches where the footing can be quite treacherous when the ground is wet or glazed with ice. Handrails and steps are bolted to the ledge to help you past the worst sections. Second, on the genuine stairway to the Pearly Gates, swimming would be allowed. Since Beaver Brook feeds a public water supply, visitors must keep out of the stream. Anyway, the water is too busy falling to form good pools.

A visit to the beautiful cascades on Beaver Brook can be combined with a number of excellent side excursions. These include continuing up the trail to the summit of Moosilauke, finding Lost River and Paradise Falls, or stopping to admire Indian Leap at Agassiz Basin.

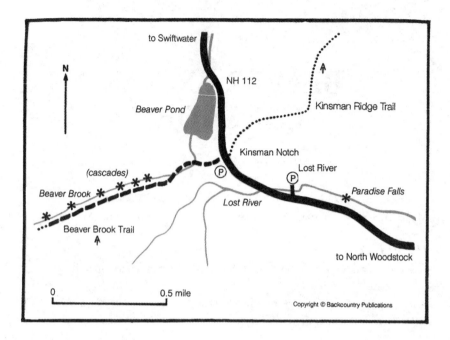

Access

The Beaver Brook Trail begins at the height of land on NH 112 in Kinsman Notch, 6 miles west of North Woodstock center. A large parking lot on the south side of the road provides access to the Beaver Brook Trail and the Kinsman Ridge Trail, both part of the Appalachian Trail.

The Trail

Beginning at the Beaver Brook Trail sign at the far end of the parking lot, the path immediately connects to the main trail that bypasses the parking lot to reach the road. Turning left on the trail, it soon crosses a brook, then a second brook on an impressively sturdy footbridge. Shortly, the trail crosses a second footbridge, beyond which an unmarked path leads left to the abandoned site of a shelter maintained by the Dartmouth Outing Club. Stay right. The DOC shelter has been relocated to the ridge above the cascades, 1.5 miles from the trailhead. A sign cautions hikers: TAKE SPECIAL CARE AT CASCADES TO AVOID TRAGIC RESULTS. Amen.

The trail is essentially level over the first 0.3 mile, then climbs and climbs and climbs alongside a nearly continuous chain of delightful cascades. After 0.8 mile the cascades taper off, but the climbing continues. For a short distance the trail stays by the brook, now just a gurgling, mossy stream. It then veers left up a small feeder stream toward the saddle between

Mount Jim and Mount Blue, 1.9 miles and 2500 vertical feet from the highway. The final 1.5 miles to the Moosilauke summit climbs only 500 feet more and includes a mercifully level stretch along the rim of Jobildunk Ravine, from which you can see the Pleiades Cascades far below on the Baker River. The trail connects to the Benton Trail just below tree line and follows an exposed ridge to the summit.

It is worth noting that Mount Moosilauke, first climbed in 1773, boasts one of the most beautiful (and windblown) summits in the White Mountains. Sunset watchers found accommodations on the summit as early as the 1840s. A carriage road provided easy access from Warren after 1870. These amenities are gone now, but the views remain.

The Cascades

By some counts over a dozen lovely, unnamed cascades adorn the precipitous ravine of Beaver Brook. To describe them all one by one would be tedious, but a sampler can provide a taste of what lies along the trail.

Shortly after the trail starts climbing, a set of bolted wooden steps leads up a slab ramp to the brink of a narrow chute that cuts through a deep cleft in the bedrock. Immediately above the chute is a small but very pretty ribbon cascade, and above this two more cascades can be seen awaiting your arrival. This prospect of cascades is characteristic of the trail: Because the ravine is so steep, as you visit one cascade you also get a preview of the coming attractions.

Farther along, the falls become more impressive. At one inviting snack stop you find a lovely cascade where the brook drops over a wall high overhead, slides down a long sloping ledge, and then drops again before disappearing over the rim of the next cascade below.

Higher, a sparkling transparent sheet ripples across a smooth slab, while 100 feet above, bright ribbons of white pour through channels in a dark wall. At your approach the ribbons turn into beautiful falls. Continuing up a short switchback, you then encounter a sheer 80-foot drop where the stream breaks into a maze of channels as it tumbles down the fractured ledge. And so it goes, a kaleidoscope of waterfall patterns.

Depending on the water level, there may be a few spots, especially higher up, where some scrambling is possible. In fact, a few fine cascades higher up the ravine can be seen only by scrambling over to the brook from the trail at opportune points. But keep in mind the DOC warning sign, as well as the restriction on swimming or bathing.

Eventually the trail enters a zone of white birch with a thick undergrowth of fir. The footing changes to a long set of irregular boulder steps, and the shoulder of the ravine becomes visible above. This is where the brook changes from cascades to gurgling steam, though there is one final treat—a small horseshoe falls cut in brown ledge—at the point where the brook divides and the trail turns toward the Mount Jim/Blue saddle.

It may be hard to imagine, but this is one long, steep climb that you will be sorry to see ending.

Lost River and Paradise Falls

A half-mile east of the Beaver Brook Trail on NH 112 is the Lost River Reservation, one of the most popular natural attractions in the White Mountains since before the First World War. If you are not heading for the summit of Moosilauke after visiting the Beaver Brook Cascades, there should be time to see Lost River while you're in the neighborhood. For waterfall chasers, the lure of Lost River is Paradise Falls and a small but extraordinary underground waterfall (once called the Falls of Proserpine) in a boulder cave named the Judgment Hall of Pluto.

At least an hour is required to visit Lost River gorge, and triple that if you also take advantage of the Geology Center, Ecology Center, Nature Garden, and Ecology Trail, as well as the gift shop and cafeteria. All of these facilities are owned and maintained by the Society for the Protection of New Hampshire Forests.

The Lost River Reservation is open to the public from mid-May through mid-October from 9 to 5 (open until 6 PM in July and August). For the trip through the gorge (as of 1998) there is a charge of $8.00 per adult and $4.50 per child, though children under 6 years old are free. (For comparison, the fee was 25¢ back in 1938.) Tickets are not sold in the last hour that the reservation is open. Off-season and off-hour visits are not permitted. The Lost River trail starts near the gift shop, descends 300 feet, and then climbs wooden stairs and walkways through the fascinating gorge. Overall, the circuit is about 0.75 mile in length.

Paradise Falls is located near the base of the gorge. Emerging from the caverns, the stream drops over a small dike wall and then plunges over a higher wall to a large pothole pool below. The Lost River brochure claims that the falls are 35 feet high, but a 1938 pamphlet calls it 20 feet, which seems to be a more accurate figure. In any case the beauty of Paradise Falls is in its magnificent setting, not its height.

A boardwalk spur provides a head-on view of the falls from across the pool, while the main trail climbs a narrow stair to a bridge above the falls. The bird's-eye view from this bridge is especially attractive. Paradise Falls was even more exciting for early visitors, who toured the gorge in reverse. The falls greeted them as they emerged into daylight—along with the stream—after penetrating the dark, narrow caverns of the gorge.

The underground Falls of Proserpine are located farther up the gorge along one of the many side paths leading into the wonderfully shaped caves and crevasses. This particular cave (labeled Number 16) is just barely big enough for the plume of water that gushes from a hole in the roof 15 feet overhead. In fact, during high water there is no room for visitors, and the cave is closed off.

Over the decades the pothole below Paradise Falls and the floor of the Judgment Hall of Pluto have both been filling with silt and gravel. Perhaps some great storm will wash out the gorge and add 10 feet to each of the falls.

Agassiz Basin (Indian Leap)

On the drive between North Woodstock and Kinsman Notch one more waterfall merits a visit: Agassiz Basin, or Indian Leap. This is located right behind Govoni's Restaurant, 1.7 miles west of North Woodstock center. Don't use the restaurant parking lot, unless, of course, you are hungry.

Agassiz Basin is a small, exquisite gorge of water-sculpted granitic bedrock (actually, Kinsman quartz monzonite), with a surging 10-foot waterfall at the head of the formation. The waters that carved the gorge also undercut a rock platform immediately below the falls, nearly forming a natural bridge above the swirling currents. It is said that Indians leaped across the 5-foot gap to prove their courage.

There is another roadside waterfall to visit if you are heading west from Kinsman Notch. Swiftwater Falls is located just below the long covered bridge (closed off when the road was recently rerouted) in the village of Swiftwater, 2 miles east of the terminus of NH 112 at US 302 in Bath. Swiftwater Falls lacks the natural elegance of the other waterfalls and cascades mentioned in this chapter, but on a hot summer's day this is the one to visit. Remember to bring your swimsuit!

Historical Detour

Kinsman Notch, like other major notches in the region, was carved and smoothed by passing glacial ice sheets. Its beautiful gorges were etched within the past 15,000 years by silt-laden meltwaters of the receding glaciers. Interestingly, the discovery of the Ice Age is generally credited to Louis Agassiz, a Swiss scientist after whom Agassiz Basin is named. In 1837, Agassiz shook the scientific world with a speech outlining geological evidence that

Europe's land forms had been shaped by an ancient ice sheet. On a visit to New England in 1847 Agassiz found confirming evidence of a great Ice Age. He then settled into a faculty position at Harvard as his remarkable thesis gradually gained adherents. This required profound changes in thinking. To accept Agassiz's evidence, scholars had to reject the biblical doctrine that land forms were products of the great Deluge—and that the earth had been created only 6000 years before.

Kinsman Notch itself is named after Asa Kinsman, a pioneer who received a grant of land in Easton, New Hampshire, in the 1780s. On his way north with his wife and an oxcart laden with possessions, Kinsman took a wrong turn at Plymouth. Instead of retracing his route to reach the road through Warren, he stubbornly hacked his way through the dense forest across the notch to his homestead, assisted by two strangers recruited in the valley.

For the next century Kinsman Notch was largely bypassed by the developments that flooded the White Mountain region with tourists. Thomas Starr King, for example, wrote lavish praise of the Pemigewasset valley and Franconia Notch in 1859, but he knew nothing of what lay up "Moosehillock Brook." Neither Kinsman Notch nor even Kinsman Mountain had yet been named.

The Notch did receive at least a few visitors, however. Two boys from North Woodstock, Royal and Lyman Jackman, went fishing up that way in 1855; Royal fell through a hole and discovered Lost River. Years later, Royal cut a footpath to the gorge and began leading tours in 1893. Lost River and Kinsman Notch quickly gained celebrity.

The area around the Notch also gained the attention of loggers. A very limited amount of logging had been taking place long before 1907, when timber baron George L. Johnson began building the Gordon Pond Railroad from the valley up to the Notch. A large logging camp was established at Beaver Meadow, in the heart of the Notch. Wholesale destructive cutting ensued, stimulating early conservationists to undertake an effort to save Lost River. In 1912, the newly formed Society for the Preservation of New Hampshire Forests purchased the gorge and surrounding property from the timber baron, establishing the Lost River Reservation—but not before all the virgin spruce had been removed and logging roads had been cut all the way to the top of the Beaver Brook Cascades.

In 1916 the Notch road was upgraded for autos. In that same year the major logging operations in the vicinity ceased. Kinsman Notch then began its slow readjustment from "waste land" to the beautiful natural attraction we enjoy today.

CHAPTER 2

BRIDAL VEIL FALLS

◆

Location: Off NH 116, south of Franconia village
Maps: AMC #2 Franconia Map (G/H-4); DeLorme Trail Map (F-4)

Hiking Facts
Distance: Parking area to falls, 2.5 miles
Altitude gain: 1100 feet (to altitude 2100 feet)
Difficulty: On the light side of moderate

◆

Does the name "Bridal Veil Falls" sound familiar? If so, you may be thinking of the famous waterfall in Yosemite valley, where Bridalveil Creek plunges dramatically more than 600 feet to join the Merced River. Its humble namesake on the western flank of Cannon Mountain in Franconia simply channels Coppermine Brook down 80 feet of drops and slides.

Nature, though, does not equate size with pleasure. A wildflower can be as engaging as a sequoia, a warbler can outsing a condor, and a waterfall can brighten your smile without requiring that you wrench your neck to see the top. For awesome scale, book a flight to California. But for a delightful waterfall, complete with fine pools, a hanging garden, and a long waterslide, hike up the Coppermine Trail to New Hampshire's version of Bridal Veil Falls.

One indication of the appeal of Bridal Veil Falls is the character of the trail. The 5-mile round-trip leads to no summits or panoramic overviews. The trailhead is located off a quiet country road rather than a major traffic artery, with no roadside sign to publicize the hike. And yet the trail is very well used. Coppermine Trail is exclusively for hikers out to visit a beautiful waterfall; many return over and over again to enjoy Bridal Veil Falls.

Access
To reach the trail, head south from Franconia village along NH 116, passing the Franconia airport and a zone of development properties. At the

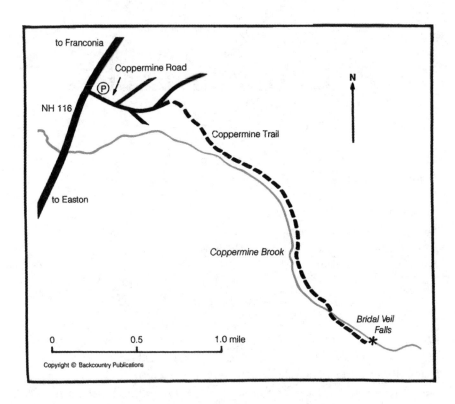

to Franconia

Coppermine Road

N

NH 116

Coppermine Trail

to Easton

Coppermine Brook

Bridal Veil
Falls

0   0.5   1.0 mile

Copyright © Backcountry Publications

airport one can arrange a short flight over the mountains in a small plane or a quiet soar in a glider! Just under 3.5 miles from Franconia village, Coppermine Road leads left into a private development. This is your turn. If you are approaching from the south, the turn will be on the right, 0.75 mile past the Easton-Franconia town line, marked by a small sign for Coppermine Village. Park on the shoulder of Coppermine Road along the 100-yard stretch between NH 116 and the sign that warns PRIVATE ROAD: NO PARKING BEYOND THIS POINT.

The Trail

On foot now, head straight up the dirt road, passing a left turn into the Coppermine Village development. Shortly thereafter the trail forks to the left, as indicated clearly by an arrow beneath a US Forest Service "hiker" sign. After passing an overgrown clearing, the trail forks right and follows an old road into the woods. This second fork is marked only by yellow paint blazes on the trees. From here on, however, the route is very straightforward and well marked.

The old road ascends steadily but gently through mixed forest. Among the many trees and wildflowers by the trail, watch for samples of striped maple. Apart from the white birch, this slender understory tree has the most attractive bark in the woods: a pattern of meandering vertical stripes of light green and white. Moose allegedly find its smooth skin especially succulent, giving the tree the nickname "moosewood." The broad three-lobed leaves of the striped maple are also quite striking.

Nearly 1.25 miles from the highway, the murmur of rushing water begins to mix with the rush of the breeze. Soon, Coppermine Brook appears below a large shelf on the right. The shelf, which has been used as a campsite, hides a small cascade and a pretty pool. Camping is also permitted just below the main waterfall at a Forest Service shelter, though there is little flat terrain in the vicinity of that site.

A few minutes farther along, the trail touches the edge of the brook at a point where the old road once crossed a wide slab of bedrock to the far side of the streambed. The trail, though, remains on the north bank here, climbing a bit more steeply and never straying far from the brook. At mile 2.2 the trail finally crosses to the south bank of the brook by a wooden footbridge. A sign indicates that the Forest Service shelter is only 0.1 mile away and the falls 0.2 mile; that first tenth is a long one, however. Still, you quickly reach the shelter, from which point the falls can be seen ahead through the trees. For its final leg the trail dips to recross the brook and ends at the edge of a pool below the falls.

Years ago the Coppermine Trail was maintained as a ski trail, which linked to other winter runs on the northern flank of Cannon Mountain. Today one can still ski in nearly to the falls, but the Coppermine Trail is an almost unrelieved ascent. In addition, the last mile has pitches that are steep enough to require a lot of tiring herringbone to climb on cross-country skis—and narrow enough to be somewhat tricky to descend.

The Falls

Bridal Veil Falls has a split personality. Viewed from the base, a feathery cascade is seen in the background, but the predominant feature is a broad, smooth bank of granite ledge that slopes down to a green pool at the foot of the falls. As the brook spreads across the face of the ledge to slide to the pool, the water takes on the appearance of a thin, rippled veil, like fine gossamer. It is this feature for which the waterfall was named.

A wholly different view of the falls is obtained from a wide terrace at the

top of the waterslide. The terrace can be reached with only moderate difficulty by climbing carefully up the left corner of the lower ledge or by a steep
footpath in the woods farther to the left. Cupped in the terrace slabs is a
second pool that is not visible from the base of the waterslide. This second
pool is larger and lovelier than the one below. From the terrace the waterslide
is now almost an incidental feature. Dominating the view is a 50-foot wall
with a wide, overhanging midriff bulge. At the back corner of the wall, the
brook plunges across the mouth of a large, dark cave situated beneath the
bulge, and then cascades down steep, angled ledges to the terrace pool.

To the left of these upper falls the wall is dry and bare, except for closely
cropped lichen. In contrast, the high wall to the right of the falls has a
northern exposure that keeps the surface damp and shady. Here a garden of
wildflowers, grasses, and ferns clings to cracks and sloping surfaces. Yellow
birch trees line the brow of the wall.

Except when the sun is at its midsummer peak, the high wall behind the
terrace keeps the upper falls and most of the terrace pool in the shade. Also,
on sunny days the temperature differential between the cold currents and
the sunny ledges alongside the pool causes a cool breeze to drift across the
terrace. The combination of shade, breeze, and cold water is enough to chill
a hiker's ardor for swimming. Still, some hardy visitors can't resist the
temptation to play in the inviting pools—a temptation heightened by the
waterslide feeding into the bottom pool. The last dozen feet of the slide are
negotiable if you take care to stay in the smooth part of the channel.

There is temptation for scramblers, as well—namely, to find a way up
and around the high wall to the top of the waterfall. This is indeed possible,
but the route is quite steep (we have seen technical rock climbers on sections
of the cliff). For extra adventure you can search for two obscure small waterfalls lying higher up Coppermine Brook. The two are identified as Holden
Falls and Noble Falls ("well above Bridal Veil Falls") in old photos that
appear in Sarah Welch's *History of Franconia* (1973).

Historical Detour

Whereas the Franconia Notch side of Cannon Mountain has been a major
tourist attraction since the first rough road from Plymouth was cut in the early
nineteenth century, the western slope along the Ham Branch of the Gale
River was more hospitable to the settlers and industries that built the town
of Franconia. The first settlement in 1774—when the area was known as
Morristown—was located just south of the present Coppermine trailhead.

The settlers turned immediately to farming, supplemented by good

Bridal Veil

fishing, plus intermittent (and quickly depleted) supplies of bear, deer, moose, beaver, and other wildlife for hunting and trapping. In addition, maple sugar could be obtained from the trees, and meager rations of edible plants and berries could be gathered in season. Yet it took rugged, determined people to struggle against the wilderness in a land of long, bitter winters and glacial-till soil that never was suited for plowing.

Ernest Poole provides a marvelous description of the life of the Ham Branch hill farmers in his book, *The Great White Hills of New Hampshire* (1946). The pioneers cleared the wild forests for land on which to build their sturdy homes, plant their corn and potatoes, and graze their sheep and cattle. The women gardened, cooked, raised the children, and kept the family stocked with necessities, such as candles, clothes, soap, baskets, blankets, and hooked rugs.

Dismayed by paying taxes to finance the coastal barons who controlled the state's plutocratic government, the farming communities west of the mountains actually chose to secede from New Hampshire and join the independent republic of Vermont after the Revolutionary War. George Washington settled this early tax revolt in 1782 by negotiating with the counties along the east bank of the Connecticut River to rejoin New Hampshire, while Vermont remained independent until 1791.

Although grouped into small communities, the hill farmers remained virtually self-sufficient well into the nineteenth century. No one would hop into the family buggy for a trip to town to buy milk or to purchase a new coat. Apart from the trading activities at the annual county fair market, the farmers' only regular commercial contacts were with itinerant peddlers who offered such commodities as hardware, tobacco, medicines (including 120-proof alcohol and opium gum), and dyes, as well as ballads and devious swindles.

Farming continued to be a major industry in the hill country west of Cannon and Kinsman Mountains until about the time of the Civil War. The farm economy languished when the Erie Canal brought competition from the lush soils of the Midwest, and the war lured farmers' sons to the battlefields and the cities.

For the town of Franconia, though, the primary source of prosperity was iron. Directly across the valley northwest of the Coppermine trailhead is Ore Hill, where a large vein of iron ore was discovered in the early 1800s. It was said to be the richest ore in the country at the time. The ore was dug from shafts blasted out of solid granite and gneiss and then transported 3 miles to foundries in town. The New Hampshire Iron Factory Company, incorporated in 1805, built a large ironworks in town, complete with a blast furnace and forge. Another similar facility was built a few years later by the Haverhill and Franconia Iron Works Company. Today, it is hard to envision that Franconia was once a flourishing center for iron smelting!

Iron was not the only ore extracted in the region. You may have guessed by now that Coppermine Brook was named for a copper mine. The mine was worked during the years before the Civil War, when a shaft penetrated 100 feet below the brook. Other copper mines dotted the surrounding hills. Like the iron ore, the copper ore was smelted and forged in the Franconia foundries. The hills were also mined for lead, zinc, silver, tin, cobalt, garnet, quartz, and mica.

And gold. Although the ironworks were put out of business by 1865 as a result of competition from the Midwest, that year John Henry Allen dug up gold-bearing quartz crystals near Lisbon, across Ore Hill. A brief gold boom ensued. No major veins were ever discovered, but diligent prospectors continue to find placer deposits and small nuggets in rivers of the area to this day (Foley, 1980).

The region's most enduring treasure, though, is undoubtedly the beauty of the mountains, the forests, and the watercourses. Treasure seekers will find an especially nice nugget up at the end of the Coppermine Trail.

CHAPTER 3

WATERFALLS AT THE GATE OF THE NOTCH

◆

Silver and Flume Cascades
Beecher and Pearl Cascades
Gibbs Falls

Location: Head of Crawford Notch on US 302
Maps: AMC #2 Franconia-Pemigewasset Map (G-7/8); DeLorme Trail Map (E-9)

◆

Andrew Jackson was in Washington awaiting his inauguration when the first hotel opened its doors at the Gate of the Notch—the height of land separating the Ammonoosuc and Saco watersheds. America then was on a binge of economic growth, geographic expansion, and demographic mobility. The frontier was luring pioneers westward, while "the White Mountain Notch" was attracting more and more tourists to its spectacular cliffs and beautiful cascades. One unique attraction at the Gate of the Notch was the path that Abel and Ethan Allen Crawford had blazed to the summit ridge of the Presidential Range in 1819.

The growing traffic of tourists and teamsters prompted the Crawfords to open a hotel near the Crawford Path trailhead in early 1829. In 1852 the Crawfords began building a larger hotel next door, but financial difficulties forced them to sell out to J.L. Gibb, after whom Gibbs Falls and Gibbs Brook are named. Gibb completed construction of the larger hotel, later called Crawford House. One of his early guests, Reverend Henry Ward Beecher, popularized a nearby cascade that now bears his name.

The cascades at the Gate of the Notch were major drawing cards for nineteenth-century tourists. Silver and Flume Cascades, hardly a mile down the road, ranked among the most famous of the White Mountain waterfalls. Gibbs Falls and Beecher Cascade were popular as short strolls for the gentle-

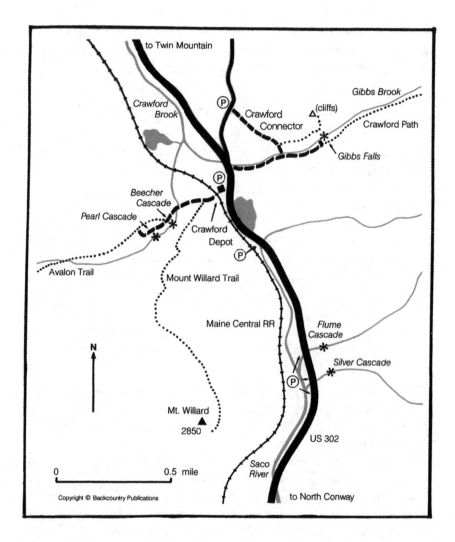

men in bowler hats and ladies in hooped skirts who frequented the luxurious Crawford House hotel.

   Today the notch is named for the Crawfords. Crawford House is gone,
having burned down in 1977. Yet visitors still flock to the Gate of the
Notch to view the cliffs and waterfalls and to hike up Crawford Path. Some-
how the waterfalls seem less remarkable now than they must have appeared
150 years ago when the first hotels were literally carved out of the wilderness. Many travelers zoom past Silver and Flume Cascades at 55 miles per
hour with hardly a glance, and the smaller cascades are often treated by

hikers in the same category as a convenient boulder—a spot for a quick rest en route to the summits. But the falls at the Gate of the Notch are always charming, often very pretty, and fun to explore.

SILVER AND FLUME CASCADES

Hiking Facts
Distance: At the roadside
Altitude gain: Zero (altitude 1700 feet)
Difficulty: Easy

Side by side on the eastern wall of Crawford Notch, the Silver and Flume Cascades feed the nascent Saco River less than a mile below the Gate of the Notch. Early writers were exceedingly impressed by the scenery here. Benjamin Willey, for instance, wrote in 1856:

> The sublime and awful grandeur of the Notch baffles all description. . . . No words can tell the emotions of the soul, as it looks upwards and views the almost perpendicular precipices which line the narrow space. . . .

Willey claimed that the cascades were "unrivaled in their romantic beauty" and that Silver Cascade, in particular, was to be considered "one of the most beautiful in the world." His florid description is rather difficult for a modern reader to stomach.

Other nineteenth-century accounts described Silver Cascade as a long, graceful silver braid gliding down the sheer cliffs of Mount Jackson. (The mountain is named after geologist Charles T. Jackson, not President Andrew Jackson.) The cascade was variously reported to be anywhere from 300 feet to 1000 feet in height. When the railroad opened in 1875, Silver Cascade was called its "brightest jewel." Observation cars provided passengers with full views from across the valley—views sullied by smoke and cinders blown back from the locomotive. Ladies wore veils to keep the grit out of their eyes.

More objectively, the Silver Cascade is attractive, but far from world-class. To reach the falls, park at either of the two large lots on the west side of US 302, 0.9 mile below Crawford Depot. The foot of the cascade is just across the highway. From the roadside Silver Cascade appears as a long, slender ribbon that glides down the ledges, dropping from one inclined

Silver Cascade

terrace to the next, and finally rushing through a bedrock chute under the highway.

To see more of the cascade or simply to get a better look, take a short hike up the rocky ledge to visit the lower falls. With some effort, plus a dash of daring, you can transform a two-minute "oh-my-isn't-that-nice" waterfall into an enjoyable adventure.

The same comment applies even more strongly to Flume Cascade. This meager waterfall is hardly worth a bother if you only want a quick view from the roadside, but a careful scramble up the ledge can be rewarding. The prettiest sections are higher up the headwall and barely noticeable from the road.

Dr. Timothy Dwight, president of Yale, had the right idea when he visited Flume Cascade back in 1797:

> Alighting from our horses, we walked up the acclivity, perhaps a furlong. The stream fell from a height of 240– 250 ft. over three precipices. . . . It is impossible for a brook of this size [puny!] to be modelled into more diversified or delightful forms.

BEECHER AND PEARL CASCADES

Hiking Data
Distance: From parking area to Pearl Cascade, 0.4 mile
Altitude gain: 200 feet (to altitude 2100 feet)
Difficulty: Easy

The name Beecher's Cascades (plural) originally referred to a series of small waterfalls and pools along Crawford Brook, which descends from Mount Field and runs past Crawford Depot to join the Ammonoosuc River at Bretton Woods. Nowadays the name Beecher Cascade (singular) applies to a particular waterfall near the bottom of the hill. Just upstream, a second small waterfall now bears the name Pearl Cascade, while the rest of the lot are unnamed.

Reverend Henry Ward Beecher, the famous abolitionist pastor of the Plymouth Church in Brooklyn, was the first to describe in writing this "avenue of cascades." A guest at Crawford House in 1856, Beecher had fled the city to escape his hay fever. He later spent every summer in the fresh mountain air, and drew hundreds of worshipers to Sunday sermons held under a great tent at Twin Mountain. Beecher was a fine writer as well as a powerful speaker. In one delightful passage from his essay on the cascades, he captured perfectly the sensual thrill of swimming in a mountain pool:

> This was my pool. It waited for me. How deliciously it opened its flood to my coming. It rushed up to every pore, and sheeted my skin with an aqueous covering, prepared in the mountain water-looms. Ah, the coldness;—every drop was molten hail. It was the very brother of ice.

Access
To reach Beecher's Cascades, park at the Crawford visitors parking lot, below the AMC Crawford Hostel.

The Trail
The Avalon Trail begins across the railroad tracks behind the Crawford Depot, where the AMC runs an information center, but the parking at the depot itself is limited to half an hour. After 100 yards the Mount Willard Trail splits off left and climbs to the brink of spectacular cliffs at the head of the Notch. This trail, a former carriage road constructed by Thomas Crawford in 1846, is perhaps the best short hike in all of the White Mountains.

The Avalon Trail continues ahead, soon crossing Crawford Brook. Less than 200 feet farther on, the Cascade Loop Trail forks left to the cascades. After a brief, easy climb you reach a small sign pointing left to a spur path for Beecher Cascade. The spur emerges on a weathered ledge of pink-brown Conway granite. The stream funnels through a narrow channel and tumbles 30 feet down a chute into a rock-bound glen. If the water is not running high, adept scramblers can climb down into the glen or explore up the ledges and waterslides above the cascade.

Continuing up the loop trail 0.1 mile, you come to another sign on the left pointing to an overlook below Pearl Cascade. Except when the water level is unusually low, Pearl Cascade is quite beautiful. A 20-foot-high cone of bubbling water dances down a mossy headwall at the back of a small gorge. The stream then traverses the gorge in a series of short steps before pouring over a 4-foot ledge into a broad pool lined with colorful cobbles. If it's a hot day, take off your shoes and wade right up the waterfall—taking care, of course, to gain secure footing on wet surfaces.

Above Pearl Cascade the path loops up to rejoin the Avalon Trail. This junction is clearly posted. More of Beecher's Cascades (plural again) appear farther up the trail. About 0.2 mile above the junction, where the trail once more touches the brook, is an unnamed twin of (the) Beecher Cascade. In some ways this one is even more attractive than the original down below. It has wider "sittin' rocks," and a splendid rifle-barrel-shaped pool at the foot of the chute. Without going into detail, suffice it to say that enterprising explorers will find other fine, nameless cascades along the streambed.

Beyond the cascades the Avalon Trail climbs steeply to Mount Avalon (at 1.8 miles) and Mount Field (2.8 miles). Unless you are bagging 4000-footers, Mount Avalon is an excellent destination—a rocky spur with panoramic views of the Notch and the Presidentials, plus good blueberries in August.

GIBBS FALLS

Hiking Data
Distance: From parking area to falls, 0.6 mile
Attitude gain: 400 feet (to altitude 2300 feet)
Difficulty: Easy, but a bit of a climb

Gibbs Falls is a short walk (0.4 mile) up Crawford Path, which begins directly across the highway from the AMC hostel beside Crawford Depot. Trailhead parking, formerly on Route 302, has been moved. Continue north on Route 302 past the hostel to Mt. Clinton Road. A parking lot lies a short distance up this road. Follow the Crawford Connector Trail across the road, climbing slightly to cross Gibbs Brook at 0.4 mile. If you want a nice view of the notch, a side trail diverges left immediately before the bridge and climbs steeply for 0.5 mile to an overlook atop Crawford Cliffs. Crossing the brook after passing this side trail will bring you to the original Crawford path. Follow the trail left, up the brook at a steady, moderate grade. Until late summer, the soft murmur of Gibbs Brook is accompanied by robins and Swainson's thrushes singing from the thick forest. Another 0.2 mile along Crawford Path, you reach the short spur down to Gibbs Falls.

The spur descends into a lovely glen shaded by virgin spruce and yellow birch. The waterfall—a sparkling silver feather ornament on a dark-gray wall of ancient gneiss—lies at the back of the glen, across a small triangular pool lined with smooth stones. Starting from ledges hidden behind a protruding knob above the pool, Gibbs Falls drops about 35 feet. The brook first sweeps through a cleft wrapped around the base of the knob and then spills down the wall to the pool.

Even on the hottest summer day the glen is refreshingly cool. (On one of our trips the temperature at the depot was nearly 100 degrees, but the glen was a comfy 75 degrees.) The ledges just above the falls are open and sunny, though, with fine channels and small pools in which to swim—including one incredible chest-deep, lime-green pothole bathtub. This pool can make your day!

The problem is reaching the upper ledges. When dry, the channel to the right of the falls has just enough toeholds for an experienced friction climber to scramble up, exiting onto the knob in front of the first spruce tree. More prudent visitors, though, will prefer to hike up Crawford Path another 100 yards to a point where the ledges can be seen through the woods below. You can then pick your way down through prickly spruce and fallen logs.

One word of warning: If you are continuing up Crawford Path to Mount Washington, don't linger too long at the falls. The summit is still 7.8 miles (and nearly 4000 vertical feet) away.

Historical Detour
Along with exhilarating scenery, the road through the Gate of the Notch also has a fascinating history.

Although there are indications that Crawford Notch was used by the Indians to transport captives during the French and Indian War, discovery of the notch is generally dated to 1771. That year Timothy Nash of Lancaster spotted the narrow gap in the wall of mountains to the southeast while out hunting moose on Cherry Mountain. He worked his way through the dense forest wilderness to explore the gap and continued all the way down the Saco to the coast.

Nash reported his discovery to New Hampshire Governor Benning Wentworth, who immediately recognized the enormous value of a direct route from the Maine coast to the upper Connecticut valley. He asked Nash to prove his claim by leading a horse from Lancaster to Portsmouth. With a friend, Benjamin Sawyer, Nash succeeded in dragging a horse down the notch, even though doing so required using a rope cradle to ease the poor animal over steep slabs at the Gate. Nash and Sawyer were rewarded with a 2000-acre grant of land just above the notch and, some say, a bag of gold.

One condition of the land grant was that a road be built. By 1785 a rough route had been constructed, but very badly. The route zigzagged across the river no less than thirty-two times, and was so steep in sections that horses and wagons still had to be pulled up with ropes. The first trade commodity to pass along the road was a barrel of rum that Captain Eleazer Rosebrook, of Guildhall, Vermont, hauled from Portland to Lancaster to exchange for a barrel of tobacco.

In 1792, the same enterprising captain moved with his family to a small log cabin at what is now Fabyan. He cleared over 100 acres of wilderness for a farm, and began taking in travelers. The log cabin had first been occupied by Rosebrook's son-in-law, Abel Crawford. But that pioneering settler soon moved 12 miles down the notch, "rather than to be crowded by neighbors." There he welcomed travelers, guided hikers, and later built the first hostel in the notch, which became known as Mount Crawford House.

The atrocious condition of the original road led in 1803 to the incorporation of a turnpike authority, which rerouted and improved the road at a cost of $40,000, raised by a lottery. The new road cut the Portland to Lancaster round-trip from twenty-two days to as few as eight. Thus, despite travelers' having to pay turnpike tolls, the volume of traffic through the notch grew rapidly. Even in winter, half-mile-long lines of horse-drawn sleighs laden with pork, cheese, butter, lard, and other freight could be seen fighting the bitter northwest winds on their way up the turnpike.

For nearly three-quarters of a century, the turnpike was the main thoroughfare through the mountains. The turnpike's importance waned—and tolls disappeared—only after the Portland & Ogdensburg Railroad (later the Maine Central) pushed a rail line through from Bartlett to Fabyan in 1875. The track up the side wall of the notch was in operation for over a century before succumbing to the internal combustion engine and modernization of the highway. The railroad has recently reopened to carry tourists from a station in North Conway up into the notch.

Because the glaciers left the Gate of the Notch only 26 feet wide, the railroad builders blasted a second gate just to the west. Moses Sweetser (1887) mentioned a proposal to span the two gates "by a double triumphal arch" commemorating victory over the mountain barrier, first by ice and later by man. The true victory is that the beauty of the Gate managed to survive the onslaught.

CHAPTER 4

THE AMMONOOSUC RAVINE TRAIL

◆

Location: From Mount Washington Cog Railroad base station
Maps: AMC #1 Presidential Range Map (F-8/9); DeLorme Trail Map (D-10)

Hiking Data

Distance: Hikers' parking area to Gem Pool, 2.1 miles; to the Gorge, 2.3 miles; to upper ledges, 2.5 miles.
Altitude gain: 2000 feet to the ledges (altitude 4500 feet)
Difficulty: Moderate to Gem Pool; strenuous beyond

◆

When the AMC opened the Ammonoosuc Ravine Trail in 1915, the trail was intended to provide visitors to Lakes-of-the-Clouds Hut and hikers along Crawford Path with a badly needed escape route from the alpine zone during the frequent bouts of extreme weather. Indeed, the early AMC trail descriptions were written from the hut down; it was presumed that trampers would be discouraged from ascending the steep, rough grade in the vicinity of the Gorge except in an emergency.

But the normally restrained AMC guidebook also mentioned that the trail had "spectacular" views, a "sensational" 600-foot waterslide, "precipitous" ledges, and "a beautiful pool at the foot of some fine little cascades" (AMC, 1922). In addition, the new trail provided one of the shortest routes to the summit of Mount Washington. Little wonder, then, that the emergency escape route turned into one of the most heavily used paths in the Whites.

Access

The usual route to the Cog Railway Base Station (also called Marshfield) is by the Base Road that runs north from US 302 at Fabyan. Alternatively, one can take the Mount Clinton Road north from US 302 at Crawford Depot,

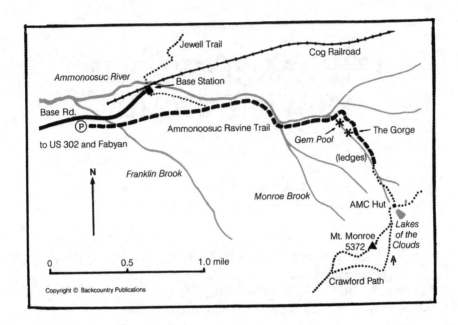

intercepting the Base Road 1.5 miles below Marshfield. Driving along the Base Road, you will see a US Forest Service parking lot for hikers on the right 0.5 mile before the Cog Railway station.

The Trail

The trail proceeds through some very pretty woods, crosses a brook, and bypasses the Base Station. The trail merges with the old trail from the Base Station 1 mile from the hikers' lot (0.3 mile above the Base Station). Continuing up the south bank of the Ammonoosuc, the gradient is steady but moderate. The footing, however, is rough and uneven much of the way.

The river here has the appearance of a typical tumbling stream, dotted with small pools and strewn with rocks. Streams on the far side of the Presidential Range drain enormous glacial bowls and therefore tend to flow strongly much of the year. In contrast the streams on the western slopes did not benefit from glacial excavation. They have carved steep V-shaped ravines that generate a high spring runoff but less water volume later in the season. The shade of the narrow ravine encourages a rich growth of moss, sorrel, and fern beneath the boreal forest.

Near the top of this lower stretch of trail the steep headwall of the Ammonoosuc Ravine comes into view at points where snow slides and heavy rains have mowed down swaths of timber. At 2.1 miles from the hikers' parking lot the trail crosses the Ammonoosuc—now just a small stream—at the foot of Gem Pool and the first cascade. This idyllic scene is a good place to rest because the trail immediately becomes very steep, climbing 1000 vertical feet in the next 0.4 mile. If you like scaling long flights of stairs, you should enjoy the next leg of the hike (and it is more scenic than a Stairmaster). And if not, just plod on step by step, pausing for frequent sips of water. Your effort will be amply rewarded.

The side path over to the Gorge is on the right 0.2 mile above the pool (though it feels farther). Don't be fooled by dead-end side paths tramped down by wishful thinkers who felt that they had reached the Gorge path. The correct path is marked by a carved wooden sign placed on a tree at head level, where it will not be noticed by hikers who are busy watching their footing. Fortunately the side path itself is easy to spot.

The main trail continues steeply up the ravine headwall. Soon you are scrambling up slabs of bedrock instead of dirty boulder steps. At one point a rock ramp leads to the edge of a precipitous drop down to the Gorge. As the trail flattens out, it reaches the first of the upper ledges, with superb views to the west. On a clear day you can see all the way across to the dark ridge of the Adirondack Mountains in New York.

As the ledges broaden out, the trail crosses back over the Ammonoosuc, now just a pretty rivulet cascading over high rock walls. The trail then passes into stunted evergreen forest and turns left to follow the course of the stream up the ledges. Looming above, the massive rock-pile cone of Mount Washington appears deceptively near at hand.

Mountain Ash

Falls in Ammonoosuc Ravine, near Mt. Washington

Although the waterfall excursion ends at the ledges, the trail continues up to Lakes-of-the-Clouds Hut, 0.6 mile beyond the stream crossing at the ledges. At the hut you can rest, have a snack, buy a souvenir T-shirt, and decide whether to push on farther. The summit of Mount Washington, with its buildings, crowds, parking lot, and rail terminal, is still a stiff hike of 1.4 miles and 1200 vertical feet. Those continuing toward the summit can make a long loop by returning to the Base Station via the Jewell Trail to the north. An excellent alternative hike is the jaunt up to the craggy summit of Mount Monroe, just south of the hut.

The Falls

Curiously, the three sets of waterfalls along the Ammonoosuc Ravine Trail have no proper names. Yet each is distinctively beautiful.

Gem Pool, just before the trail steepens, might well be the pool you see when you close your eyes to daydream about mountain streams. Its clear, shallow waters form a perfect crystal fan, bound in banks of ancient rock. The handle of the fan is a silvery cascade that emerges from the forest through a narrow chute carved in the ravine wall.

Lying in a shady hollow that opens toward the northwest, Gem Pool gets little direct sunlight. Also, the pool often harbors a fair supply of blackflies, making it difficult to linger too long in its grace. Fortunately, though, there is a lot more to see farther up the trail.

The Gorge is one of the finest waterfall spectacles in the White Mountains. Here the river, a sparkling ribbon of water, completes a 600-foot tumble in a long series of bold leaps down the lofty headwall of the ravine (only a portion of which is visible from the rocky rampart at the Gorge). The cascade terminates with a straight plunge into the corner of a dark pool at the base of the Gorge's sheer walls of weathered schist. From the left a small side stream mimics the main cascade, tumbling down its own narrow channel of the headwall to join the Ammonoosuc at the pool. If the rocks are dry, you can scramble down to the poolside to inspect the Gorge and the talus pile that dams the stream's outlet in low water.

One feature contributing to the spectacle is that you get a very intimate view of the Gorge from atop the crag opposite the falls. It is like looking at a splendid work of architecture from a third-story window across a narrow street—with the glistening pool serving admirably as the street. Don't miss it, especially if there has recently been rain. A word of warning, though: Despite the bone-chillingly cold water, this pool may be irresistable on a hot day, so expect to get wet.

The hike's third waterfall formation is less clearly demarcated. It begins where the trail crosses the stream at the upper ledges and continues for about 0.3 mile. Here, the pint-sized stream teams up with rugged, crystal-embedded schist and quartzite ledges to form a long, variegated series of thin falls, waterslides, and cascades. Add in bracing mountain air, warm sunlight bathing the smooth rock, and panoramic vistas, and you have a captivating spot for a hiker's picnic!

At the ledges the water flow is highly variable. During dry spells the upper cascades can slow to a trickle. But the ledges themselves are ever beautiful. And unlike the confined conditions in the ravine below, the ledges offer room to explore.

Historical Detour

The name "Ammonoosuc" is derived from the Abenaki Indian word for "fish-place." To the early settlers this name was quite appropriate; the river provided a bounty of trout and salmon, as well as a favorite hunting ground. Ethan Allen Crawford is reported to have pulled 600 to 700 pounds of trout and salmon out of the river each year to serve to his family and guests. Today the river below Marshfield remains a favorite spot for anglers. Recent years have even seen the return of the salmon as a result of successful pollution-control efforts and stocking by the state Fish and Game Department.

The value of the Ammonoosuc Ravine as an emergency exit from the alpine zone at Lakes of the Clouds (then called Blue Pond) was evident almost as soon as Abel Crawford cleared the first path from Crawford Notch to the summit ridge in 1819. In her *History of the White Mountains,* Lucy Crawford describes how two "gentlemen from Boston" were forced down what they called "Escape Glen" to retreat from a storm in 1823. One nearly lost his life when a tree root came loose at the top of a 50-foot precipice. Two years later the noted biologist William Oakes also fled down "Amanoosuc" Ravine, which he referred to as "the most villainous breakneck route."

Another climber cited by Lucy Crawford wrote in 1825 of the fearsome weather encountered above the tree line:

> I have experienced gales in the Gulf Stream, tempests off Cape Hatteras, tornadoes in the West Indies, and been surrounded by water spouts in the Gulf of Mexico, but I never saw anything more furious or dreadful than this.

One of the earliest recorded fatalities among White Mountain climbers occurred on an emergency retreat down the Ammonoosuc Ravine. In October 1851, the son of an English member of Parliament died trying to escape from snow and high winds that he encountered during a hike up Crawford Path.

It is surprising, then, that no formal route down the ravine was established until the AMC opened both the trail and the Lakes-of-the-Clouds Hut in 1915. This is especially so considering that Ethan Allen Crawford cut a path up what is now the Base Road all the way back in 1823. This road provided a means of ascending Mount Washington—essentially establishing the Cog Railway route—that was more protected than the Crawford Path. The latter continued to be popular, though, and the new path was on the wrong side of the summit to provide a quick exit when storms struck the ridge.

One early hiker to ascend the route from the Base Road was Sylvester Marsh, a Campton native who made a fortune in meat packing in Chicago. His climb in 1852 inspired the idea of building a cog railway to the summit. Marsh convinced the New Hampshire legislature to grant a charter in 1858. Construction was then delayed by the Civil War, but the line was completed and opened to the public in 1869. A small hotel was established at Marshfield station, which lodged logging crews during the winter months. For nearly fifty more years hikers climbed alongside the railbed, and the waterfalls of Ammonoosuc Ravine continued to be neglected.

Bonus Falls of the Ammonoosuc
Between Marshfield and the Zealand Campground (on US 302) the picturesque Ammonoosuc River is graced with long stretches of rapids, etched exposures of fine granite, beautiful pools, small cascades, and two excellent waterfalls that were once major attractions in their own right.

The Upper Falls of the Ammonoosuc, beside the Base Road 2.3 miles from US 302 (no signpost), is a strong candidate for the most beautiful formation in the whole region. Here the river has chiseled the fine-grained granite with a dazzling composition of potholes, grottoes, and curved walls, including a unique underwater arch. The clear waters surge down a smooth chute and plummet into a deep pothole pool about 20 feet in diameter. The swollen, gritty, glacial outwash which carved this gorge seems to have had a fine artistic sense. To reach the falls, look for the long and often heavily used gravel shoulder on the side of the Base Road. The falls are just next to the road.

According to one forest ranger a number of people have drowned here when pinned underwater by powerful whirlpool currents beneath the falls. Many more have been pulled out unconscious or deeply frightened by their near-death encounters with this current. Some swimmers are tempted to leap off the cliffs into the deep pool. As attractive or adrenaline inducing as it may seem, *swimming at this waterfall has resulted in a large number of tragedies. This is easily the most dangerous waterfall in the region, so please play it safe.* Until recently this was private property and swimming was prohibited. Now that it is public land once more, swimming is not prohibited, but it remains as treacherous as ever: If you swim, you SWIM AT YOUR OWN RISK!

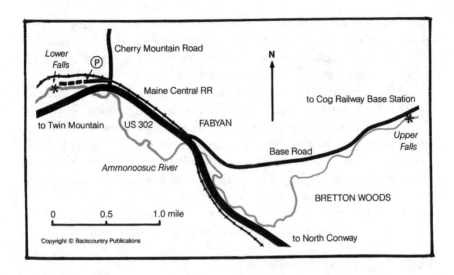

The Lower Falls of the Ammonoosuc is reached by turning north off US 302 onto the Old Cherry Mountain Road, 0.9 mile west of the Base Road, and 1.4 miles east of Zealand Road. There is a sign for the falls, but you need keen eyes to spot it. A large parking area is located at the end of a paved road on your left immediately after the turn off US 302 (before the railroad tracks). Hiking along the dirt road at the end of the parking area, you will find the river sandy and shallow at first. Only 0.1 mile from the parking area the current quickens. Large boulders appear in the riverbed, and then smooth reddish-brown ledges mark the top of the falls. Access is easiest at the foot of the falls, 100 yards farther down the road.

At Lower Falls the river glides down a long, broad channel of gently sloped granite shelves, deeply undercutting a granite wall that is jointed like fine masonry. Though the biggest single drop in the river is not more than 3 feet, the overall effect is quite beautiful. Because of the shallows above the falls and the broad, sunny ledges, the water temperature here is much less frigid than farther upstream. On the other hand the water is also less clear, and the ledges tend to be slippery.

Moses Sweetser, writing in 1887, warned tourists to stay away from Lower Falls because a nearby sawmill ruined the view. This early case of overdevelopment has long since disappeared, so tourists today are warned not to miss this easy side trip.

CHAPTER 5

CASCADE RAVINE (MOUNT ADAMS)

◆

Location: From Bowman, on US 2 on the west side of Randolph
Maps: AMC #1 Presidential Range Map (E-8/9); DeLorme Trail Map (10-B)

Hiking Data
Distance: Parking area to First Cascade, 2.5 miles; to Second Cascade, 2.7 miles
Altitude gain: 1500 feet to the Second Cascade (altitude 3000 feet)
Difficulty: Moderate, but the last mile is rough

◆

Cascade Ravine is a narrow cut on the steep northwest shoulder of Mount Adams, separating the tongue of Israel Ridge from the broad massif of Nowell Ridge. Cascade Brook dashes down the ravine to join Castle Brook and form the Israel River. Both the ravine and the brook take their name from a long string of cascades that line a band of exposed ledges tucked in high virgin forests midway up the mountain flank.

The Israel Ridge Path to the cascades was cut in 1892 by J. Rayner Edmands, a researcher at the Harvard Observatory and an early president of the Appalachian Mountain Club. He was also the premier trail builder of the Presidential Range. In addition to the Israel Ridge Path up Mount Adams, Edmands established the Gulfside Trail along the summit ridge; the Randolph Path to the saddle (now Edmands Col) between Mount Adams and Mount Jefferson; the Edmands Path up what is now Mount Eisenhower; the Link trail that slabs up the northern slopes, connecting all of the trails out of Randolph; and the West Side Trail around Mount Washington's summit cone. Much of this work was done largely at his own expense.

Edmands had explored Cascade Ravine in 1868 while still a student at the Massachusetts Institute of Technology. Later he devoted special efforts

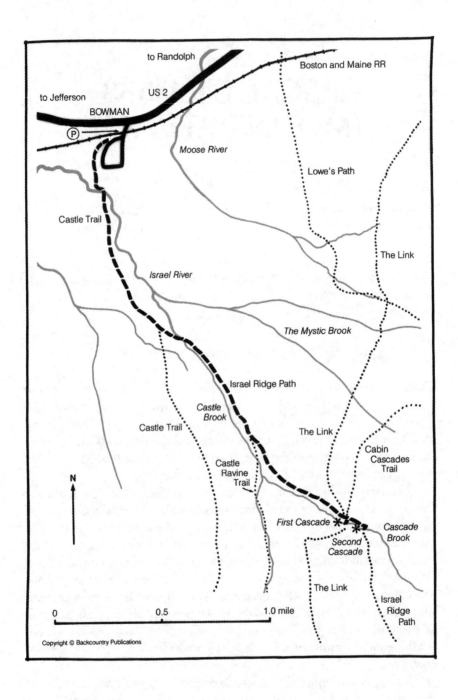

to Randolph

Boston and Maine RR

to Jefferson

US 2

BOWMAN

Ⓟ

Moose River

Lowe's Path

Castle Trail

The Link

Israel River

The Mystic Brook

Israel Ridge Path

Castle Brook

Castle Trail

The Link

Cabin Cascades Trail

Castle Ravine Trail

N

First Cascade ✳

✳

Cascade Brook

Second Cascade

The Link

Israel Ridge Path

0   0.5   1.0 mile

to helping others enjoy the ravine and its attractive cascades. Although the cascades were already accessible as early as 1880 by a long spur off Lowe's Path, Edmands chose the Israel Ridge Path up Cascade Ravine as his very first trail project. At the foot of the Second Cascade he constructed Cascade Camp, with one cabin for the ladies and one for the gentlemen, along with a set of scenic trails that became known as the "pleasure paths in Cascade Ravine." One of these paths climbed along the brook past six cascades in the vicinity of Cascade Camp. Edmands also routed his Link trail past the cascades, providing a well-graded route from the Old Ravine House in Randolph, a favorite stopover for visiting mountaineers.

The cabins at the Second Cascade were highly popular until they were swept away by floods and slides unleashed by a severe storm in November 1927. Hardly a decade later the pleasure paths of Cascade Ravine were obliterated by the Great Hurricane of 1938, which closed 700 miles of trails throughout the White Mountains.

Today only the First Cascade and Second Cascade remain accessible by trail. Even these cascades, which saw a lot of traffic around the turn of the century, are infrequently visited. Cascades three through six can be reached only by a rough bushwhack. The pleasure path has not been restored.

Access

The hike begins on the Castle Trail from Bowman, a tiny settlement where US 2 edges the Boston and Maine railroad track 1 mile west of Lowe's Store, and 4.3 miles east of the junction with NH 115 at Jefferson Highlands. A small "hiker" sign on the south side of US 2 marks the turn-off. There is also a trailhead sign for the Castle Trail beside the gravel parking area between US 2 and the railroad track.

The Trail

After checking to make sure your car lights are off (a step we once forgot!), walk across the tracks and follow the right-hand gravel driveway, which has a wonderful view of the twin ravines and the Castellated Ridge up to Mount Jefferson. The ravine on the right is Castle Ravine; that on the left is Cascade Ravine, your objective.

The Castle Trail quickly turns off the driveway and enters the woods. The property owners have posted very conspicuous signs to make sure that you spot the turn. In about 100 yards the trail passes into the national forest and soon crosses a power-line clearing. The Israel River is just past the clearing. The trail follows the river a short distance before crossing (at mile 0.4).

In high water the crossing is quite tricky to manage with dry feet.

The Castle Trail climbs gradually through the hardwood forest by an old logging road to fork (mile 1.3) where the Israel Ridge Path begins. The river runs parallel to the logging road out of view. Listen, though, for the rush of the Israel Rapids off to the left about 0.2 mile after the initial river crossing. There is no path down to the river here, but this lovely run of small cascades and pools is well worth a short detour. In its trail guide the Randolph Mountaineering Club recommends the rapids for trout fishing and picnicking.

From the trail junction the Israel Ridge Path splits off to the left on another logging road and soon recrosses the river. If there has been much recent rain, this second crossing may require wading. After an extended heat wave had been broken by thundershowers in August 1988, the water was a bone-chilling 49 degrees Fahrenheit when we waded through. In fact the river here never gets very warm because of its high catchment basin, its heavy forest cover, and its northern exposure. Betty Flanders Thompson (1958) points out that a gradient of just 5 degrees on a north-facing slope reduces the sun's intensity to the equivalent of conditions 300 miles farther north.

On the east bank now, the Israel Ridge Path hugs the river's edge for a short distance and then angles up the foot of Nowell Ridge to a junction where the Castle Ravine Trail forks to the right (mile 1.7). From this point the Israel Ridge Path enters Cascade Ravine. The climb gets steeper, and the path becomes narrower and rougher as it ascends high on the flank of the sharp V-shaped ravine.

If you fall into a hiking trance on sustained uphill slogs, you will not notice the Link coming in from the left at mile 2.5. But around the next corner you won't miss the well-marked junction where the Israel Ridge Path climbs to the left and the Link continues on ahead. A confusing sign at the junction, TO CABIN-CASCADES TRAIL, refers to a side trail a few dozen yards up the Israel Ridge Path.

Once this junction is reached, your work is nearly done. The head of the First Cascade is a hop, skip, and jump down the Link. The head of the Second Cascade just 0.2 mile above the junction up the Israel Ridge Path, which passes some slippery ledges along the way.

The maze of trails on the northern apron of the Presidentials provides a variety of attractive alternatives to a simple up-and-back-down-again day trip to the cascades. For example you can follow the Israel Ridge Path through the virgin forest beyond the cascades to Mount Jefferson, and then

Boulders at the top of Second Cascade

loop back to Bowman by the spectacular Castle Trail. Or, turning in the opposite direction, you can climb Mount Adams and loop home by way of Lowe's Path and the Cabin-Cascades Trail. If you prefer more brookside scenery, you can contour around Israel Ridge on the wild Link path and descend Castle Ravine Trail. This trail crosses Castle Brook four times and passes a small, pretty cascade on the short stretch between crossings two and three. In high water all four crossings require getting your feet wet.

The Cascades

On leaving the Israel Ridge Path, the Link trail drops to the crest of the First Cascade, the boldest formation in the ravine. Here Cascade Brook tumbles out from a thick cloak of forest, rushes over a narrow rim where the trail crosses, and bounds down a long flight of giant bedrock steps totaling roughly 100 feet in height. The view across the ravine from the top of cascade ledge is as fresh and unspoiled as the cool breeze that drifts down the bed of the brook.

From top to bottom the pitch of the cascade is about 45 degrees, but each individual step is a steep drop. This means that the bottom of the cascade is hidden from view, and it isn't easy to scramble down the ledge. With a bit of pluck, a few rock-climbing moves, and a considerable amount of caution, it is possible to clamber down the eastern (near) corner of the ledge. It is unfortunate that the scramble is so treacherous because the loveliest cascades are at the base of the formation.

The Second Cascade runs down another long, broad slab of ledge. This one slopes much less steeply and lacks the staircase plunges that characterize the First Cascade. Consequently, the Second Cascade is not as lofty or as dramatic as the First, but it is a much friendlier place to stop for a fig bar, to bask in the sun, and to explore. With little difficulty one can scramble from the narrow crossing at the top of the cascade all the way to the small pool at the bottom, where Cascade Camp was located. The cascade itself tumbles past large boulders below the trail crossing and then slides down the corner of the long ledge below a rocky bank hedged with small birch, mountain ash, spruce, and fir.

The Second Cascade is high enough up the ravine to offer an excellent view out to the northwest. From the ledge one can see across Israel Ridge to

Young Male Moose

Jefferson and across to the Pliny Range. This is also a good place to admire the bedrock. At this altitude the rock consists of interbedded quartzite and schist, both metamorphic descendants of ancient seabed sediments. Curved pressure patterns are clearly visible, along with veins of minerals such as mica, garnet, and sillimanite. This tough, weathered rock becomes very slippery when wet.

To reach the Second Cascade it is not necessary to stay on the Israel Ridge Path to where it crosses the brook. In fact, the easiest access is to step out onto the shoulder of the broad ledge when it is first seen off to the right, just before the point where the trail mounts a bare slab of rock set with spikes (showing that there used to be wooden steps bolted to the rock).

Cascades three through six, which once were reached by Edmands' Pleasure Path, have returned to a state of wild splendor. They are crowded closely by dense forests, strewn with timber felled by decades of storms and carpeted with thick beds of lush, fragile moss. Unless and until the old Pleasure Path is restored, these upper cascades will remain inaccessible to all but experienced and well-prepared bushwhackers. If you continue up the Israel Ridge Path, however, you can catch a glimpse of the top cascade. About 0.6 mile and 900 feet above the Second Cascade you can look across the ravine and see in the distance a silvery plume dashing grandly down the dark facade of the remote headwall.

Historical Detour
The Israel River forms at the confluence of Cascade Brook and Castle Brook. The Indian name for this river was some variation of Siwoog-a-nac or Singrawac. These names have been translated to mean "a place where we return in the spring" or "foaming stream with white rock." Either interpretation makes clear that the Indians considered the river to be a place of great beauty. The English renamed the river for a pioneer named Israel Glines, who visited the region to hunt and trap along its banks sometime before 1750.

Prior to the end of the French and Indian War in 1763 there were no settlements in the north country. Yet legend has it that in 1759 nine men met their doom somewhere up in a deep ravine at the head of the Israel River—where, it is said, they may have concealed a silver statue of the Virgin Mary weighing as much as eight pounds.

The legend is well grounded in historical facts, which are recounted in Solon Colby's *Indian History*. In September 1759, two British officers who had been sent to Saint Francis, Quebec, to request neutrality of the Indians were imprisoned and turned over to the French. In response, the angry General

Jeffery Amherst issued orders to a company of two hundred elite fighters led by Major Robert Rogers to punish the Indians for their maltreatment of the emissaries and to inflict revenge for many years of Indian raids.

Although spotted and pursued, Rogers' Rangers succeeded in taking the Indian village at Saint Francis by surprise in a dawn raid. The raiders killed dozens of Indians and destroyed the village—wherein they found hundreds of poles bearing white scalps. Among the buildings destroyed was an elaborately decorated chapel. Before burning the chapel the raiders cleaned it of valuables, including the silver icon. It is said that by raiding this chapel the rangers brought on themselves a curse that haunted their return to British territory.

Evading both French and Indian forces on their tail, the retreating rangers detoured toward the Connecticut River. With supplies running low and the weather deteriorating, the company split up into small groups. Along the way some men died of starvation and some of exposure, while other rangers were overtaken by pursuing Indians. One group of nine men—the group with the silver statue—planned to follow the Israel River and escape through Jefferson Notch. According to Colby, they were never seen again, though their rusted muskets and rotting knapsacks were later found along the banks of the Israel River. Over the years many objects stolen from the church at Saint Francis have been found at various locations around northern Vermont, but the icon of the Virgin Mary was never seen again.

Some of the details omitted by history have been filled in by legend. A deceitful Indian guide, it is said, misled the company bearing the silver statue. He brought them high up the Israel River into a ravine, where he poisoned the leader with a rattlesnake fang. The other men scattered and perished in the early winter snow. By some accounts one man managed to reach a settlement, where he told the story of his comrades' fate and revealed that the silver statue lay hidden in a cave, high in the unmapped ravine.

The raid on Saint Francis and its aftermath are all the more tragic because the decisive battle in the French and Indian War had already been fought and won when Rogers' Rangers fell on the Indian village. On the very day that orders were issued for Rogers to proceed north, the British forces under General James Wolfe were defeating the French at Quebec.

Even if a silver statue does lie buried in Cascade Ravine it is not likely ever to be found unless some future landslide happens to unearth the cache. Until that day, however, the silver cascades themselves are a treasure we all can enjoy.

CHAPTER 6

POND BROOK FALLS

◆

Location: Nash Stream valley, north of Stark (via NH 110)
Map: USGS Percy Quadrangle

Hiking Data
Distance: Parking area to falls, 0.1 mile
Altitude gain: 100 feet (to altitude 1500 feet)
Difficulty: Easy

◆

If certain European financiers had not decided to liquidate some corporate assets, this waterfall trip might have remained a north-country secret. Therein lies a tale.

When work on this book was beginning I asked a friend from the north country to pick his favorite White Mountain waterfall. His response was quite unexpected: "The cascades off Nash Stream. Wonderful place!" I had never heard of it. "Not many people have," he explained, "and it's hard to find unless you know where to look." He was vague on the directions: a crude footpath up a side stream north of Percy Peaks.

A few weeks later, in mid-August, I hiked up Percy Peaks with a visitor from Boston. I promised him that the mountain's immense granite dome would be bursting with juicy blueberries. The views would be splendid. And, I added, we could explore a wonderful waterfall nearby. The hike went according to plan, but our exploration of side streams north of Percy Peaks turned up only muck and briars. My waterfall notebook sums it up concisely: "Nope." Further investigation revealed that none of the guidebooks, old or new, mentioned any such cascades or falls off Nash Stream. Nor was any waterfall shown on any maps. Surely we hadn't missed much.

Then a second friend identified the same spot as her favorite White Mountain waterfall. She was reluctant to elaborate because she did not want the secret publicized. Anyhow, she pointed out, the waterfall did not belong in this book because the property was private timberland.

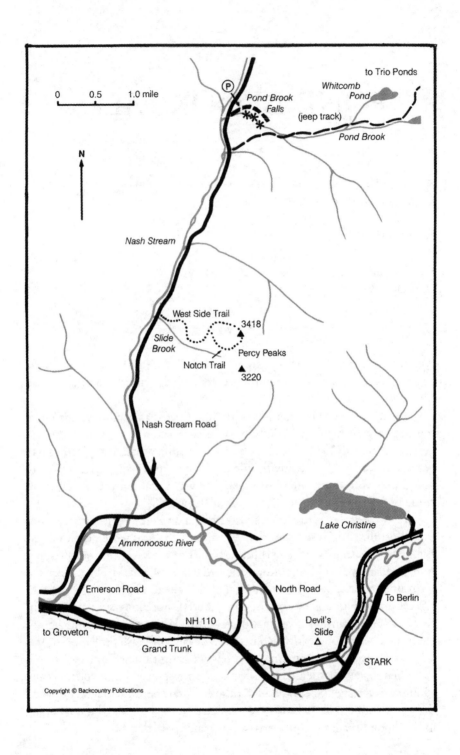

to Trio Ponds

Whitcomb Pond

P

Pond Brook Falls

(jeep track)

Pond Brook

0   0.5   1.0 mile

N

Nash Stream

West Side Trail

3418

Slide Brook

Percy Peaks

Notch Trail

3220

Nash Stream Road

Lake Christine

Ammonoosuc River

Emerson Road

North Road

To Berlin

to Groveton

NH 110

Devil's Slide
△

STARK

Grand Trunk

Copyright © Backcountry Publications

Enter the financiers. Since the turn of the century the Nash Stream watershed had been owned and logged by timber companies. The most recent owner was Diamond International, which in turn was acquired by Generale Occidental, a European conglomerate. In 1987 the corporate financiers concluded that the Diamond properties were worth more in cash than in trees. Consequently, in May 1988, over 67,000 acres of Diamond forestlands in northern New England were sold to Rancourt Associates, a land developer. Gravely concerned conservation groups and public officials quickly organized a scheme for public acquisition of 45,000 acres of prime recreation land including the Nash Stream watershed. (More on this below.)

Since the Nash Stream lands were about to become a public reserve, the elusive waterfall regained the list of prospects to be explored. A bit of map detective work revealed that the most likely location for the waterfall was on Pond Brook, a feeder stream draining four ponds cupped in a high valley between Long and Whitcomb Mountains (obviously not household names). On my initial venture I had not driven far enough north of Percy Peaks. A second trip, though, revealed a backcountry bonanza.

Access

From Groveton follow NH 110 east for 2 miles through the winding valley of the Upper Ammonoosuc River to a left (north) turn onto Emerson Road at a sign for Nash Stream. After 1.25 miles Emerson Road crosses the river and turns sharply to the right. When the road turns right a second time at an intersection 2.2 miles from NH 110, you turn left (north) onto Nash Stream Road. This turn takes you onto a logging road that penetrates a dozen miles up the remote Nash Stream valley. The surface is rough dirt and gravel, but the road is generally passable after the spring mud season ends.

At 2.6 miles along the Nash Stream Road, you will pass the trailhead for the hike up Percy Peaks. Prior to 1989, the only marking for the trailhead was a large rock overgrown with vegetation. Now a signpost marks the beginning of the trail.

Side Trip: Percy Peaks Trail

The climb up North Percy Peak is just over 2 miles long by the Notch Trail, with some steep and slippery stretches along the way. The West Side variation becomes especially treacherous when wet. The summit offers a spectacular panorama of the north country, with excellent views south across the Pilot Range to Mount Washington, and unrivaled blueberry picking. Consult the AMC guide for a detailed trail description.

Access

Beyond the Percy Peaks trailhead the logging road continues north through the narrow valley, passing forests in various stages of regeneration. This mixed habitat is excellent birding territory. Our visit seemed to coincide with an abundance of yellow-shafted flickers. Other visitors have reported numerous hawks and falcons, perhaps feasting on scrumptious flickers.

If you stop alongside Nash Stream to birdwatch or to explore, you may notice that the banks are stony and denuded of soil. In May 1969—after a hard winter with more than 7 feet of snow accumulation—meltwater and rain burst a dam that held back 240 acres of Nash Bog Pond. It is said that a 20-foot-high wall of water surged downstream to Groveton, scouring everything in its path. The scars remain visible today. The stony gravel banks you see in the Nash Stream valley, exposed by the flood, are a fascinating relict left by glacial retreat depositing large amounts of sand, gravel, and cobbles.

At mile 4.9 (measured from the turn off Emerson Road) you pass a dirt track that diverges up a ridge to the right. This rugged jeep track leads to Little Bog Pond and Trio Ponds. It is *not* passable in standard vehicles. At mile 5.6 Nash Stream Road crosses a culvert over Pond Brook. Park just beyond the culvert on the right side of the road. A footpath marked by a sign for Pond Brook Falls climbs from the parking area. The path makes a soft right turn and soon reaches the foot of the lower cascades.

As a detour, consider driving a few miles out of your way to see the village of Stark. Dwarfing the picturesque hamlet is Devil's Slide, a massive ledge rising nearly 800 feet above the constricted valley of the Upper Ammonoosuc River. During World War II Stark was the site of a German prisoner-of-war camp, an interesting account of which can be found in the recent book *Stark Decency,* by Allen Koop. Today it is best known for its annual fiddler's festival.

The Waterfall

A "wonderful place," my friend said. Take him at his word. Pond Brook collects the waters of numerous feeder streams and four remote trout ponds that cover more than 120 acres of highland shelf. On exiting its mountain vale, the brook tumbles and slides down a long corridor of granite ledge, creating a fascinating tapestry of cascades and small waterfalls.

The initial view you get of the waterfall is merely a pleasant teaser. The path first reaches a minor cascade pouring through a sluice at the back of a pothole pool, churning the tea-colored waters to a white foam. By scram-

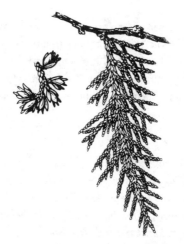

Northern White Cedar

bling up one tier of granite blocks, you reach a small waterslide terminating in another sparkling pool, where the brook undercuts a large table rock to form a low, dark grotto.

One tier higher the falls change character entirely. The brook spreads out and crisscrosses an angular banked ledge 75 feet in width and triple that in length. The granite is fashioned with assorted scoops, dips, ridges, and flakes. In spots the rock itself ripples under a glassy liquid veil. On one side of the ledge a long "ski jump" contour sweeps down from the forest crest. The inner edge of the ski jump drops off abruptly, forming an unusual lateral water curtain in the middle of the broad ledge. Though the polished granite is not steep—it inclines about 25 degrees—the surface is quite slippery when wet, so caution is required when exploring the formation.

Climbing farther to the top of the ski jump ledge, you will reach a marvelous water plume that actually spouts above the horizontal. Higher still, a lacy curtain of water drapes across the mouth of a deep cavern. Capping the display are waterfalls draped over large angular blocks of granite. Surely these falls were meant for frolicking woodland elves.

The path to the waterfall runs up through the woods all the way to the top, allowing one to explore without scaling slick granite ramps and tall boulders. The upper ledges offer secure perches from which to enjoy the view across Nash Stream valley to the long ridge of Stratford Mountain and the 3701-foot summit of Sugarloaf Mountain.

Above the topmost falls the gradient of Pond Brook eases, and the ledge narrows. Spruce, birch, and maple trees press against the banks. If you are curious to explore upstream, Little Bog Pond is 2 miles and 500 vertical feet farther on. The trout will be waiting for you, and perhaps a few moose as well.

Our visit to Pond Brook Falls took place in late August on a day when the forecast called for sunny weather and highs around 70 degrees. It turned out to be cloudy and 49 degrees. In better weather the open ledges get plenty of sun to encourage visitors to test the chilly pools, showers, and slides.

Historical Detour

> *The narrow valley of Nash's Stream*
> *is cloven through this rugged and desolate region. . . .*
> *The character of the view in this direction is wild*
> *and primeval, the mountain forests being as yet*
> *unbroken by tilled clearings or roads,*
> *and no vestige of civilization is visible.*

—Moses Sweetser, 1887

While settlement and development spread quickly along the Connecticut River valley after the French and Indian War, only a trickle of migration reached the isolated town of Percy (later Stark), which was incorporated in 1795. For three generations the quiet village remained the domain of remote hill farms and small local mills.

The town's quiet isolation ended when the Atlantic & St. Lawrence Railroad ran its Portland-to-Montreal trunk line through the valley in 1852. (The following year the Grand Trunk Railroad took over the line.) Stark was transformed into a railroad boom town, and heavy logging began consuming the neighboring forests. Sweetser's description of the view north from Percy Peak, quoted above, indicates that the remote kingdom of spruce and pine along Nash Stream did not succumb quickly to the woodsman's ax, but these forests were not long to remain "wild and primeval."

Shortly after Sweetser climbed Percy Peaks, the era of the great log drives reached the north country (see chapter 7). Like other backcountry watercourses Nash Stream became a spring thoroughfare for the winter's harvest of softwood logs. According to Robert Pike in *Tall Trees, Tough Men,* the Nash Stream valley was logged initially by the Odell Manufacturing Company, a predecessor of the Groveton Paper Company. Later the Groveton operations were acquired by Diamond, which retained the land until 1988.

As modern forestry practices evolved after the turn of the century, the timber companies proved to be capable stewards of the northern woodlands. John Porterfield explained in a *New Hampshire Spirit* article (January/Febru-

Pond Brook

ary 1989) that "paper company ownership of the land meant stability." Indeed he described the Nash Stream "wildlands" as "untamed, defiant of the 20th century realities south of the notches"—echoing Sweetser's words a hundred years earlier.

Because Nash Stream was still untamed, its sale in May 1988, along with the other Diamond timberlands, produced an anguished outcry of concern. Conservation groups and public agencies had been negotiating with Diamond to acquire the Nash Stream property, but they were out-hustled and outbid by Rancourt Associates, who offered over $19 million for 67,000 acres of forestland—far more than the land's appraised value. When Rancourt announced that all but 2,000 acres would be auctioned off that September, subdivision and development seemed imminent—and more threatening to public recreation than the destructive logging that occurred back around the turn of the century elsewhere in the White Mountains.

Even politicians disinclined to accept government interference in private markets joined hands with conservationists to protect Nash Stream. Senator Warren Rudman introduced legislation in Congress raising the threat of federal eminent domain. Governor John Sununu worked to arrange state funding for land purchases, while pressing Rancourt to reach an accommodation.

An expensive bargain was struck. The state of New Hampshire purchased 45,000 acres for $12.75 million, of which $7.65 million would come from the state's Land Conservation Investment Fund and the balance from the federal purchase of a conservation easement to the land. Interim financing was provided by the Society for the Protection of New Hampshire Forests, a pioneer in preserving the state's natural treasures, and by The Nature Conservancy.

Part of the cost will be recovered through a lease of the gravel and timber rights. This means that forest harvests and gravel mining will continue in the Nash Stream valley. Still, the public achieved the single most important purchase of recreational forestland since the north-country wilderness was sold to private interests more than a century ago. On October 27, 1988, the title changed hands.

We all enjoy happy endings, but the Nash Stream acquisition is not the end of the saga. Faced with a combination of takeover threats and rising development values for timberlands, edgy corporate managers are likely to place other large tracts of timberland on the auction block in the future. As one executive explained to the *Boston Globe* (September 14, 1988), "The MBAs come into the paper companies and say we've got to make the assets perform." A concerted and sustained effort will be needed to ensure that the public interest in forest recreation land is expressed effectively in the market.

Back in 1832 the town of Percy was renamed Stark in honor of General John Stark, the hero of Bunker Hill and the Battle of Bennington. It was General Stark who uttered New Hampshire's state motto: "Live free or die." In a way, the state's purchase of the Nash Stream watershed extends the principle to the great wildlands and forests of the north country.

CHAPTER 7

BEAVER BROOK FALLS

◆——————◆

Location: On NH 145, just northwest of Colebrook
Map: USGS Dixville Quadrangle

Hiking Data
Distance: Roadside
Altitude gain: Zero (altitude 1200 feet)
Difficulty: Easy

————————————◆

The main tourist centers of the White Mountains are concentrated to the south of US 2, which runs from Lancaster through Gorham. The entire White Mountain National Forest lies to the south of NH 110, which runs from Groveton to Berlin. But in terms of both tradition and at least some geology books, the White Mountain region extends up through the vast timberlands of northern New Hampshire.

The mountains of the far north are quite different from the great peaks in the tourist centers to the south. Summits are generally rounded and wooded, and few points north of the Nash Stream headlands (see chapter 6) exceed 3000 feet. Even by these modest northland standards, the low hills above the Connecticut River valley outside Colebrook are hardly more than bumps on the map. This is not a setting where one would expect to find a major waterfall, any more than one would expect the sparsely populated north country to field a baseball team to compete with the Red Sox. Yet Beaver Brook Falls matches up well against the major-league waterfalls of the higher White Mountains. And it is conveniently located alongside one of the few paved roads in the district.

To avoid confusion it is important to distinguish our present subject, Beaver Brook Falls in Colebrook, from the Beaver Brook Cascades covered in chapter 1. There are at least five Beaver Brooks scattered throughout the state, so it is not entirely coincidental that two important waterfalls share the Beaver label.

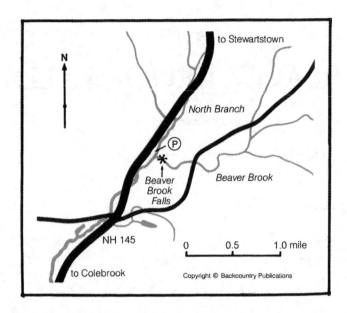

Judging from the frequent use of this name, it would appear that the pioneer settlers were far more impressed with the beaver than with other common denizens of the mountain streambeds, such as blackflies, bullfrogs, or kingfishers. (Although one obscure waterfall is named Muscanigra, after the blackfly; see chapter 29.) This is no surprise, considering how important the cute rodent was to early inhabitants of the north woods. The beaver supplied meat, clothing, barter pelts, and medicines to the Indians. Early settlers so prized the pelt that they hunted the poor *Castor canadensis* nearly to extermination in the region. Only in recent decades has the beaver returned in significant numbers. Today, the animal is valued for its ecological contributions more than its fur. Beaver ponds regulate the water flow in mountain streams and create excellent habitat for a variety of wildlife. But when beavers move too close to human activity, their dedication to cutting trees and building ponds can be a terrific nuisance. There was even a train wreck in Vermont a few years back that was blamed on a beaver pond that undermined the railbed.

Along with the moose, the beaver is a symbol of the north woods. So it is fitting that Beaver Brook Falls provides a handy excuse for waterfall seekers to visit the north country. To make the most of the long drive, a trip to the falls can be combined with a visit to Quebec Province (to practice your French), a canoe trip on the Connecticut Lakes, or a tour of Dixville Notch State Park. The Dixville side trip is described briefly below because each wall of the notch hosts an attractive waterfall.

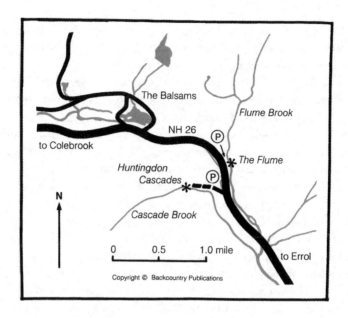

Access

The town of Colebrook is located 36 miles north of Lancaster on US 3, 10 miles below the forty-fifth parallel (the halfway point between the equator and the North Pole) and 11 miles from the international border crossing at Beecher Falls, Vermont.

To reach Beaver Brook Falls (heading north), stay on US 3 for one block beyond the junction with NH 26, Colebrook's main intersection. Then turn right onto NH 145, which is marked with a large sign for Stewartstown and Clarksville and a small sign for the waterfall. Route 145 winds through the outskirts of town, with fine views to the high pyramid of Vermont's Mount Monadnock across the Connecticut River. The road then enters the shallow valley of Beaver Brook and reaches the waterfall 2.5 miles from US 3. Truly, you can't miss it. There is a large sign on the right saying BEAVER BROOK FALLS SCENIC AREA, a conspicuous pullout on either side of the road for parking, and a splendid view of the falls directly across a broad, terraced lawn.

The Falls

Flanked by tall evergreen spires that climb the valley wall, Beaver Brook dashes down more than seven stories of dark ledge. The top half of the falls is quite steep, while the bottom portion is more of a cascade than a direct fall. During high water, the scene is especially beautiful as the brook spreads across the whole face of the ledge and plunges over the upper cliffs in a clear leap of nearly 30 feet. In more typical summer conditions the falls are less dramatic, but then recreational opportunities are at their best.

Below the foot of the cascade the brook runs 30 yards through weedy shallows and then turns a 90-degree corner to parallel the highway. It merges at this point with a side stream coming down from Stewartstown Hollow. Both below the cascades and around the corner in the woods are wading pools where children can play safely, including spots with sandy bottoms. Keep an eye out for deer tracks along the banks. There are also interesting old foundations to investigate in the woods. These are the remains of an electric powerhouse built about 1890.

The Colebrook Kiwanis Club maintains picnic facilities for the public as well as walkways along the stream to the foot of the falls. From the end of the walkways, informal paths climb through the forest on either side of the falls to the top of the ledge. These paths are steep and eroded but passable. The one on the right provides the best views of the falls, since the foliage on this side has been trimmed. One reward for exploring up the falls is a close-up view of sinuous veins of quartz embedded in the ancient phyllite and schist ledge rock. Another bonus is the sweet, subtle fragrance of white cedar (arborvitae), which is abundant on the steep slopes alongside the falls.

Even though you can get a fine view right from your car, Beaver Brook Falls is not there just to *see*. It is also for picnicking, strolling, wading, swimming, and exploring. Have fun.

Side Trip: Waterfalls of Dixville Notch

Dixville, New Hampshire, had a population of only fifty people in 1990. Yet the town boasts four claims to fame: It is the home of one of the grandest resort hotels in the northeast, the Balsams, built in 1873; it is the first precinct in the country to finish counting ballots in each presidential election (always going Republican); it produces most of the nation's rubber balloons; and it encompasses a beautiful notch that is geologically unique among New England's mountain passes. Only Dixville Notch is cut from ancient shales that have been buckled to nearly vertical strata and eroded to create jagged walls and pinnacled ridges.

There are two picnic areas at the lower end of the notch—one on Flume Brook, which descends from the north, and one along Cascade Brook, which approaches from the south. As the names suggest each brook contributes a waterfall to the scenery of Dixville Notch.

To reach Dixville Notch from Beaver Brook Falls, double back to

Colebrook and turn east on NH 26. The highway climbs gradually up the shallow valley of the Mohawk River for 11 miles to the height-of-land where the stunning Balsams Hotel is located. The Flume Brook picnic area is on the left 1 mile east of the height-of-land. The Dixville Flume is right beside the lower end of the picnic area. Although metamorphic schists and phyllites dominate the upper reaches of the Notch, here the brook crosses onto an intrusion of granite, carving a sheer gorge about 250 feet long and as much as 40 feet deep. Rushing through a narrow constriction at the neck of the flume, the brook tumbles down a series of cascades to an abrupt 15-foot drop over a bank of ledge. Since there is little underbrush below the thick canopy of conifers alongside the brook, one can walk along the rim of the gorge for a bird's-eye view of the waterfall.

Another 0.25 mile down the notch, at the lower boundary of the state park, a second picnic area lies off to the right (south) behind a green equipment shed. Cascade Brook is a 0.1 mile walk back into the forest. According to the 1896 edition of Moses Sweetser's travel guide, excursion parties stopped to dine at this rest spot and then walked up the brook for fifteen minutes to where "a cliff-side seat is reached, from which a noble series of falls are seen, descending sheer from the precipice above." These are called Huntingdon Cascades. Today, paths lead from the picnic area to a moss-lined ravine at the foot of a pretty set of small cascades. No "precipice" or "noble falls" is in sight. The position described by Sweetser might be higher up the ravine, but no maintained paths lead the way.

In addition to the two waterfalls and the spectacle of the notch itself, there are a number of short hiking trails to outcrops or ridges with excellent scenic views. For example, the Sanguinari Ridge Trail leads from the Flume Brook picnic area to a pinnacle 1 mile up the ridge. For more information,

Beaver

consult the *AMC White Mountain Guide,* or stop for a map at the information booth across from the Balsams (summer season only).

Historical Detour

For White Mountain waterfall seekers the trip to Beaver Brook Falls may seem a bit off the beaten path. This was literally true back around 1774, when Eleazer Rosebrook led his wife, Hannah, his two young daughters, and the family cow up the Connecticut River to settle in the Colebrook wilderness. Although a charter had been issued in 1770 to Sir George Colebrooke, chairman of the board of the British East India Company, no other settlements were to be found within 30 miles of Rosebrook's small log cabin.

A vivid portrait of the early settlers' isolated life at Colebrook is given by Rosebrook's granddaughter, Lucy Crawford, in her *History of the White Mountains.*

> Their living was principally upon animal food. . . . The woods were beautiful and well stored with game, such as moose, deer, bears, etc., and hunters might, in a short time, kill and procure a sufficient quantity of this kind of food to supply their families a long time.

Lucy Crawford describes how Rosebrook once had to walk all the way to Haverhill to procure a bushel of salt—a round-trip of 160 miles. But her greatest praise is reserved for Hannah Rosebrook: "What courage this woman must have possessed . . . changing relatives, friends, and neighbors for the woods!"

When the Revolutionary War was declared, Rosebrook moved his family down to Guildhall, Vermont, and went off to join the fight. Later, after his daughter Hannah married Abel Crawford, Rosebrook left his productive farm at Guildhall and once again took to the wilderness. This time he followed his pioneering son-in-law into the heart of the White Mountains, becoming one of the earliest and most prominent settlers in the vicinity of what later became Crawford Notch (see chapter 3).

Despite losing the Rosebrooks, Colebrook soon attracted other settlers with its vast forests and rich river-valley sediments. The town grew and prospered on a foundation of dairying and potato farming. At one time it was a major producer of potato starch, with as many as eight factories. The town also became a trading center after the road through Dixville Notch was cut in 1804, creating a land route from "Upper Coos" to Portland.

Undoubtedly the greatest drama in Colebrook history, however, was

ROBERT KOZLOW

Beaver Brook Falls

the log drive that choked the Connecticut River each spring from 1868 to 1915. During most of this period, the timberlands of the northern Connecticut River valley were monopolized by George Van Dyke, the most powerful of New Hampshire's often-vilified lumber kings. Van Dyke was known for his fondness of 160-proof "white wine," his unsavory business practices, and his motto: "Get out the logs"—often applied without regard for life or property. When he saw a worker fall into a logjam, Van Dyke would shout to the others, "To hell with the man. Save the cant dog!" (This was a stout hooked pole used to turn and control logs on the river.) And when his log drives destroyed farm buildings and railroad bridges, Van Dyke anticipated modern business practice by endlessly delaying compensation payments through legal maneuvers.

Once, thirty Colebrook farmers claimed compensation for crop damage caused by the log drive. Van Dyke met with the farmers "with a pistol on his desk" and declared, "I ain't goin' to pay a cent" (Poole, 1946). It took the farmers years to recover their losses through the courts.

If Van Dyke was fascinating, his rivermen were legendary. For a few weeks each spring, rains and melting snows would raise the north-country streams and rivers high enough to bear along the winter's accumulation of logs, which were stacked on landings along the banks. With their nail-studded calked boots, the rivermen didn't simply joyride the logs down the Connecticut. Much of their time was spent breaking mountainous logjams, dynamiting ice jams, anticipating and preventing jams, prying wayward logs off the banks or maneuvering them out of eddies, and generally cajoling the timber down the roaring river. In the process they spent long hours waist deep in ice water, "flirted with death a dozen times a day," and slept it off each night in soggy clothes and wet blankets. Their work required an incredible mix of agility, balance, strength, and judgment, as well as 7000 calories a day of pork and beans, pea soup, molasses, bread, cakes, and pies. By comparison cowboys practically had desk jobs.

A single log drive from the north country to Van Dyke's mill at Holyoke, Massachusetts, could float 50 million board feet of softwood logs past Colebrook, with timber blanketing as much as 100 miles of the Connecticut River. When paychecks were handed out at the end of the drive, many of the men would head for the river towns and go on wild, drunken sprees that often lasted for weeks. Some men would spend everything they had earned on drink and women in a matter of days. And many would leave with indelible souvenirs in the form of spike marks from getting stomped in riotous brawls. In towns such as Woodsville and North Stratford it is said that gentler citizens barred their doors while the woodsmen partied in high gear.

Much of this information about the log drives, including the unattributed quotations, comes from Robert Pike's absorbing book, *Tall Trees, Tough Men*. Pike's accounts of the rivermen add an aura of adventure to the otherwise tranquil scenery along the Connecticut River en route to Beaver Brook Falls.

The Basin

THE PEMIGEWASSET/ MERRIMACK WATERSHED

◆

CHAPTER 8

WELTON FALLS

———◆———

Location: On the Fowler River in Alexandria, just east of Cardigan State Park
Map: AMC Mount Cardigan Map (B-13)

Hiking Data
Distance: Parking area to falls, 1.2 miles
Altitude change: Minus 300 feet (to altitude 1100 feet)
Difficulty: Easy

———————————◆———————————

Admittedly, Welton Falls is not an official "White Mountain waterfall." As the raven flies, the falls are 10 miles south of the White Mountain National Forest. But it is far better to fudge the boundaries than to omit this "surpassing beauty"—as the falls are described in early editions of the *AMC White Mountain Guide*—on a geographical technicality.

The AMC Cardigan Lodge serves as home base for visiting Welton Falls. Set in a broad meadow in Shem Valley at the foot of Mount Cardigan, the year-round lodge also serves as a center for hiking, camping, snowshoeing, and cross-country skiing. Mount Cardigan, which has top billing for most visitors, is a hiker's dream. The mountain's broad, bare dome dominates the local topography. On clear days the summit view encompasses a panorama of sparkling lakes, waves of forested ridges, and a serrated skyline of high peaks to the north. The climb from the lodge is a moderate 1700-foot ascent with well-graded trails and excellent loop routes. (Pick up a map at the lodge.) The excursion is especially rewarding in August when the summit ridges host a carnival of fresh blueberries.

With an early start, a moderately ambitious hiker can reach both the mountaintop and the waterfall in a single day trip. The combined tour can be under 8 miles long, depending on the route. In hot weather it is best to schedule the climb in the cool morning hours, leaving the afternoon for sampling the fine pools below Welton Falls.

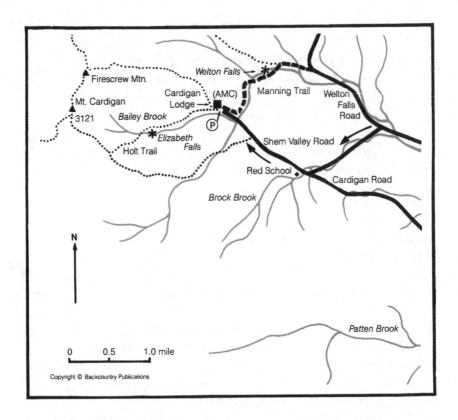

This chapter also describes Elizabeth Falls, which lies along the path up Mount Cardigan. Though it is not a major attraction, Elizabeth Falls is interesting enough to have a look at if you happen to be walking right by it anyway.

Access

The most challenging aspect of a visit to Welton Falls is negotiating the drive in to the lodge. Take NH 3A north from Bristol center for 2-plus miles to a left turn just past the large stone church at the southern tip of Newfound Lake. A road sign at the junction points to Wellington State Park. Call this junction mile 0.0. After skirting the overly developed lakeshore, once a favorite Indian haunt, continue straight (west) when the main road turns to the north at mile 1.9. Again continue straight (west) at a fork to the left (mile 3.1). You are now on Fowler River Road. At mile 6.3, watch for an unobtrusive AMC sign indicating a left turn onto a dirt road. Ascend this road to an old red schoolhouse at mile 7.5, where a final right turn takes you

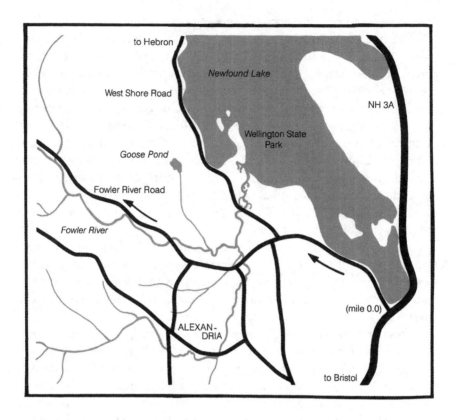

across a low ridge into Shem Valley and the AMC lodge (mile 9.0). Warning: The last 2.7 miles require careful driving when the road is muddy or icy.

The Trail

After pausing to admire the view of Mount Cardigan from the parking area, find the sign marking the Manning Trail to Welton Falls. The trail crosses the east lawn of the lodge toward a large cookout firepit and enters a grove of spruce, which conceals a number of campsites. After passing through the airy spruce stand, the path descends a small hill and swings left along a high shoulder above the west bank of the Fowler River from which you can see some small slides and pools. Clear yellow blazes mark the route, which contours through mostly hemlock forest with a dense understory of hobblebush. This broad-leaved straggly shrub bears pretty white flowers that develop into dark purplish fruits. Though the fruits are edible, I've found they taste awful—best left for the birds. Allegedly, the plant's name stems from its unpleasant way of blocking would-be buchwhackers . . . hobbling them.

The trail stays well above the river, where miniature potholes dimple colorful ledge shelves that border a narrow channel where the river's clear currents tumble over a series of tiny cascades. As seen from the trail, none of the riverbed clues presage the scene you will encounter farther downstream.

The trail continues parallel to the river, passing through stands of hemlock and young hardwood forest before descending to cross to the east bank of the river at just under 1 mile. After a stretch of fairly level hiking, the trail climbs over a low ridge to a large, rocky knob, where the river gathers speed and slides into a gorge on the left. At the knob the trail makes a sharp right turn, while a spur path continues onto a narrow shelf that leads to a small cave notched in the face of a cliff directly above the falls! Sturdy cable fencing offers comfort and protection.

The Manning Trail, meanwhile, circles the rim of a deep chasm across from the waterfall and descends to the mouth of the formation (mile 1.2). Beyond the waterfall the trail continues downstream a few hundred yards, where it fords the river and terminates at an abandoned extension of Fowler River Road.

This northern tail of the Manning Trail is unmarked, unmaintained, and circuitous. But for those who are not prone to getting lost, it provides a backdoor shortcut to Welton Falls. On the drive in, ignore the turn for the AMC lodge at mile 6.3 and bump along Fowler River Road another 1.2 miles to a sharp right turn up a hill. Here, an abandoned extension of the road runs straight into the woods. If your car has good clearance and the track is dry, you can drive in 100 yards and park just before a washed-out gully. Otherwise, park and walk from the road. About 100 yards beyond the washout a path on the left leads down to the Fowler River. Ignore this turn, and continue 20 more yards to a second left turn onto an old logging road. This is the Manning Trail, which soon fords the river and follows along the east bank to Welton Falls. By this back-door route the hike to the falls is 0.5 mile.

The Falls

To envision Welton Falls, start with a deep pool 40 feet long and 20 feet wide shaped like a wineskin, its rock-bound mouth narrow enough to jump across with only a touch of anxiety. Place the pool in a precipitous hollow with moss-covered cliffs rising 40 to 60 feet above the water. Line the rim of the hollow with a thick hemlock forest. Near the back of the ravine etch a narrow channel halfway down the cliff. Finally, send a river rushing through the channel and surging over the cliff in a foamy plume, stirring the pool to a slow swirl.

BRUCE AND DOREEN BOLNICK

Sunny slabs and pools downstream from Welton Falls

There are many vantage points for viewing Welton Falls. The most unusual is from a small cave in the face of the cliff directly above the falls. This is reached by the spur path mentioned in the trail description. Crouched in the cave with the back of your head scraping its dome, you feel like part of the landscape. From this point you have a clear view of the river sweeping around the base of the high knob and accelerating through a series of chutes and cascades to its dramatic plunge to the pool below.

More conventional views are obtained from the rim of the cliff across from the waterfall, and from the mouth of the ravine looking up to the falls.

Surely the most stimulating vantage point, however, is from the middle of the pool. This aquatic view is best appreciated in hot weather. With the waterfall facing east and the pool draining to the north, the ravine receives sunlight only in the late morning. The pool's deep water, therefore, never gets very warm.

For younger children and less adventurous swimmers, the Fowler River provides a long line of shallow, tranquil pools below the waterfall gorge. Farther downstream past the lower river crossing of Manning Trail you will find small, delightful cascades and splendid rock-lined pools. Because the river swings around to the east here, the broad ledges benefit fully from the warm midday sun.

A Waterfall Side Trip

If you hike up Mount Cardigan from the AMC lodge you will probably pass within a stone's throw of Elizabeth Falls. The popular Holt Trail crosses Bailey Brook immediately above the falls, an easy mile from the lodge. Being only 1000 feet below the forest fringe that encircles Cardigan's dome, Elizabeth Falls bears but a humble veil of water much of the year. The thin current spreads across dark slabs at the brow of a shady ravine and then separates into fine strands that dangle over 40 feet of cliff before regrouping in a wide pool at the base of the ravine. Let the summit wait a few minutes while you stop to rest, have a snack, and feel the quiet pulse of Elizabeth Falls.

One minor route complication merits attention. The Holt Trail follows a forest road for over 0.5 mile and then turns off to the right shortly before the road crosses Bailey Brook on a wooden bridge. If you happen to miss this right turn and reach the bridge, you have accidentally gotten onto the Alexandria Ski Trail. You can double back to the Holt Trail or simply continue up the south bank of the brook to rejoin the trail just above the falls. In the latter case, Elizabeth Falls will be in the ravine that drops away to your right as you are climbing.

Historical Detour

Although it is the southernmost of the major waterfalls of the White Mountain region, Welton Falls, ironically, was one of the last to catch the public eye. According to Bernard Shattuck, a town historian for Alexandria, local folk have enjoyed Welton Falls since shortly after the area was settled in 1769. In fact, the waterfall takes its name from a family that once owned a nearby farm. But as a tourist attraction the falls remained virtually unknown until after World War I—decades after the high peaks of the White Mountains had become familiar terrain for hikers and logging railroads had stripped the heart of the northern wilderness.

A rail branch reached the town of Bristol even before the Civil War, but neighboring Alexandria remained a quiet hill community of small farms and mica mines, off the beaten path for itinerant travel editors. Deep in Alexandria's backwoods, Welton Falls was uniformly overlooked in nineteenth-century guidebooks for tourists and hikers. By 1920, 2,000 acres of land around Mount Cardigan had already been acquired as state forest, and yet popular guidebooks said not a word about the waterfall.

Welton Falls finally entered the limelight in 1923 when the state obtained more than 100 acres of land to create the Welton Falls Reservation. A year later members of the AMC Merrimack Chapter built the Manning Trail from the Fowler River Road to the summit of Firescrew Mountain—named for a towering smoke spiral produced by the 1855 fire that bared the summit ledges. The first leg of the original Manning Trail was obliterated by timber operations after World War II.

The most significant development in the Mount Cardigan region occurred ten years later. Though the nation was mired in the misery of the Great Depression, interest in the novel sport of skiing was booming in New England. In a sense the economic trauma gave life to the new sport, since the Depression-born Civilian Conservation Corps (CCC) supplied the labor power for cutting the first ski trails.

True to its tradition of promoting mountain sports, the AMC was in the vanguard of the ski boom. In 1934 the club purchased over 500 acres of forest and abandoned farmland in Shem Valley (at under $2 an acre) to establish a ski center on Mount Cardigan. The purchase included a dilapidated farmhouse built before the Civil War—called the "old Shem Ackerman place," whence the name of the valley. Club volunteers set about converting the old farmhouse to "a modern ski lodge," as it was described in a *Manchester Union* article of January 11, 1935; the article is posted on the wall of the lodge.

Energetic club members promptly began building ski trails. In the words of the *Union* article, the result was "one of the most complete and satisfying winter sports centers in the state." The Cardigan Ski Reservation was such a hit that special trains were run from Boston to Canaan and Bristol. In those days a "complete and satisfying" ski center did not include a ski lift. Skiers were happy to ascend on foot. With the postwar advent of automatic lifts at commercial ski areas, the Cardigan Ski Reservation faded quickly from glory.

An article in *Appalachia* (Winter 1983–84) celebrating the fiftieth anniversary of Cardigan Lodge tells how the old Shem Ackerman place was occupied at the time of the AMC purchase by a bearded squatter, John Yegerman, and his old dog. Yegerman is described as a Latvian who had been imprisoned in Siberia and escaped by way of the Bering Strait to become a hermit in Shem Valley. To build the lodge the club had to evict Yegerman and his dog, who moved into a nearby shack—early victims of New Hampshire's ski-boom development.

CHAPTER 9

WATERVILLE CASCADES

◆

Location: Waterville Valley
Maps: AMC #2 Franconia-Pemigewasset Map (J-7); DeLorme Trail Map (L-7)

Hiking Data
Distance: Parking area to foot of falls, 1.2 miles
Altitude gain: 300 feet (to altitude 1800 feet)
Difficulty: Easy

◆

Try a quick word-association test: What is the first thing that comes to mind when you hear "Waterville Valley"? If you thought "skiing," you should be in good company. The valley's winter sports facilities are undoubtedly its best-known attraction today. One tourist leaflet sets the tone by discussing alpine skiing, ski touring, and snowmobiling before mentioning any summer recreation at all. But down the list in small print under the heading "hiking," careful readers will notice "short walks to spectacular cascades" as well as hikes to beautiful mountain ponds and several 4000-foot peaks.

Prior to the introduction of modern alpine skiing facilities, Waterville Valley was best known for its summer mountain scenery. The village was a small, secluded resort with one large inn and a handful of cottages set in the deep bowl formed by Mount Tripyramid to the east, Mounts Osceola and Kancamagus to the north, Mount Tecumseh to the west, and Sandwich Mountain to the south. Early guidebooks commended Waterville Valley to "true mountain connoisseurs."

Along with excellent fishing and splendid mountain views, the hike along Cascade Brook was always a favorite attraction. Turn-of-the-century postcards highlighted the cascades; their grainy photographs show that a wooden footbridge once spanned the ledges above the bottom cascade. Had the word-association game been played a hundred years ago, the response to "Waterville Valley" might well have been "cascades." Or perhaps "trout."

Access

To reach Waterville Valley turn off I-93 at exit 28 (Campton), and follow NH 49 for 11 miles up the valley of the Mad River. In the village the turns become a bit more confusing. Stay on NH 49 as it swings to the left past a golf course and then makes a sharp right turn (where a side road continues straight) before reaching a large parking area beside the foot of the Snow's Mountain ski lift. A large sign declares the lot to be the parking site for Cascade Path and the Norway Rapids Trail.

An alternative route into or out of the village is by the Tripoli Road (exit 31 off I-93). This gravel road climbs through Thornton Pass, between Mount Osceola and Mount Tecumseh, and descends into the village only a few yards south of the parking lot.

The Trail

The Cascade Path is maintained by the Waterville Valley Athletic & Improvement Association (WVAIA), which supports 22 miles of trails in the valley. The path begins at the north end of the parking lot. Initially the trail ascends a grassy ski slope before turning left into the woods. Don't take the first two turns into the woods, which are ski trails and usually roped off. The hiking trail cuts off the ski slope at a wooden sign for Cascade Brook above a blue hiking sign. Once the path enters the woods, intermittent yellow blazes painted on the trees mark the way.

At 0.5 mile from the parking lot the Elephant Rock Trail diverges to the right while Cascade Path continues straight on. The path contours around the flank of Snow's Mountain and then descends to a trail junction at Cascade Brook (mile 1.0). From this junction Cascade path turns right and follows up the west bank of the brook (the left turn crosses the river and leads to the Norway Rapids). Although you are heading upstream here, the path is not steep at all. Cascade Brook looks like a very ordinary forest stream for the first 0.2 mile, at which point the trail passes a lovely pool— the first hint of more interesting sights just ahead. At the base of the first cascade, the trail branches into the main Cascade Path, which crosses the river to follow its left (northeast) side, and the Cascade Path West Side.

Over the next 0.25 mile both paths climb more steeply up both sides of the brook past a nearly continuous string of beautiful cascade scenery, ending at a bridge where the Snow's Mountain service road crosses the brook (mile 1.5). Judging from the trampled soil, most hikers stay on the west bank. It is the official trail that provides better views of the upper cascades and better access to the remarkable pools.

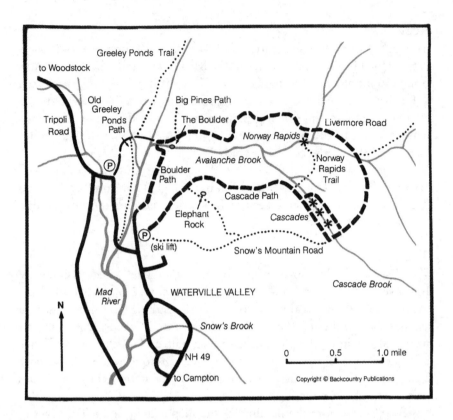

From the top of the cascades there are three ways to head for home. First, you can simply retrace your steps back along Cascade Path. Second, you can turn right above the cascades and follow the gravel road to the top of the Snow's Mountain ski lift. From there the ski slope descends directly to the parking lot at the trailhead. This route is shorter, only 2.5 miles for the circuit, and offers fine views across the valley from the top of the ski slope.

The third route is longer, but it complements the cascades with more brookside scenery. From the bridge above the top cascade, turn left and descend the Snow's Mountain service road for 0.6 mile to Livermore Road, which you will intercept just beyond a sturdy bridge over Avalanche Brook. (These "roads" are dirt tracks used primarily by hikers and skiers; vehicle traffic is very rare.) Head west (left) on Livermore Road, and watch for a Norway Rapids Trail sign on your left after 0.2 mile. A short detour over to the Norway Rapids is highly recommended.

After the detour, follow the gradual descent of Livermore Road for 1.3 miles. When Avalanche Brook next comes into sight on the left, take a side path down to see "the Boulder"—one of the most immense glacial erratics in the region. (If immensity strikes your fancy, you should also watch for the Big Pines path heading north off Livermore Road a few hundred yards before the Boulder turn. The name explains where this side path goes.)

If you can manage to wade across Avalanche Brook at the Boulder (a tricky proposition), you can pick up the Boulder Path on the south bank. This path provides a nearly straight 1-mile shot back to the parking lot, though be careful to stay on the path rather than the cross-country ski trails which join and leave this trail. Finishing by the Boulder Path, the complete circuit is a 4.5-mile hike. If you prefer to avoid fording Avalanche Brook at the Boulder, continue down Livermore Road 0.1 mile beyond the Mad River bridge. Then take the Old Greely Ponds path south toward town. At the paved road, two quick left turns will take you back to the parking lot. This option adds an extra quarter-mile to the loop hike.

The Cascades

Cascade Brook presents a visual symphony of variations on a theme. The theme is simple and appealing: pretty waterfall to a sparkling pool.

At the first cascade the brook sweeps through a high gate of heavily fractured bedrock (Norway quartz monzonite) and forms a cone of white-water as it falls over 25 feet to a dreamy pool on the floor of a shady glen. The formation is not large, but it is compellingly lovely. Thus the harmonious theme, *con grazia.*

The first two variations are small, delightful water chutes into rock-lined pools. Then comes a grand repetition of the first cascade; viewed from the west bank, the high waterfall silhouettes an overhanging profile sculpted in the rock. Just above, a wide sheet of water fans across a granite ramp and slides into a deep pothole pool. Altogether the orchestra of rock and water restates the theme eight times, ending with surging crescent cascade sluicing into a glimmering green pool. And at the end of the performance, you can replay your favorites simply by returning down the path.

Many of the deep, clear pools formed by the cascades would make wonderful swimming holes except that the brook's northeast exposure provides little direct sunlight. Moreover, most of the cascade basins have steep banks that make it difficult to reach the pools.

For water play, your best bet is to route your return trip past Norway Rapids, as outlined above. At the rapids, Avalanche Brook slides over more than 100 yards of smooth, sloping, colorful ledges, forming small chutes, plumes, and pools. Best of all, the ledges lie east to west, so they benefit fully from the midday sun. There is not really a waterfall, as such, at Norway Rapids, but on a warm summer day kids of all ages won't mind at all.

Historical Detour

A sculptor creating a statue honoring the founders of Waterville Valley might consider modeling two figures: Nathaniel Greeley and the brook trout. It was for fish and game that Indians from the lakes region and the Pemigewasset valley made excursions into the valley. The "brooks prolific in trout" also played a major role in the development of tourism. One early guidebook goes so far as to say that the valley "might have remained obscure and unknown until doomsday, had not a few anglers stumbled upon it while in pursuit of brooks and waters new" (Drake, 1881). The very name of the valley highlights the significance of the mountain streams.

In some White Mountain townships fishing was a primary source of food for the early settlers. A single spring day out on a mountain brook could yield literally hundreds of trout as well as a crop of Atlantic salmon. By drying the spring catch, Indians and settlers could accumulate enough cured provisions to last through the hungry winter—at least in a good year.

It is said that in precolonial days, the salmon runs down on the Merrimack River had the appearance of a solid mass of fish. Indians even told of walking across Salmon Falls in the southern part of the state on the backs of the ascending salmon. By 1850, though, downstream dams eliminated the Atlantic salmon from the Pemigewasset watershed altogether. After the Civil War efforts were made to modify the dams in order to restore the salmon, but overfishing, new dams, and the modern scourge of pollution again killed off the species.

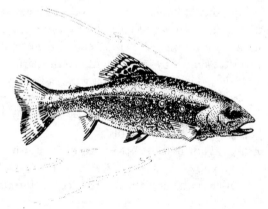

Brook Trout

Waterville Cascades

Since 1969, a group of federal and state agencies has worked to reestablish the Atlantic salmon in the Merrimack River system (as well as the Connecticut River). The Mad River is one beneficiary. In addition, the New Hampshire Fish and Game Department has been replenishing the Mad River system with trout stock since 1939. The stocking programs include rainbow trout and brown trout, but the eastern brook trout is the only species native to the cold White Mountain streams, where it rarely grows to even six inches in length.

And then there is Nathaniel Greeley, the most successful of the early settlers who tried carving farms out of the valley wilderness beginning in 1820. Considering the terrain, it is not surprising that most of these efforts failed. According to Anderson and Morse (1930), the town had only 20 acres of cleared land in 1831, when seventeen poll taxes were assessed. By 1833, the year Greeley began lodging boarders, the population was down to just six.

Eventually Greeley acquired all of the cleared land in the valley. In 1865 he opened an inn, which for many years was called Greeley's Summer Boarding-House, or simply Greeley's. A handful of cottages was added shortly thereafter, and a system of trails was developed, including the path to the cascades. This path was also the first leg of the original trail up Mount Tripyramid, the area's greatest marvel. Writing about it in 1881, Samuel Adams Drake was struck silly with awe: "Hail to thee, mountain of the high heroic crest. . . . None approach thy forest courts but do thee homage." Great landslides on Mount Tripyramid in 1869 and 1885 (hence the name Avalanche Brook) added to its renown.

The Cascade Path also connected Waterville Valley to the original Livermore Road when it opened in 1879, providing a direct bridle path from the valley to Mount Washington. An earlier Waterville-to-Crawfords path through Mad River Notch, cut in 1860, had been much more circuitous.

During Greeley's stewardship there was no problem of overdevelopment in Waterville Valley. The tourist facilities remained modest in scale, as Campton, not Waterville, received most of the traffic, most of the attention of the landscape painters and poets, and most of the ink in the tourist guides. Greeley's was considered a resort for fishermen and for those who sought "seclusion and fine mountain scenery" rather than the comforts of a grand hotel.

Greeley was succeeded by Silas Elliot (the inn was called Elliot's Hotel for many years) and then by an association of guests who bought the property at the end of World War I. Throughout this era, development of Waterville Valley was evidently dominated by the philosophy of small is beautiful. From 1880 to 1930 the town's population merely swapped digits from 32 to 23 people, although a few new cottages were added to the village street map. Though much of the valley fell into the hands of timber interests, no logging railroads ever penetrated into the valley. The forests were still in healthy shape in 1928 when the government bought nearly 23,000 acres from the Woodstock Lumber Company for inclusion in the White Mountain National Forest. Not long thereafter the first ski slopes were cut to add a winter season to the mountain resort. The seeds of the modern Waterville Valley had been planted.

The end of the era might be dated, however, to the late 1960s when modern alpine skiing blossomed, the grand Waterville Inn burned down, and the first condominiums were built in the village. Since then the valley has developed rapidly. But with the national forest owning most of the land in the township, Waterville Valley should still be a lure for the "true mountain connoisseurs" of future generations.

CHAPTER 10

GEORGIANA FALLS

◆

Location: Just below the Indian Head Profile, south of Franconia Notch
Maps: AMC #2 Franconia-Pemigewasset (J-4); DeLorme Trail Map (H-4)

Hiking Data

Distance: Parking area to Lower Georgiana Falls, 0.8 mile; to Upper Georgiana
   (Harvard) Falls, 1.3 miles
Altitude gain: 600 feet (to altitude 1600 feet)
Difficulty: Moderate

◆

Visitors to Georgiana Falls face an unusual problem: locating the falls! The difficulty stems from the fact that different sources provide conflicting accounts about which of the waterfalls gracing the steep ledges along Harvard Brook is the real Georgiana. The twenty-fifth edition of the *AMC White Mountain Guide* pins the label on the lower cascades, while using the name Harvard Falls for the uppermost drop. But the book's map, like most maps, locates Georgiana at the top of the ledges. Thomas Starr King's 1859 description ("One of the grandest cascades of the mountain region ... making two leaps of eighty feet each, one right after the other") is a clear but exaggerated reference to the upper set of falls. Then again, the 1922 AMC guide refers to both the lower and upper cascades as Georgiana Falls, while acknowledging that the latter is "sometimes known as Harvard Fall." Curiously, though, the 1922 map labels only the *bottom* as Georgiana. The 1998 AMC guide (the twenty-sixth edition) applies the Georgiana/Harvard names, while admitting that it may be more historically appropriate to call them the Upper and Lower Georgiana Falls.

   An authoritative description by M. Isabella Stone in an early issue of *Appalachia* (Volume IV, 1885) indicates the genuine Georgiana Falls as the precipitous cascade at the top of the long ramp of ledge; the name Harvard Cascade was given to a beautiful small waterfall 0.2 mile farther

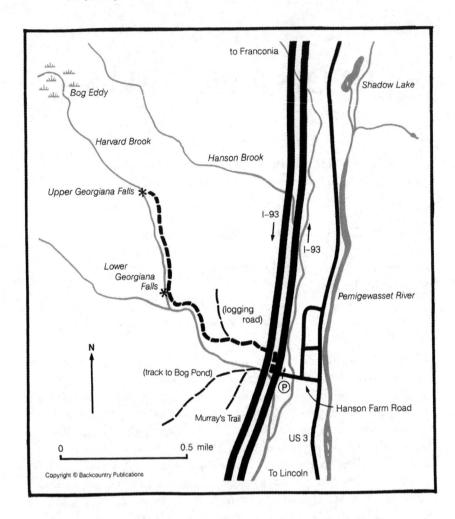

Copyright © Backcountry Publications

up Harvard Brook. For clarity, the bottom section of the brook's rapid descent will be referred to here as Lower Georgiana Falls.

Although labels have been applied inconsistently during the past century of maps and trails descriptions, there is no confusion about what you should see on your hike: You should explore the whole stretch of cascades. However, Upper Georgiana Falls proper is certainly the highlight of the trip.

Access

To begin the hike to Georgiana Falls you must first find Hanson Farm Road, which turns off the west side of US 3 in North Lincoln, across from the

Longhorn Restaurant. For orientation, the location is between exit 33 on Interstate 93 and exit 1 (for the Flume) on the Franconia Notch Parkway. Northbound drivers on I-93 can get a wide-angle preview of Georgiana Falls—a narrow white ribbon splitting a verdant expanse of undulating hillside—by scanning the ravines south of the Indian Head cliff from the top of the long hill above exit 32 (one exit south of North Lincoln).

The Trail

The first path to Georgiana Falls was cleared in 1877. Earlier in the present century the Forest Service maintained the Bog Pond Trail past Georgiana Falls. Today no official trail is maintained, but a good footpath still climbs alongside Harvard Brook up to the falls. The footpath starts at an unmarked gravel parking area at the end of Hanson Farm Road, 0.1 mile west of US 3. Walk through the gate in the chain-link fence on the west side of the parking area, and follow dirt logging road through a pair of tunnels under I-93, passing a side trail on the left, Murray's Trail. About 0.3 mile beyond the highway and 100 yards after crossing a metal culvert, you will reach a small grassy clearing where the path cuts into the woods on the left. Watch carefully because the turn here is easy to miss. (The logging road continues climbing up to the right.) From this point blazes mark the way, though there seems to be a mix of yellow, red, and orange blazes.

Once off the logging road, you will find that the scenery changes to a pretty forest with tumbling brook. The path is quite easy to follow as it parallels Harvard Brook upstream for 0.3 mile through a mixed company of trees. Soon you arrive at the base of an open gray ledge encrusted with lichen and moss. The path climbs one flight of blazed rocks past some small introductory cascades to a broad shelf at the foot of Lower Georgiana Falls.

According to a local fisherman who passed us on his way to Bog Pond to try his luck on the brown trout, most visitors stop at this point and turn back, not realizing that the main waterfall is higher up the trail. According to the old *Appalachia* article, hikers were making the same mistake a century ago!

Above the pool the blazed trail steepens considerably as it ascends through the woods to the right of the brook, with obstructed views. In this stretch, the trail deteriorates to a network of paths. Don't worry too much about staying on the correct one, as they all follow closely up the stream to reach the Upper Falls. As an alternative to following the trail, you can climb right up the ledges (if they are dry) to enjoy the line of cascades that runs nearly 0.5 mile from the bottom pool to the cliffs at Georgiana Falls. The last leg of this climb, however, is too sheer to negotiate without rejoining the footpath, which itself has some tricky footing. After maneuvering up a steep, wooded slope, the path emerges atop a bluff that faces directly into the midsection of the main waterfall.

The trail continues a short distance further, descending a small gully and then mounting the corner of a cliff to reach the rock slabs above the falls. Beyond this point, Harvard Brook flattens out on broad ledges punctuated by several smaller cascades and pools. A rough informal path, often marked with moose tracks, continues along the north side of the brook for half a mile to a lovely marsh called Bog Eddy. Anyone venturing another 1.25 mucky miles and 500 vertical feet up Harvard Brook will reach Bog Pond, a remote crystal lake at the foot of the Kinsman Ridge. This idyllic wilderness scene is best viewed from the Kinsman Ridge Trail, below Eliza Brook Shelter. About half a mile below Bog Pond, Harvard Brook tumbles through a lattice of cascades formerly called the Upper Falls. Under present conditions, this cannot be reached without great difficulty.

In *Walks and Climbs in the White Mountains* (1926), Karl Harrington devoted a full chapter to describing in great detail the entire hike up Harvard Brook, despite the fact that his photos show hardly a trickle of water at the Upper Falls! One is tempted to agree with Isabella Stone that "few visitors would care to go so far."

The Falls

Lower Georgiana Falls consists of a sheet of cascades draped across a wide ledge 30 feet high. Near the bottom of the cascade a large cleft boulder stands sentry above a tea-colored pool that is cupped in a broad shelf of bedrock. The rock here was described a century ago by Professor Huntington, the state geologist, as a breccia of gneiss, hornblende, and other silicates cemented by a light feldspar paste. Translated, this means that the tough ledge rock is embedded with a fascinating variety of minerals. It is also a very inviting ledge for brookside scrambling, and its sunny southeastern exposure creates a pleasant environment for a waterfall picnic.

Ascending the ledge one flight up from the bottom pool, you can see the brook gush through a chute that undercuts a bank of ledge before sliding into a second fine pool. Farther on, the waters have etched a narrow channel down the base of a large, steep slab. As you climb higher, the hemlock forest closes in more tightly on the ledge. Soon you reach a small, boulder-strewn pool at the foot of another narrow cascade. High above, a slender reed of whitewater angles across the dark forest backdrop. This is Georgiana Falls, from afar.

Farther up at the bluff you will be gazing straight into the heart of the falls with a full frontal view. The brook slides directly toward you over a sloping ledge before plunging down a sheer cliff into a deep, narrow chasm at your feet. Down in the confined basin the turbulent waters make a sharp right turn and embark on their long descent to the bottom pool. Beyond the bluff the footpath drops into a gully before climbing the corner to the top of the cliff. The gully offers an altogether different perspective on the waterfall: a close-up side view looking down the narrow basin and out across the Pemigewasset valley to the south.

The flat stretch of brook above Georgiana Falls is quite safe to explore, but the precipitous formation itself is not a good place for sporting. It is instead a visual and spiritual playground, offering the rugged geometry of rock and brook, the complex dynamics of the falls, and the tranquil valley panorama beyond.

When the brook runs high, Georgiana Falls is quite a spectacle, with powerful currents surging across the full face of the steep cliffs. Viewing the falls from the bluff at such times, one can almost imagine how a small fish must feel looking into the baleen of an approaching whale's jaw. When the brook is low, the falls are less commanding, but then there are better opportunities for exploring the ledges above and below.

Historical Detour

Georgiana Falls lies under the watchful gaze of the Indian Head on Mount Pemigewasset. Down in the valley, its waters swell the river bearing that same ancient Indian name. Like the exact location of Georgiana Falls, the name Pemigewasset (pronounced with a soft "g") is attributed to different origins in different books. Some sources claim that the name comes from an Indian tribe that lived near what is now Plymouth before fleeing to Canada following a massacre in 1712. Others recount the legend of a great chief, whose very profile is carved in the Indian Head cliff on the nearby mountain that now bears his name. According to the legend Chief Pemigewasset used the top of this mountain as a lookout to watch for campfires of marauding Algonquins. In one version of the folktale, the chief died on the mountaintop one frigid winter while watching for his wife to return from a visit to her Mohawk homeland.

In more serious reference books, though, one finds no mention of Chief Pemigewasset, and the local Indian subtribe seems to have been named after the river rather than the other way around. The river, it seems, derives its colorful name from an Abenaki Indian word that simply means "swift, extended current" or "extensive rapids."

ROBERT KOZLOW

Lower Georgiana Falls

As for Georgiana itself, the source of the name is quite obscure. Might it have been intended as a feminized tribute to our first president? Thomas Starr King (1859) merely lamented that the name was not very appropriate for such a grand cascade. Moses Sweetser's usually informative guidebook, *The White Mountains: Handbook for Travellers* (1887) is no more helpful and indeed fuels confusion about what is Georgiana and what is Harvard Falls.

In his description of Georgiana Falls, Sweetser noted, "The Falls have been visited very rarely for several years past, on account of their secluded position." The "position" was not to remain secluded much longer. Even as Sweetser was writing, George B. James, of Roxbury, Massachusetts, was in the process of consolidating land holdings in order to sell large parcels to the loggers. According to C. Francis Belcher (1980), George James was a self-proclaimed conservationist whose shocking strong-arm tactics in acquiring timberlands earned him the title of "Vampire of the White Mountains," among other epithets.

In 1896 the Boston and Maine Railroad was authorized to run a branch line from North Woodstock to a sawmill at Whitehouse Brook near the Flume. This indicates that logging operations had by that time penetrated into Franconia Notch. In 1904, George L. Johnson established a sawmill and a bustling company town (named Johnson) nearly at the base of the present trail to Georgiana Falls. Johnson's crews quickly stripped the timber in the surrounding territory, sparing only the trees that framed the Indian Head. In 1907, after securing a ten-year contact to timber rights farther south, Johnson built the Gordon Pond Railroad to haul logs from the flanks of Kinsman Mountain. The trackbed ran right across the lower section of Georgiana Falls.

This railroad shut down in 1916, and the town of Johnson soon disappeared. Logging around Georgiana Falls continued many years thereafter but without the wholesale destruction wrought by the earlier operations. In 1983 the property around the falls was purchased by the State of New Hampshire, as part of the land acquisition for the Franconia Notch Parkway project.

Today, the resurgence of moose and beaver populations in the headlands above Georgiana Falls testify that the forests are regaining their health. Old Chief Pemigewasset must be pleased to gaze once again across verdant ridges rather than scrub and slash. One wonders, though, what his impression might be of the sprawling commercial developments in the valley below.

CHAPTER 11

THE FLUME-POOL LOOP

◆

Location: Franconia Notch
Maps: AMC #2 Franconia-Pemigewasset Map (H-4); DeLorme Trail Map
  (G/H-4)

Hiking Data

Distance: Parking area to Avalanche Falls, 0.8 mile; to Liberty Gorge Cascade,
  1.4 miles; to The Pool, 1.5 miles; round-trip, 2.1 miles. (Subtract 0.5 mile
  from each figure if you take the shuttle bus to Boulder Cabin.)
Altitude gain: 250 feet from covered bridge (low point) to Avalanche Falls
  (altitude 1500 feet)
Difficulty: Easy (particularly with shuttle bus to Boulder Cabin)

◆

"This natural curiosity fills the beholder with amazement and admiration."
So Lucy Crawford, in her *History of the White Mountains,* reacted to the
Flume. Ever since its discovery in 1808, the Flume has been a favorite tourist
stopover. It has been celebrated by writers, artists, poets, photographers, post-
card companies, and tour operators.

Flume formations are actually fairly commonplace in the White Mountains. Among the better known are those in Dixville Notch, at Sabbaday
Falls, and on Kedron Brook in Crawford Notch. In geological terms a flume
is formed from a narrow band, or dike, of softer rock, such as basalt, that has
plugged a fissure in harder bedrock. When exposed to running water, the
dike erodes much more rapidly than the surrounding bedrock. The result is
a narrow, sheer gorge that is gradually widened by frost action. The Flume
in Franconia Notch, therefore, is not really a curiosity. What accounts for
its notoriety is its size: 800 feet long and 12 to 20 feet wide, with vertical
walls 7 to 9 stories high.

Since the Flume gets so much publicity in its own right there is no need
to discuss it at length in a book on waterfalls. There is a need, however, to

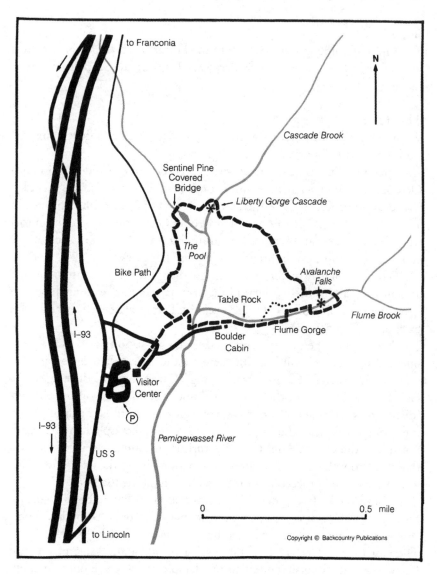

tell about the three fine falls that lie along a pleasant loop hike, which just happens to pass through the Flume. It should be noted that these waterfall attractions are for spectators rather than explorers. The trail leads to overlooks offering excellent views, but off-trail recreational adventures are not permitted here due to the heavy tourist use of the area.

Access

The Flume-Pool loop trail starts from the Flume Visitors Center, which is reached off exit 1 of the Notch Parkway (I-93) or by US 3 from North Lincoln.

The Trail

From the vast parking area there are three ways to get to Boulder Cabin, 500 yards below the Flume.

First, when the state-operated visitors center is open (mid-May to mid-October, 9 to 5:30) a 0.5-mile shuttle bus ride to Boulder Cabin is included in the entrance fee. In 1998 the entrance fee was $7—up from 25 cents in 1938 (children ages 6 to 12 are $4, and under 6 are free). In addition to a ticket booth, the visitors center has information exhibits, a gift shop, a cafeteria, and a short film on Franconia Notch State Park.

Second, you may prefer to leg it rather than ride the bus. Just follow the asphalt footpath to the left behind the visitors center. Continue down the gravel path to the covered bridge over the Pemigewasset River and then back up to Boulder Cabin.

Third, when the visitors center is closed—off-season or off-hours—the hike is a bit more circuitous. But these are the times when the area is less crowded and therefore especially engaging. (Offsetting this advantage is the fact that the boardwalk through the Flume is dismantled during the off-season and barricaded off hours, so you can't see quite as much of the famous gorge.) Park at the highest lot and follow the asphalt bicycle path north into the woods. After 0.1 mile, turn right onto a paved service road that runs from the Liberty Springs Trail parking lot to the back of the visitors center. Then proceed to Boulder Cabin along the footpath.

From Boulder Cabin the trail ascends sharply to Flume Brook, which it follows for a short distance upstream before crossing on a footbridge. Flume Brook at this point offers a splendid bonus attraction known as Table Rock. The glistening waters slip smoothly over a broad, sunny ledge of polished Conway granite: a total contrast to the damp, narrow gorge only yards upstream. Access to the steeper part of the ledge is restricted by a wooden rail fence.

Past the footbridge the trail splits. The fork to the right leads into the mouth of the Flume gorge. The fork to the left is the usual descent route from the head of the Flume. But when the Flume boardwalk is closed, take the left-hand fork to the head of the gorge for views of Avalanche Falls. It might be tempting in the off-season to scramble up the gorge without benefit of the boardwalk. This is quite unsafe, though, because the rocks are slippery when wet and extremely treacherous when iced. Indeed, in the winter fully equipped ice climbers can occasionally be found practicing technical moves on the tremendous icicles that drape the vertical walls of the gorge.

The boardwalk into the Flume traverses the length of the gorge to the foot of Avalanche Falls, where a ramp climbs to the outlet at the head of the falls. En route to Avalanche Falls the walkway passes two very pretty small cascades at the narrowest part of the gorge. From the steps at this point you can see a band of dark basalt in the gorge wall to the left.

At the top end of the Flume there is an interesting cave, which is guarded by jack-in-the-pulpits during the late spring. A wooden shelter provides a rest stop for weary visitors, and toilets are located behind the shelter. As you begin to descend from the shelter, you will confront another fork in the trail. The path to the left returns to the bottom of the Flume and Boulder Cabin, while the wide dirt trail heading straight into the woods ahead is the loop trail to the Pool.

This trail contours around the side of a long ridge and then drops gently through a fine hardwood forest. The large trees include stately white ash, which can be recognized by their compound leaves and deeply furrowed bark. In the spring the forest floor is dotted with wildflowers, highlighted by bright white hobblebush bouquets. In the summer, thrushes, robins, and chickadees fill the air with gay song. After just over 0. 5 mile the trail crosses a stream and reaches a gravel path on the left, which leads down a set of steps to the overlook at Liberty Gorge Cascade.

Continuing along the main trail, you quickly reach a second set of steps on the left. These descend to a sturdily railed viewing platform perched atop a 130-foot-high cliff that forms the northeastern wall of the Pool. The trail then drops and curls around to cross the Sentinel Pine Bridge, a picturesque span over a gorge cut by the Pemigewasset as it cascades into the Pool. The bridge takes its name from a 175-foot-tall white pine that towered above the gorge until falling victim to the hurricane of 1938. This pine now forms the main beam for the bridge.

Across on the southwestern rim of the gorge, a side path leads down to another railed platform with picture-perfect views across the Pool to the high wall of cliffs and the cascades beneath the Sentinel Pine Bridge.

To finish the loop just follow the main trail over a small ridge and back to the visitors center (or to the parking lot, off-season). This final leg of the hike features a garden of massive boulders called glacial erratics. These boulders were plucked off mountains and transported south by passing glaciers, then deposited at their present location when the ice sheets melted away.

The Falls

Avalanche Falls, once called Flume Cascade, is located at the head of the Flume. It is not a waterfall giant, but the setting is hard to beat. Flume Brook emerges from the woods on the hillside, dashes across bare slabs of smooth Conway granite, and plunges over the lip of the gorge. When the stream is low, the waters tumble steeply down large granite steps into an alcove carved in the side of the gorge, and then leap to the bottom of the Flume. When the stream is running high the water surges over the edge in a single 45-foot drop. Viewed from alongside, on the ramp that leads out of the gorge, the falls form a sparkling mare's tail, with soft rainbows afloat in the spray.

In early winter or early spring, when the gorge is bedecked with ice, Avalanche Falls can be unusually beautiful. (Only tremendous self-restraint prevents us from calling it "gorgeous.") Frozen spray builds up to form a rippled translucent mask for the falling water. Ice and snow linger well into May in a deep cave just above the falls. The cave is formed by the collapsed wall of what was once an extension of the gorge. In the roof at the back of the cave there is a secret exit just large enough for kids to climb through.

Liberty Gorge Cascade is generally overshadowed by its famous neighbors along the loop trail. Compared to the falls at the Flume and the Pool, the Liberty Gorge Cascade lacks drama. But this is easily the highest of the falls. The stairs from the trail lead to a railing set on a bluff halfway down a steep ravine. Across the ravine the cascades sweep in a long, arching chute down a steep cut of bedrock, framed with spruce, yellow birch, and hemlock trees. At the base of the long rock slab the waters fan out to form a broad sash that drops into a crystal pool. Below, the stream continues its steep tumble down the heart of the ravine. Unhappily there is not much to do at Liberty Gorge Cascade other than spend a few minutes admiring the scene from the viewing rail.

The Pool is not itself a waterfall. Rather, like the Flume, it is the name for a grandly impressive formation, with cascades at the upper end. Whereas the Flume is long and confining, the Pool is an enormous basin—150 feet in diameter, 40 feet deep, under granite walls 13 stories high. And whereas everyone expects to be impressed by the Flume, the Pool generally comes as a very pleasant surprise. As one young girl shrieked at first sight of the Pool, "Whoooo! That's beautiful!"

The best views of the cascades are from the middle of the breezy Sentinel Pine Bridge, from the trail on the side path just past the bridge, and from the viewing rail at the end of this side path. Seen across the waters of the Pool from a high viewing rail, the cascades may appear rather insig-

ROBERT KOZLOW

Avalanche Falls

nificant. But the ring of turbulent foam they stir up in the Pool suggests that the cascades would be impressive closer up, especially when the Pemigewasset River is running high. From 1853 to 1887 an eccentric country philosopher named "Professor" John Merrill earned a living operating a rowboat in the Pool, providing summer visitors with a close-up view of these cascades. Today visitors are essentially confined to sightseeing from various high perches.

Another effect of being high above the Pool, across from the cascades, is that their song is strangely muffled. John Anderson and Stearns Morse (1930) described the feeling: "It seems oppressively quiet, in spite of the noise of the water, as if some secret wood cult kept here a shrine of silence."

Historical Detour

"How wild the spot is!" exclaimed Thomas Starr King of the Flume, in his book *The White Hills*, published in 1859. Even then the statement was not meant in a literal sense. The Flume House, a hundred-room resort hotel, had been built in 1848 not far from the site occupied by the visitors center today. In fact, King went on to caution his readers that the best time for a visit was in the early morning or the evening, "in order to be able to see the Flume without the large parties."

The Flume was discovered about 1808 by 93-year-old Jessie Guernsey, who reportedly came upon the gorge while fishing up the brook from her pioneer homestead a mile south. At the Guernsey farm was a blockhouse where settlers reportedly fended off a fierce attack by Abenaki Indians from Canada, who allegedly had been incited by the British during the War of 1812. (Solon Colby, in his *Indian History*, denies that any Indian attacks occurred in New Hampshire during that war.) With construction of the road through the Notch—the bridge below Boulder Cabin dates back to 1820—the Flume and the Old Man Profile quickly became major attractions for nature-loving travelers and curiosity seekers.

Surprisingly, the geological formation seen by early visitors to the Flume differed rather dramatically from what we see today. Most notably, an enormous boulder was wedged between the narrow walls of the Flume until it was washed away by tremendous flood on June 20, 1883. Visitors walking along the crude plank predecessor to today's boardwalk would shudder as they passed directly under the massive boulder. The same storm cleaned out ages of accumulated rubble. This made the gorge longer and deeper—and gave birth to both Avalanche Falls and Table Rock. Even now the geology is visibly dynamic: Visitors in the spring can see fresh flakes of granite lying on top of last fall's leaves.

The original Flume House burned down in 1870 but was replaced in 1872 with an even grander hotel. The latter, in turn, burned down in 1918. It was replaced by a restaurant, then a tourist center. The contemporary visitors center was built as part of the Notch Parkway project in 1986.

CHAPTER 12

THE BASIN-CASCADES TRAIL

◆

Location: Franconia Notch
Maps: AMC #2 Franconia-Pemigewasset Map (H-4); DeLorme Trail Map (G-4)

Hiking Data

Distance: Parking area to the Basin; 0.1 mile, to the Cascades, 0.2 mile; to Kinsman Falls, 0.5 mile; to Rocky Glen Falls, 1.1 miles
Altitude gain: 600 feet to Rocky Glen Falls (altitude 2000 feet)
Difficulty: Easy to Kinsman Falls; moderate thereafter

◆

If there were a delight meter for measuring the splendor of waterfalls, its reading for the Basin would be surprisingly low, considering the spot's great popularity. This large pothole pool set in a riverbed sculpture of polished Conway granite is a fascinating natural feature, to be sure, but not much of a waterfall. Most visitors gaze at the swirling currents for a few minutes, snap a photo, and then tramp back to their cars. Adventurers who leave the crowds behind and forge up the Basin-Cascades Trail, however, quickly find their delight meter swinging high into the "lovely" zone. Dr. William Prime, who was known as America's Izaak Walton for his popular nineteenth-century book *I Go A-Fishing,* called Cascade Brook "the finest brook in America for scenery as well as for trout."

Cascade Brook is a delight not only in terms of lovely views. The cascades and waterfalls that extend for a mile along the brook are also great fun to explore, offering a mixture of broad ledges, cool glens, and tempting pools. If you bring any rambunctious kids along, it will be hard to hold them back! They'll find the urge to scamper up the ledges nearly irresistible. And on a warm summer day they might "accidentally" get pretty wet investigating the clear pools.

A visit to the falls can be combined with a hike to Lonesome Lake, which occupies a picturesque basin beneath the high bluffs of Cannon Mountain, 1000 feet above the floor of Franconia Notch. Best of all would be to combine the waterfall hike with an overnight stay at the Lonesome Lake AMC hut. The hut offers visitors hearty home cooking, fine hospitality, and a perfect view of evening alpenglow shimmering on the cliffs of Franconia Ridge across the notch.

Access

Both lanes of the Notch Parkway (I-93) have large, well-marked exits to parking for the Basin. Heading north, you will reach the turn-off 1.5 miles past the Flume.

The Trail

A footpath passes through a tunnel under the parkway and then follows the Pemigewasset River—here just a sparkling stream—a short distance upstream. Cross the footbridge to the west bank for the best view of the Basin and access to the trailhead.

Driving southbound, you will find the turn-off 1.5 miles below Lafayette Campground. The walk in from this direction is more interesting, as the Pemi here exhibits a fine collection of scoured granite molds—the best being the Basin itself. An asphalt path along the east bank of the river provides access to the Basin for handicapped persons. For the best view, though, cross the first footbridge and continue along the west bank path to the Basin. Anyone camping at Lafayette Campground can hike along the river all the way to the Basin, via the Pemi Trail.

After visiting the Basin, follow the path across the footbridge behind the viewing deck, past an information sign about the mammals of Franconia Notch. Dogleg to the right along the clearly marked pathway. Only about 50 yards from the Basin you will reach a large sign identifying the Basin-Cascades trailhead.

Very quickly after you start up the trail the lower ledges of Cascade Brook appear off to the left. Smooth granite slabs slope hundreds of yards upstream, bedecked with an assortment of cascades. The ledges can be reached from the trail almost anywhere along this stretch. In fact, it is most enjoyable to leave the trail altogether and scramble up the sloping streambed or the woods immediately alongside. Since the trail parallels the cascades, meeting the ledge at a number of points, you won't get lost.

Immediately above the ledges Cascade Brook becomes a boulder-

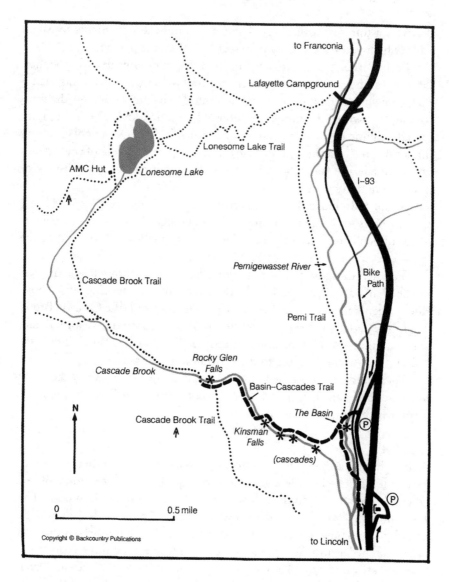

strewn mountain stream. The trail here slants into the woods and mounts the side of a ridge above the north bank of the brook, climbing steadily. At 0.4 mile from the trailhead an unmarked side path leads down to Kinsman Falls, which can't be seen until you reach the bottom of the ravine. Slightly farther up the main trail another side path runs to the top of the falls. Soon thereafter the trail fords to the south bank of the brook at the base of a pretty, but unremarkable gorge. Here, a sign misleadingly marks Kinsman Falls (which you have already passed at least 0.1 mile below).

Beyond the stream crossing the trail becomes considerably rougher. Footing can be tricky in spots where the trail passes over slick roots, damp rocks, small side streams, or stretches of mud. To compensate for the poor footing, you will find a running exhibit of brook treasures. There is a pretty cascade spilling over a steep granite wall into a shady gorge; a pool glittering like a tiny green starburst; a pothole tub serviced by a shower of cold stream water. Beside the trail, the damp forest floor puts on its own display of mushrooms and mosses.

At 0.4 mile above the stream crossing a Forest Service sign nailed to a spruce points to Rocky Glen Falls. This is one sign that is hardly needed. It is not difficult to discern the identity of the formation to the right of the trail—a rocky glen split by a beautiful set of falls.

To reach the ledge platform to the falls, climb up through a damp cleft in the glen wall off to the left, being careful of slick footing. Just above Rocky Glen Falls the Basin-Cascades Trail merges with the Cascade Brook Trail. The latter proceeds across the brook and continues at a moderate grade another 1.4 miles to Lonesome Lake. The Cascade Brook Trail also links up with routes leading to the surrounding summits.

For a moderate 5.4-mile loop, you can hike up to the lake by the route just described and then descend by the Lonesome Lake Trail to the Pemi Trail, which returns to the Basin.

The Falls

Although the Basin is only a minor-league waterfall, it shouldn't be missed. Here the crystal-clear Pemigewasset—old guidebooks were fond of the adjective "pellucid"—funnels down a narrow chute into a deep pool. The force and angle of the cascade incessantly stir the pool's cold jade waters, creating a sweeping whirlpool that has undercut a granite shelf to form an elegant arched grotto. Watching the current revolve around the Basin pool, you can easily understand how waterborne sand and stones could carve such potholes in the solid granite bedrock. Geologists estimate that the Basin has been formed during the past 25,000 years, with most of the cutting being done as the retreating ice cap swelled the Pemi with grit-laden meltwater.

Whereas the Basin is for viewing, the cascades are for playing. For the price of a very short hike you get lovely, sunny ledges that have been bared by the stream and then scalloped, grooved, beveled, and polished by thousands of years of freshets. Near the base of the formation the stream is con-

A section of the Cascade Brook's ledges

fined to a narrow channel along the left edge of the ledge (except when the water is high). Here the rock is smooth and level enough that even a toddler (under close supervision) can have a safe romp in dry conditions.

Scrambling up and over a granite hump, you will find pretty waterslides and small, shallow pools dotting the long, sloped cut of rockbed. Higher, the views across the notch improve as the rock becomes more angular and ornamented with lacy cascades. Altogether there are more than a half-dozen distinct levels of cascades and pools stacked along the ledge. The entire stretch is custom-made for exploring.

At Kinsman Falls exploring is less easy. The side path from the main trail descends steeply into a cool ravine. At the head of the ravine a 20-foot-high ribbon of whitewater pours through a narrow chute flanked by dark cliffs that rise nearly three stories above an oval pool. The ravine forms a cool, breezy amphitheater with the falls at center stage and a mural of mosses and lichens adorning the walls. Rounded boulders at the foot of the pool provide ample seating for the audience, which is generally quite small in number. Indeed, you might have the theater all to yourself, even on days when the Basin below is jammed with tourists.

If you are not content being a spectator, it is possible to hop boulders to the left bank of the stream and climb carefully to the slabs atop Kinsman Falls. Considering the strength of the current and the dangerous plunge just below, attempts to leap the channel above the falls are definitely inadvisable.

Rocky Glen, the last of the waterfalls along the trail, is the most lovely of the lot—though it has keen competition for the honor. The dictionary defines a "glen" as a secluded, narrow valley. In this instance the valley is a narrow gorge carved into a large outcrop of frost-fractured rock. The formation looks as if some great force had pulled at the sides of the outcrop until it split along a zigzag fissure, providing a channel for the tumbling brook.

At the bottom of the falls you can approach the mouth of the glen and peer up the lower tongue of cascades, but the sheer cliffs make it difficult to get very far. The best view is obtained from the flat-topped boulders and ledges flanking the brook just above the falls. From this vantage point you can see the wide whitewater curtain cascading into the glen, forming a large pool at the center. The walls below amplify the lilting music of the brook. Altogether it is a wonderful place to sit a spell and absorb the woodland atmosphere.

Historical Detour

While Mount Washington attracted explorers within decades after the arrival of the Pilgrims, there is no record of Franconia Notch being explored until after the French and Indian War. Even the Indians seem not to have frequented the notch, perhaps because of their belief that the mountains were abodes of the gods. Since the township of Woodstock received its grant in 1763 and Franconia was settled in 1774, the Notch evidently had visitors already. But not until early in the nineteenth century was the first narrow road cleared through the primeval forest.

With the road came pony-express mail service to the north country, followed by stagecoach service from Plymouth (New Hampshire). With the coach service came the tourists. Just after midcentury, grand hotels were attracting thousands of well-heeled tourists to see the "savage and startling forms in which cliffs and forest are combined," as Thomas Starr King described Franconia Notch in 1859. King glowingly recounted for his readers the beauty of the Basin and urged visitors to hike up the cascades "that slide along a mile of the slope of the mountain at the west." The formal trail, however, was not established for another century.

Anyone feeling that the natural serenity of the Basin is blighted today by the nearby traffic might find comfort in knowing that the problem is not exclusively a product of the auto age. King, too, remarked about the traffic more than a century ago: "if it [the Basin] did not lie so near the dusty road . . .," he lamented.

As in most of the region, tourists were followed by loggers who gained access to the land when it was sold off by the state after the Civil War. In fact, the Cascade Brook Trail up to Lonesome Lake ascends along old logging roads for much of its length.

After the elegant Profile House at the head of Franconia Notch was destroyed by fire in 1923, conservationists pressed for the property to be reacquired by the state for public recreation. In 1927 the notch became a forest reservation, financed by a grant of $200,000 from the state and matching contributions from the public—including a popular "buy-a-tree" campaign operated by the Society for the Preservation of New Hampshire Forests. The society managed the notch reservation until 1948, when it became a state park.

This entire span of history had been witnessed by a grand old white pine tree that until recently stood three-fourths of the way up the lower cascades. The tree's tall spire, now fallen across the river, towered above the surrounding treetops. This forest elder was one of the few precolonial white pines remaining in New England. In 1668, long before the White Mountain region was settled, all white pines large enough to be made into ship masts 2 feet in diameter and 72 feet long were claimed by the king for the Royal Navy. Thereafter deputies of the royal surveyor general combed the countryside to brand the "mast pines," some of which were reported to be as large as 264 feet high and 7 feet in diameter.

The colonists, who did not accept royal directives complacently, generally cut what they liked, anyway. They sometimes mobbed and beat royal agents who tried to enforce the mast laws. Robert Pike (1967) estimates that for every mast pine to reach England, another five hundred were cut for timber by the colonists. Pike contends nevertheless that resentment over the mast pine laws "did more to cause the American Revolution than the Stamp Act and the tea tax put together."

Today the White Mountain forests are graced by many tall and beautiful white pines, but the giants of the past are gone.

CHAPTER 13

THE FALLING
WATERS TRAIL

◆

Location: Franconia Notch; trail begins at Lafayette Place parking lots
Maps: AMC #2 Franconia-Pemigewasset Map (H-4/5); DeLorme Trail
Map: (G-5)

Hiking Data
Distance: Parking area to Stairs Falls, 0.8 mile; to Swiftwater Falls, 1.0 mile; to
Cloudland Falls, 1.4 miles
Altitude gain: 1100 feet to Cloudland Falls (altitude 2900 feet)
Difficulty: Moderate

─────────────────── ◆ ───────────────────

To summit baggers, Falling Waters Trail is the southern leg of a grueling but popular 8-mile loop traversing the craggy alpine ridge that runs across Mounts Lafayette, Lincoln, and Little Haystack. Even hikers preoccupied with thoughts of the spectacular summit ridge are captivated, however, by the beautiful waterfalls they encounter in Dry Brook ravine. They may pause at the falls only briefly on their long hike—time enough for a breather and a snack—but the spell of the waterfalls beckons them to return.

To travelers through Franconia Notch, Falling Waters Trail provides easy access to mountain forests, frolicking streams, and a string of fine falls and cascades, including Cloudland Falls, the highest in the vicinity. The hike could hardly be more convenient, with trailhead parking right off the Notch Parkway (I-93). Since we pass through the notch quite often, the convenience and beauty of Falling Waters has made it our most frequented trail. We have been drawn back over and over again to visit our pet falls in all their moods.

Access
Traveling south, pull off the Notch Parkway at the sign for Lafayette Place, just under 2 miles past the Old Man viewing points. Swing to the right and

park near the footpath tunnel that crosses under the Parkway to reach the trailhead. Heading north, watch for the TRAILHEAD PARKING sign about 1.5 miles beyond the Basin. There are picnicking facilities on both sides of the highway.

The Trail

The Falling Waters Trail and the Old Bridle Path Trail (up Mount Lafayette) start together behind the toilets at the northbound parking area. If you are planning to hike beyond the falls to the summit ridge, check for a report on the mountain weather. One blustery July morning after the passage of a stormy cold front, we were informed that the summits would have below-zero (Fahrenheit) windchills all day with a chance of snow squalls. Clad in shorts, we were quite grateful for the news and altered our hiking plans accordingly.

At 0.2 mile the Falling Waters Trail splits off to the right from the Old Bridle path across a footbridge over Walker Brook. Even if you intend to get no farther, it is worth a trip to the bridge just to spend a few moments

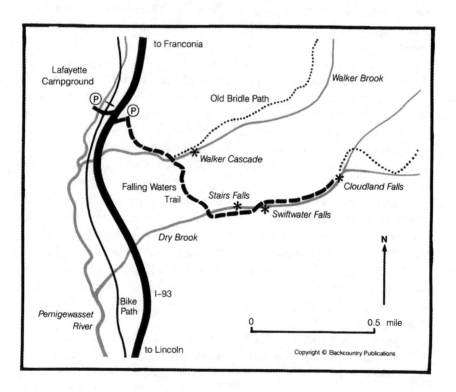

listening to the brook's lilting music and watching its crystal-clear waters swirl over smooth boulders to small, sparkling pools. By bushwhacking 100 yards up the north side of the brook you can reach Walker Cascades. Here, clear brook waters slide 50 yards down sloping banks of burnished granite ledge, where a wide part in the forest canopy admits the noonday sun. The highest cascade is a 10-foot drop over a block midway up the ledge. Though not as grand as the well-known waterfalls along the Falling Waters Trail, Walker Cascades has better pools and fewer visitors. You might even find that you have the spot to yourself for a picnic or a cold swim.

Past the footbridge the Falling Waters Trail turns left and climbs parallel to Walker Brook for a short distance. Just off the trail near the top of this first hump, you can catch sight of silvery cascades below, but the descent to the brook from this point is rough. The trail then veers to the southeast, traversing a forest of slender hardwood trees with an abundance of yellow birch and white birch. Apart from some muddy spots here, the trail is in fine condition all the way to the top of the falls.

Dry Brook is reached at 0.7 mile. Unless the brook is low some deft rock-hopping is needed to get across the series of small cascades and pools. The boulders here invite passersby to pause and enjoy the woodland atmosphere.

Across the brook the trail climbs above the south bank, turns left, and ascends a short distance to the foot of Stairs Falls. This is the smallest of the three main waterfalls along the trail—not quite 20 feet high—but it is by far the prettiest. Here the brook spreads out and drapes a broad curtain of white ribbons over a tier of angular granite steps. An open patch of stony ground by the trail is a good place to sit and meditate on the mantra of the falling waters. Another good rest spot is a rock perch on the smooth ledge at the top of the falls.

Above Stairs Falls the trail skirts a jagged rock wall known as the Sawteeth Ledges. Very quickly then you reach Swiftwater Falls, which churns down 60 feet of weathered bedrock chutes to a rippling pool that cuts directly across your path. To get to the granite ramp on the other side of the stream, you can either do another rock-hop or balance across on a birch log that spans the stream—if it hasn't yet washed away. Once across, be careful going up the rock slab; it is treacherous when slick with spray, drizzle, or ice.

During dry weather Swiftwater Falls snakes down a long curved channel above the crossing, while in high water the brook splits to form a frothing white necklace around a large outcrop of rock at the top of the falls.

Stairs Falls

Though Swiftwater Falls can be impressive at times it is less graceful than its neighbors above and below. Also, there is little room for scrambling around to explore the steep and confined ravine.

The trail next climbs steeply along the north side of Swiftwater Falls, providing an opportunity to clamber to a cluster of boulders midway up the falls. Some ledges at the top of the falls can also be reached with a bit of climbing. Above this steep pitch the trail steadily ascends the flank of a deep V-shaped ravine. Dry Brook tumbles down a long series of leaps and slides, usually well below the trail. At a few points the trail edges closer to the stream, providing access to fine "sitting rocks" with views up and down the ravine. One stretch of trail follows an old logging road, confirming that even the walls of the notch were invaded by the loggers around the turn of the century.

Because of the trail's steady grade, the hike above Swiftwater Falls seems longer than the indicated mileage. Just as you begin to doubt your guidebook, however, the trail crosses a rough outcrop of rock and descends to the climax of your waterfall hunt. In front of you Cloudland Falls tumbles over a fractured cliff, fanning into an endlessly animated white cone 80 feet tall. It is easy to scramble down the rocky bank to the stream-bed for a neck-stretching view from the bottom. When the water is high, the cold draft of spray rushing down the narrow ravine and the echoing roar of the falls will chase you back onto the trail long before you tire of the view.

Although Cloudland Falls is the climax of the trip, don't stop at the bottom. The scene just above the falls is not to be missed. The trail again becomes quite steep as it works its way up the left side of the falls beneath high overhanging ledges that sprout gigantic icicles from autumn until spring. The climb here makes it easy to appreciate the full stature of the falls, which may not look so tall when seen from below. At the top of the climb you will reach flat ledges that run out to the edge of the vertiginous lip of the waterfall ledge. This high terrace also provides an excellent view across Franconia Notch to the Kinsman ridge and the broad crest of Mount Moosilauke looming in the west. As a delightful bonus, a side stream gushes from the dark forest on the far side ledge and spills over a 15-foot-high wall to join the cascades and waterslides in the main channel.

The picturesque terrace above Cloudland Falls is a logical terminus for your waterfall trip. Beyond, the trail climbs alongside the north branch of Dry Brook and then crosses to a series of tedious, increasingly rugged switchbacks through dense evergreen forest. Until one reaches the stunted balsams just below the summit of Little Haystack, there is little more to see along the remaining 1.8 miles of the trail. The only exception is about 0.5 mile below the summit ridge, where a spur trail leads down to the base of a vast, exfoliated slab of bare granite, called Shining Rock. A trip to the summits would be incomplete without spending a few minutes investigating this impressive formation. Last but not least, the ridge across to the Lincoln and Lafayette summits is one of the most splendid walks in the White Mountains. From the north end of the ridge traverse you can descend by way of the AMC Greenleaf Hut (hot chocolate!) and the Old Bridle Path,

Balsam Fir

arriving right back at your car.

In the winter the Falling Waters Trail usually has enough snowshoe traffic to permit anyone with warm, lined boots to hike in as far as Stairs Falls. Before being blanketed by deep snow, the molded green and blue ice formations of Walker Cascades and Stairs Falls are also fascinating to visit—carefully. Beyond Stairs Falls the steeper sections of trail generally require proper winter hiking equipment.

Historical Detour

Long after Crawford Notch began to suffer the blights of civilization—a turnpike, a railroad, logging operations, fires, landslides—Franconia Notch was still being celebrated for its "pleasing aspect of primeval quietude and tranquil beauty" (Sweetser, 1887). The Profile House at the head of Franconia Notch was one of the grandest and most elegant tourist hotels of the region, yet only a narrow carriage road cut through the dense, undefiled forests of the Notch itself. Most visitors to Profile House arrived from the north by a narrow-gauge rail link out of Bethlehem. The railroad from Boston swung west from Plymouth through Warren and Haverhill, bypassing the high mountains.

Lafayette Place, at the base of the present Falling Waters Trail, is the site of a tavern built in 1835. Only ten years earlier the highest peak of the Franconia Range had been rechristened Lafayette in honor of the French general, who was visiting the United States at the time. Formerly it had been called Great Haystack, which explains why there is no big brother to Little Haystack along the ridge. Just before the Civil War the tavern was expanded into a tourist hotel called Lafayette House, which burned down only a few years later.

Most early guidebooks gave lavish and detailed descriptions of the Notch, the Flume, and the Basin but said not a word about the waterfalls along the present Falling Waters Trail. The one early description is found in Moses Sweetser's guidebook (1887), which referred collectively to the trio of falls along Dry Brook as "Walkers Falls." Thereafter the waterfalls seem to have disappeared from public view for nearly eight decades. Not even the *AMC White Mountain Guide* mentioned the falls until after the Falling Waters Trail was established in the late 1950s by Clyde F. Smith, a watchman at Cannon Mountain.

One cause for this long neglect was the devastating arrival of the lumberjacks in the forests and ravines on the western flanks of Franconia Ridge. Testimony to this effect is given in early editions of the AMC guide, which described how the Old Bridle Path from Lafayette Place had "long been disused and portions have been obliterated by logging." (This trail was reestablished in 1929.)

In 1918 the newly created White Mountain National Forest purchased the property up the ravine of Dry Brook from the Johnson Lumber Company (see chapter 10). Franconia Notch itself was acquired by the State of New Hampshire in 1927. Since then Sweetser's "primeval quietude" has not exactly been restored, but you can once again enjoy the "tranquil beauty" of the regenerated forests and the long-lost waterfalls along the Falling Waters Trail.

CHAPTER 14

FRANCONIA FALLS

◆

Location: Off the Lincoln Woods Trail, which starts on the Kancamagus
  Highway east of Lincoln
Maps: AMC #2 Franconia-Pemigewasset Map (H-5/6); DeLorme Trail Map (H-6)

Hiking Data
Distance: Parking area to falls, 3.2 miles
Altitude gain: 300 feet (to altitude 1500 feet)
Difficulty: Moderate. The round trip is more than 6 miles, but the trail is very
  level and easy.

◆

On a sunny summer's day when Franconia Brook is not running too high and
the broad slabs of rock alongside the falls are dry, Franconia Falls is a perfectly
delightful spot for a water frolic. You can take a quick swim in a cold, clear
pool. Or you might muster the courage for a fast ride down a hip-wide water
chute that spouts over the lip of a 10-foot-high cliff into the swirling current
of a deep pothole pool. You can choose a cold Jacuzzi in the foaming wash
at the base of a smaller cascade, or you can just take off your shoes and wade
in more tranquil pools above or below the falls. Whatever your choice, the
smooth, open ledges of colorful Conway granite soak up the warmth of the
sun well past noon, providing a ready recovery from the chill of the brook
waters.

At other times of the year you will be less inclined to go for a swim, but
these beautiful falls are always a pleasure to visit and explore.

Access
Traveling east along the Kancamagus Highway, the parking lot for the
Lincoln Woods Trail will be on your left 4.7 miles east of Lincoln,
immediately after the highway crosses the bridge over the East Branch of
the Pemigewassset River.

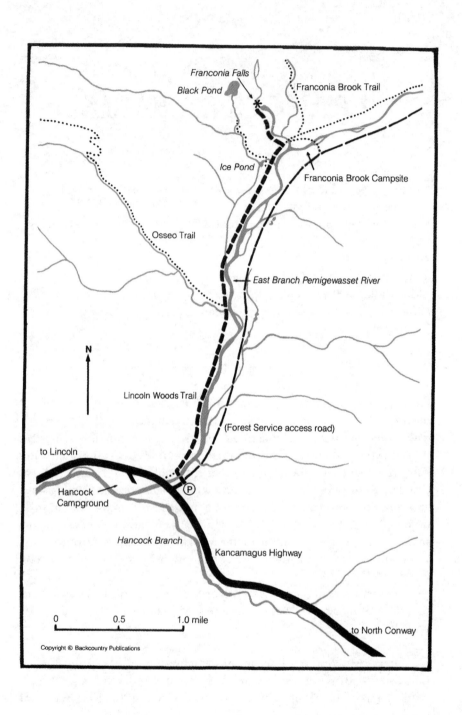

Franconia Falls

Black Pond

Franconia Brook Trail

Ice Pond

Franconia Brook Campsite

Osseo Trail

East Branch Pemigewasset River

N

Lincoln Woods Trail

(Forest Service access road)

to Lincoln

P

Hancock
Campground

Hancock Branch

Kancamagus Highway

0   0.5   1.0 mile

to North Conway

Copyright © Backcountry Publications

A Note to Trail Users

Although this trailhead lot is one of the largest in the White Mountains, it is often packed full—attesting to the popularity of the trails along the East Branch. With the rapid development of Lincoln and Loon Mountain, these trails have become as popular among cross-country skiers as among hikers. This skyrocketing popularity has led to severe degradation of the area around the falls and the campsite near them. High numbers of people have trampled the soil and damaged the forest. Many of the visitors do not properly deal with their wastes (the nearest toilet is at the campsite), which has led to what the Forest Service calls "an unacceptable sanitary condition." To allow this area to recover, the Forest Service has introduced a day-use passport system. All visitors to the falls must check in at the visitors center at the Lincoln Woods parking lot to receive a free day pass, where they are educated regarding proper disposal of human waste. There is a limit of sixty visitors per day to the falls. If you arrive late and do not get a pass, look to chapter 18 for similar alternatives: remember that this policy is trying to allow a beautiful part of our national forest to recover. Also, rangers check passes and identification at the falls, so do not try to slip in. This policy is currently being revised and is likely to change when a better waste management system is developed.

The Trail

From the parking area, cross the river on the footbridge. Pause at the center of the swaying bridge and watch the river's mesmerizing currents sweep through the maze of polished boulders below. At the end of the bridge, simply turn right and follow the trail for 2.8 miles to a smaller wooden footbridge spanning Franconia Brook, just past the recently closed Franconia Brook Campsite. The new campsite is across the river, accessible by crossing Franconia Brook and taking a trail which branches to the right off the Wilderness Trail to cross the Pemigewasset River. Fording the Pemigewasset is done by hopping large rocks placed by the Forest Service—and sometimes displaced by the river. To reach the falls, turn onto the spur trail that branches to your left just before the bridge over Franconia Brook. The falls are 0.4 mile up the spur. Each essential turn is clearly marked by a wooden sign.

You will notice that the Lincoln Woods Trail is unusually straight and level. The reason becomes apparent once you begin to see railroad ties down the middle of the trail: You are hiking the route of an old logging railroad. The route runs through mixed forest, essentially parallel to the East Branch of the Pemi. At spots where the river edges the trail you can walk to the bank and find large, smooth boulders to rest on, with views north up the

BRUCE AND DOREEN BOLNICK

Franconia Falls

riverbed toward the distant Bond ridge. In late July and early August another excellent place to stop for a rest, even if none is needed, is a huge raspberry patch on the left just past the Osseo Trail cutoff (leading up to the high peaks of Franconia Ridge), 1.4 miles from the parking lot.

One mile past the Osseo Trail, another trail branches off to the left. This one follows a small stream for 0.8 mile to tranquil Black Pond. Just beyond this turn for Black Pond, you reach the closed Franconia Brook Campground, amidst a stand of tall spruce, pine, and hemlock trees. The spur trail to Franconia Falls is only a hop, skip, and a jump ahead.

In the winter the Lincoln Woods Trail is heavily used for cross-country skiing. The ski trip to Franconia Falls is very easy all the way to the lower section of the spur trail. The last 0.25 mile to the falls, however, is quite narrow and steep for negotiating on skis. It is also anticlimactic, since in midwinter the falls are disguised under a thick mask of ice and snow. On one winter trip we encountered a party descending the spur trail. They told us that the trail was not passable far enough to reach the falls. Yet as they spoke the falls were less than 100 yards away, and their tracks confirmed that they had reached their destination without recognizing it!

The Falls

If it weren't for the bone-chilling water, you could hardly wish for a more fascinating waterfall playground than Franconia Falls. Here the crystal waters of Franconia Brook descend across an acre of smooth, sunny ledges in surging leaps and graceful slides, broken by deep, clear pools and gouged granite potholes, foaming with current.

The beauty of the entire formation lies in its long mosaic of narrow channels and silvery water veils cast amidst sculpted granite beds. The tallest free drop, midway up the cascades on the trail side of the ledges, is hardly more than 10 feet, yet it is of stunning design. A swift current rushes down from a small pool above and pours through a shallow water chute about hip wide and 20 feet long. At the base of the chute the water spouts over an abrupt drop into a deep, clear, swirling pool, ringed by steep, smooth granite walls on three sides. A second channel of water tumbles down another corner of the pool, its currents buffeting those spawned by the spout. Brave and hardy (or foolhardy?) adventurers enter the long chute well above the spout and ride the swelling current to the pool below. At the far end of the pool a fairly level slab offers the best exit. But be warned that the strong current in the pool is somewhat disorienting, and the pool's deep waters are shockingly frigid. When the water is high, restrictions on swimming may be posted by the Forest Service. It is wise to check the information board in the parking area before hitting the trail.

Telling about Franconia Falls by describing the water spout is like telling about a three-ring circus by describing a favorite clown: There is a lot more to see, as well. The ledges are custom-made for careful exploring or carefree relaxing, with open views to the southeast across the valley of the East Branch of the Pemigewasset toward Mount Hancock.

Red Raspberry

If you choose to explore, watch out for rock surfaces that have been polished by the current to the point of being slippery even when dry. This is not an idle warning: Serious injuries have happened here. If you are careful, however, and if the water level is not too high, you can negotiate your way safely up and down the full length of the falls—and beyond. For example, around a right-hand bend not far upstream from the falls, you can find an exquisite, crystal-green pool that has undercut a house-sized ledge to form a large grotto fringed with spruce.

Because of the gentle hike in, the campsite nearby, and the growth of tourism in the Lincoln area, you can expect to find a small crowd of visitors at Franconia Falls on any fine hiking day. Campers have the best opportunity to enjoy the falls at their leisure. The hike in to the Franconia Brook Campsite (now relocated to the east side of the river) is one of the easiest trips for beginning backpackers. Except at this national forest campsite, no camping is permitted within 0.25 mile of the Lincoln Woods Trail.

Historical Detour

The area you traverse to reach Franconia Falls has a fascinating history that dates back barely a hundred years. The description of the area in Moses Sweetser's *The White Mountains: Handbook for Travellers* (1887) states simply that "this great wild land is virgin soil for the fisherman and hunter, and the brooks and ponds are swarming with trout." Though still pristine wilderness, the land was already in private hands as a result of a New Hampshire General Court decision in 1867 to sell off the state's undeveloped lands for a trifle, on the pretext of financing public schools.

After trunk-line rail links connected the White Mountain region with the major eastern urban markets, the loggers swarmed in to the back-country. In 1892, virtually overnight, the present town center of Lincoln was transformed from the site of a small, remote mountain lodge amidst dense wild forests to the center of operations for timber baron—or wood butcher, depending on your point of view—James Everell Henry.

Earlier in life Henry had failed at drilling for oil in Canada, growing wheat in Minnesota, and scratching for gold in California, but his success at mining New Hampshire's forests was legendary. In his 1980 book on the old logging railroads, C. Francis Belcher cites a quotation attributed to J.E. Henry in a 1908 *Collier's* article: "I never see the tree yit that didn't mean a damned sight more to me goin' under the saw than it did standin' on a mountain." Whether the quotation is authentic or not, it certainly characterized Henry's attitude as he set about penetrating the wilderness with

72 miles of railroad lines to haul the timber out and supplies in. On summer Sundays Henry earned pocket change by running a flatcar full of "excursionists" into the heart of his mountain logging empire.

Incredibly, within fifteen years the area was virtually barren; it was first stripped clean of its towering spruce and fir, and then it was devastated by an awesome 1907 inferno that burned for over ten days on residual "slash" from the logging operations. Thereafter logging activity along the East Branch of the Pemigewasset ebbed. The federal government bought the land from near-bankrupt loggers in 1936, but only after more than 1 *billion* board feet of timber had been removed from the 66,000-acre watershed. The East Branch & Lincoln Railroad lines into the erstwhile wilderness continued to be used until 1948, when the last tracks were pulled up.

Equally incredible has been the verdant recovery of the East Branch forests so evident today. Indeed, Belcher contends that the very deeds of "wood butchers" were the spark that ignited public opinion, leading to the passage of the Weeks Act in 1911 authorizing the federal purchase of land for the White Mountain National Forest. The story came full circle in 1984 when federal legislation established full wilderness protection for the Pemigewasset Wilderness area.

As you stride along the Lincoln Woods Trail across the surviving hemlock ties, look around at the youthful forest and let your thoughts drift back to the days of the East Branch & Lincoln Railroad. One of the old workhorse engines can be visited nearby at the entrance to Loon Mountain.

CHAPTER 15

NO. 13 FALLS

◆

Location: In the Pemigewasset Wilderness, south of the Garfield Ridge
Maps: AMC #2 Franconia-Pemigewasset Map (H-5/6); DeLorme Trail Map (F-6)

Hiking Data

Distance: To falls from Kancamagus Highway, 8.0 miles; from NH 3 via
 Galehead Hut, 7.3 miles
Altitude gain: From Kancamagus Highway to falls, 600 feet (to altitude 1600
 feet); from NH 3 via Galehead Hut to falls, 0 feet (up a 2200-foot ridge
 then down 2200 feet on the far side)
Difficulty: Strenuous

◆

Around the turn of the century Camp #13 was the terminus of the Franconia
branch of the East Branch & Lincoln Railroad, which hauled in supplies to the
remote logging camp and hauled out the timber. On occasional summer
Sundays, flatbed cars carried tourists on excursions from Lincoln into the interior.
Gentlemen in dress coats and ladies in ruffled blouses and full-length skirts would
ride into Camp #13 and marvel "at the completeness of the removal of all the trees
that once stood upon these mountains" (Harrington, 1926).

 Now that lightweight hiking boots have replaced flatcars as the primary
mode of transportation in the area, the falls and cascades high on Franconia
Brook still bear the name of the former lumber camp. Located at the foot of
Mount Garfield, deep in the heart of the Pemigewasset Wilderness, No. 13
Falls is the most remote of all the major waterfalls in the White Mountains.
From the south the hike in is easy, but the round-trip is 16 miles long; from
the north the trail is very rough and only slightly shorter. Consequently,
No. 13 Falls is impractical as a single day trip from the road for all but the
hardy hiker who relishes a long, tiring trek.

 For the rest of us, No. 13 Falls can best be reached by spending a night
or two out on the trail. The most comfortable option is to establish a home

base at Galehead Hut—itself the most remote of the AMC mountain huts—and then take a day hike down to the falls. If you stay more than one night at the hut, you can also fit in a day trip up Twin Mountain and over to the summits of the Bond ridge. This is another superb excursion.

A second option for reaching No. 13 falls is to backpack and camp. There is a national forest tentsite with nine tent platforms right next to the falls. An easier alternative is to set up base camp at the Franconia Brook campground (see chapter 14) and then make a pilgrimage to No. 13 Falls as a day hike. Experienced campers may prefer to push on into the Pemigewasset Wilderness to find an off-trail site for low-impact camping en route to the falls.

If you find yourself asking whether the trip to No. 13 Falls is worth all the trouble, the answer is a resounding "yes." The falls and cascades are beautiful, and there is a subtle magic to the wilderness. Also, your nights out in the mountains will be treasured memories. But be sure to pray for decent weather.

Access

The easiest route in to No. 13 Falls is from the Kancamagus Highway via the Lincoln Woods Trail and the Franconia Brook Trail. The previous chapter described the first 2.8 miles from the trailhead parking lot to the footbridge over Franconia Brook. This time cross the footbridge to the Wilderness Trail and make a quick left turn onto the Franconia Brook Trail at mile 2.9.

The Trail

The Franconia Brook Trail begins by climbing a low hill and entering the Pemigewasset Wilderness Area. For the next 3 miles the trail follows the gentle gradient of the old logging railroad bed, except at stream crossings and at one rough detour just south of the Lincoln Brook Trail cutoff (mile 4.6). This detour bypasses the site of old Camp #9, which has been flooded by a beaver pond. Gray ghosts of trees killed by the rising pond waters are visible from the path. The detour is also the point where a young man lost his way returning from No. 13 Falls in July 1988 and died of exposure before being found. This tragic incident serves to remind us that the vast forest tracts of the Pemi Wilderness—though deeply satisfying to explore—are inhospitable places to get lost and dangerous places for parties to become separated.

Shortly after passing the Lincoln Brook Trail cutoff the Franconia Brook Trail edges another large beaver pond where the air is filled with swallows; kingfishers may also be seen perching on bleached gray snags. Look for the

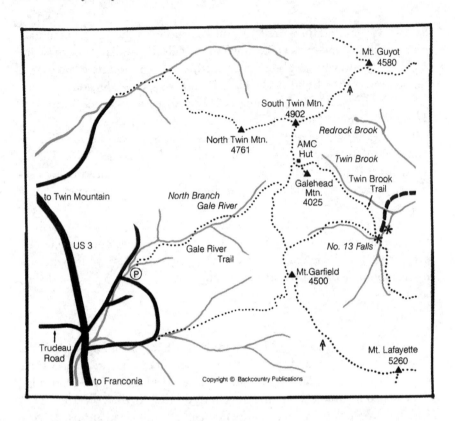

beavers' lodge, a mound of sticks and branches, in the middle of the pond. Beyond the beaver pond the trail passes through an *Alice in Wonderland* corridor beneath a canopy of spruce and fir trees and then crosses Hellgate Brook (mile 5.4) and Redrock Brook (mile 6.4). Past Redrock Brook, where old Camp #10 was located, the trail climbs more persistently, though it never gets very steep. The crossing of Twin Brook at mile 7.4, near old Camp #12, marks the beginning of the home stretch to No. 13 Falls.

The alternative approach, from the north, ascends the Gale River Trail past Galehead Hut and then descends to No. 13 Falls by the Twin Brook Trail. To get to the Gale River Trail from US 3, watch for Trudeau Road about halfway between Franconia and Twin Mountain. A sign at this intersection points north to the Ammonoosuc District Ranger Station, where national forest information can be obtained. You want to turn south, however, onto the bumpy gravel road opposite Trudeau Road.

Once on the gravel road, continue straight for 1.35 miles to a right turn. From this turn it is just a 0.25-mile drive to the trailhead information

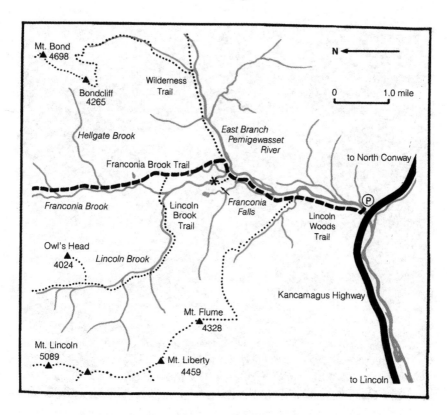

sign and parking area. The Gale River Trail first passes through a broad belt of northern hardwood forest, crossing a sturdy footbridge over the North Branch of the Gale River at mile 1.5. This is a beautiful rest spot. Bear in mind, however, that the river feeds a public water supply, so swimming and wading are prohibited here.

The trail gradient remains moderate for another 1.5 miles, during which the river is crossed back to the west bank. Gradually you will notice the forest being conquered by conifers. Then comes the crunch: a steep, rough, 1000-foot climb to the Garfield Ridge Trail (mile 4.1). At the top of the steep climb turn left. The hut is 0.5 mile farther on and 400 feet higher.

To reach the falls from the hut, start off on the Frost Trail, a short spur that brings 4000-foot-peak baggers up Galehead Mountain. In only 0.1 mile the Twin Brook Trail branches to the left. Pull up your knee bandages and head on down. It's a sustained drop of 2.6 miles and 2200 feet down to No. 13 Falls. Obviously this means you will have a hard slog back to the hut, but a hearty hut dinner and the panoramic twilight view of the

One of the many cascades at No. 13

Pemigewasset Wilderness should be enough to revive your spirits.

In addition to the two routes described above, No. 13 Falls can also be reached by the Lincoln Brook Trail, or by *descending* along the Franconia Brook Trail from the Garfield Ridge Trail just east of the Garfield Ridge Campsite. If you are interested in these alternate routes, consult the *AMC White Mountain Guide* for details.

The Falls

So what do you get in return for all the effort required to reach No. 13 Falls? Nothing grand or dramatic. Your reward is simply a delightful package of cascades, waterfalls, and pools, all wrapped in tranquil wilderness. In fact, the very name of the place is often truncated to "13 Falls," which is descriptive of what you will find.

Approaching by the Franconia Brook Trail from the south, your first contact with the falls will be the muffled undertone of falling water harmonizing with the rushing breeze. Very soon the forest to the left opens up to reveal a broad, sloping ledge that invites you to climb down from the trail. Go right ahead and accept the invitation. You will be greeted by a long slide of water that tumbles down a smooth bedrock ramp and pours over a 10-foot block of ledge into a clear green horseshoe-shaped pool. Stop for a snack and a rest. Dunk your head in the cold stream, cool your tired feet, or take a quick dip in the pool. Then get ready for some exploring.

Upstream the exposed bedrock (metagraywacke and then Kinsman quartz monzonite) stretches on for hundreds of feet, providing a wide selection of small chutes and slides, shallow pothole pools, scalloped tubs, and sunning rocks on which to recover from a cold dunk. Partway up the sloping ledge the streambed forks. To the right—in the direction of the campground and the trail junction—a maze of thin cascades slips down a broad expanse of broken slabs. Here are found the sunniest and warmest basking rocks. Along the left-hand fork the ledge narrows. You can follow the slabs up alongside a waterslide to a lovely mare's tail waterfall 20 feet high. Above this the forest closes in more tightly, providing a deep green frame for a picturesque water spout that empties into a split-level pair of pools.

Now explore downstream. Just below the horseshoe pool a beautiful triple-ribbon cascade feeds into an enormous oval pool set in a cool glen. This is surely one of the most impressive pools in the whole region. We like to call it the Olympic Pool. Because it is so large and deep, this pool is very cold; it would be wise to check with your cardiologist before going for a swim here. Below the Olympic Pool you will find the brook tumbling to one pool after another, splitting the forest with a deep ravine.

You can't help but enjoy yourself at No. 13 Falls. You can scramble around and explore the ledge, or splash around in the brook, or just bask in the sun and relish a hard-earned rest—while gathering strength for the long hike out.

Historical Detour

In addition to the railbed and the scars of old logging roads traced on the hillsides, physical remnants of the old lumber camps in the Pemigewasset Wilderness can still be found. At No. 13 Falls the most apparent sign is a set of thick iron spikes that protrude here and there from the ledge. Elsewhere we have stumbled on half-rotted spiked logging boots, a fancy cast-iron oven door, rusted iron wheels, and even a well-preserved rail.

In his book *Logging Railroads of the White Mountains,* C. Francis Belcher describes the character of J.E. Henry's logging camps along the East

Branch & Lincoln Railroad. A typical camp was a small community that included "stables, living quarters, cook shacks, blacksmith shops, and allied structures for many horses, 150 or so lumberjacks, and their bosses." All Henry's buildings were red-painted frame-and-board structures that could be dismantled and hauled by rail to another camp as logging operations shifted.

The barracks often slept one hundred exhausted, snoring lumberjacks at a time, two per bunk. This was relative comfort compared to the primitive lumber camps portrayed by Richard Pinette in *Northwoods Echoes* (1986). In the earlier camps a dozen men slept on their sides stacked like spoons under a single quilt, conserving space and providing a feast for the lice.

The lumberjacks were well fed, with large variations in quality depending on the cook. Supply trains arrived each Tuesday and Friday, so fresh beef was available regularly. Meals were eaten in silence in compliance with the standard cook's rule: "Feed your guts and get through" (Poole, 1946). Other company rules were equally strict. Most dealt with the care of horses, with safety, and with economy. On the latter point, workers were routinely charged for broken equipment and fined for all manner of rule violations. Consequently the tough, spirited lumberjacks often found payday to be quite an unpleasant surprise. To settle any arguments over these punitive sanctions, it is said, J.E. Henry himself handed out the monthly paychecks armed with a gun.

Tote roads from the main camps were cut into the mountainsides during the summer, providing access to timber high up the slopes. Most of the actual logging was done in the winter when the tote roads were smoothed over with ice and snow. The 12-hour workdays began and ended in frigid darkness. The job was physically demanding, tightly disciplined, and very dangerous.

In this context, the hike into No. 13 Falls doesn't seem so tough after all.

CHAPTER 16

THOREAU FALLS

◆

Location: At the far end of Zealand Notch from Zealand Road, off US 302
Maps: AMC #2 Franconia-Pemigewasset Map (G-7); DeLorme Trail Map (F-8)

Hiking Data
Distance: Parking area to Zealand Falls, 2.8 miles; to Thoreau Falls, 4.8 miles
Altitude gain: 650 feet to Zealand Falls (altitude 2650 feet) but only 350 feet to Thoreau Falls (altitude 2350 feet)
Difficulty: Moderate, but long

◆

Henry David Thoreau, the renowned New England writer, naturalist, and philosopher, is honored in the White Mountains by one wonderfully fitting tribute: a waterfall of sweeping beauty, located in the most distant corner of the Merrimack watershed. Moses Sweetser chose to name these falls for Thoreau in part because the poet of Concord had "so often written lovingly of the Merrimack River and its fountains in the wilderness."

Thoreau visited the White Mountains and climbed Mount Washington in 1839 and again in 1858 but never saw the particular "fountain in the wilderness" that now bears his name. Although Ethan Allen Crawford was leading parties to Ethan Pond as early as 1830, the vast forest tracts down the North Fork of the Pemigewasset River's East Branch were still essentially terra incognita. Today dozens of hikers visit the falls each weekend when the weather is clear and mild. Many even ski in during the winter.

Unlike Thoreau, we now have the advantage of a well-graded trail as well as books and maps to direct us to the falls. But we are at a keen disadvantage as students of Nature. Who today can match Thoreau's patience and diligence in absorbing the lessons of the forest? In a eulogy delivered at Thoreau's funeral, Ralph Waldo Emerson described how his friend took to the woods:

> He knew how to sit immovable, a part of the rock he rested
> on, until the bird, the reptile, the fish, which had retired from
> him, should come back and resume its habits. . . . He knew

every track in the snow or on the ground, and what creature had taken this path before him. . . . Under his arm he carried an old music-book to press plants; in his pocket, his diary and pencil, a spy-glass for birds, microscope, jack-knife and twine. He wore a straw hat, stout shoes, strong gray trousers, to brave scrub-oaks and smilax, and to climb a tree for a hawk's or a squirrel's nest. He waded into the pool for the water-plants. . . .

To Thoreau the wilds were a tonic. He found beauty at each step, heard music in the stillness of the forest, and delighted in fresh fragrances borne by the breeze. As much as the man himself, Thoreau Falls honors Nature— with a capital *N*.

One very enjoyable way to visit Thoreau Falls is to spend a night or two at the AMC Zealand Falls Hut. From that base Thoreau Falls is an easy day trip, leaving plenty of time for imbibing the heady tonic of the wilds.

Access

The Zealand Road turns off US 302 at the Zealand Campground, nearly midway between Twin Mountain and Bretton Woods. Drive in 3.6 miles to the parking area and trailhead sign at the end of the road. This road is closed in the winter, so if you are snowshoeing or skiing in, park on Route 302 and be sure to add an extra 3.6 miles each way when calculating the distance.

The Trail

From the trailhead, the route to the falls runs straight through Zealand Notch for 4.6 miles via the Zealand Trail and then the Ethan Pond Trail. For the final 0.25 mile you follow the Thoreau Falls Trail down to the falls. An alternative route to Thoreau Falls is to start on the other end of the Ethan Pond Trail at Willey House Station in Crawford Notch. This hike is favored by many backpackers, who spend a night at the Ethan Pond shelter, but it is a bit longer than the hike through Zealand Notch and involves an extra 1400-foot-climb over the Willey ridge.

From the end of the Zealand Road, the Zealand Trail crosses a bridge over Hoxie Brook and ascends slowly through evergreen forest. Look for blue blazes at spots where the direction of the trail is not readily apparent. At 0.7 mile the trail takes a hard right turn and picks up the smooth, well-graded bed of the old Zealand Valley logging railroad.

Soon the character of the forest changes dramatically as the trail approaches a marshy tableland at the head of the notch. Long sections of plank walkway bridge shallow beaver ponds, where stunted but sturdy white birch and feathery mountain ash replace the conifers. In early summer redstarts and white-throated sparrows flutter in the undergrowth, whistling greetings. In the spring, when the wildflowers are in bloom, you might also surprise a garter snake out basking in the sun.

The woods soon open out to provide a magnificent view of Zealand Notch, a U-shaped gap carved out of an ancient mountain pass by the Pleistocene glaciers. This is what Franconia Notch must have looked like 200 years ago, before it was "improved" for tourists and travelers!

After passing the terminus of the A-Z Trail (from Crawford Depot) at mile 2.3, the Zealand Trail circles placid Zealand Pond. It is hard to resist stopping to take a photograph of the large beaver lodge in the foreground. On the forested slope behind the pond a dark green stripe of conifer spires marks the location of Whitewall Brook and Zealand Falls, which can be seen glinting silver in the sun. At 2.5 miles the Zealand Trail ends, and the Ethan Pond Trail begins. To the right, the Twinway Trail leads up a 10-story flight of steep rock steps to Zealand Falls and the AMC hut (0.2 mile).

Continuing along the Ethan Pond Trail, you now enter one of the loveliest forests in the region. All around you are gleaming white birch with twisted boughs—a legacy of catastrophic fires that ravaged the notch around the turn of the century. Soft yellow-green crowns of birch also blanket the steep mountain wall to the west, which is capped by the gray crags of Zeacliff, 1300 feet overhead.

The trail contours along the eastern wall of the notch 200 feet above Whitewall Brook and 600 feet beneath the stark, crumbling cliffs of Whitewall Mountain. Although the path generally follows the old railroad grade it is not exactly level. Nearly a century of slides, storms, and rockfalls have buried some sections of the old railbed and washed away others. The slides also opened up superb views of the notch and created corridors where thrive a new generation of young spruce, blueberries(!), and colorful wildflowers such as the splendid rhodora. From one fresh rockslide you can even spot a huge (and heretofore undocumented) natural rock profile of a female moose at the crest of the Whitewall cliffs. Admittedly this requires a bit of imagination—as well as a proper angle.

The Zeacliff Trail cuts off right at mile 3.8 (just past the moose profile). Not far beyond, the notch widens out and the trail passes into immature boreal forest. Soon you reach the junction with Thoreau Falls Trail. The sign at the junction gives the distance to the waterfall as 0.3 mile, but it is even nearer than that.

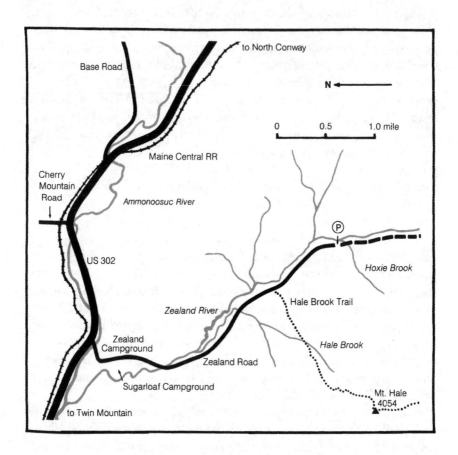

The Falls

On a clear day your first impression at Thoreau Falls probably won't be of the waterfall itself but rather of the magnificent view to the southwest across the deep, wild valley of the North Fork to the high ridge of Mount Bond. Very likely the second feature to catch your eye will be the clear stream sliding across a broad, smooth shelf of Conway granite, dimpled with potholes. When you walk to the edge of the shelf, however, the waterfall will command your attention. At your feet the stream dances in a sweeping arc down long, sloping terraces of weathered granite, undercutting a high concave wall topped with slender birches that sway in the constant updraft.

Moses Sweetser (1887) described Thoreau Falls as being 200 feet high

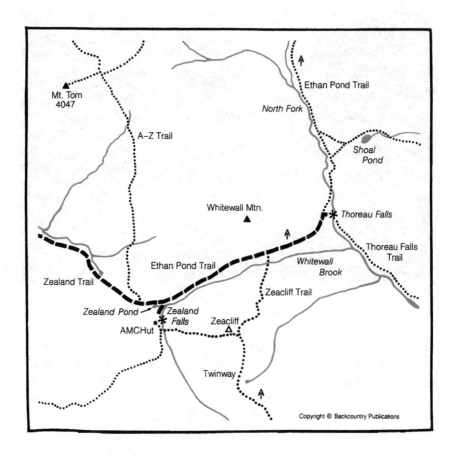

and 0.5 mile long. These figures might have included some of the cascades above and below the main waterfall, but they do convey the impressive scale of the whole formation. The grandeur of Thoreau Falls was extolled in Karl Harrington's *Walks and Climbs in the White Mountains* (1926): "None of the others has the massive wildness, the long splashing descent . . . , the lonely isolation, the poetic atmosphere. . . ."

For the best view, work your way to the bottom of the ledge, from which point the long dogleg cascade is especially lovely. When the rock is dry, it is normally possible to scramble right down the ledge. In fact, the angle of the rock makes the scramble very delightful—or very scary, depending on your predilection! (The topmost incline is a bit steep, but it can

ROBERT KOZLOW

Boulders at the base of Zealand Falls

be bypassed easily on the right.) If you prefer to avoid scampering down smooth, airy ledges, you can reach the bottom of the falls by the trail, which crosses the stream at the top of the ledge and descends through the woods.

Exploring above and below the falls is great fun. There are small cascades with pretty pools, large tumbled boulders, and interesting rock formations. Downstream, watch for a natural bridge in the bed of the stream and a large wedged boulder that appears to be supporting an overhanging outcrop.

Compared to Thoreau Falls, Zealand Falls is a minor attraction. It can be quite pretty with a good current, but you wouldn't want to walk a 6-mile round-trip just for this. Still, Zealand Falls is a pleasant treat for hut guests and weary hikers passing by. The brook that tumbles down the ledges alongside the Zealand Falls Hut is named Whitewall Brook, which is a bit strange considering that Whitewall Mountain is on the *other* side of the notch. Maybe someone got tired of having everything named Zealand.

Spaced along the ledges beside the hut are small cascades, rippled waterslides, crystal pools, and etched channels that resemble miniature flumes. The open slabs also provide excellent views through the notch to distant Mount Carrigain. The main falls are below the hut, where the ledge abruptly drops two stories into a shady ravine. Large angular blocks of granite that have been wedged from the wall by frost clutter the base of the falls.

On a warm summer day the atmosphere at Zealand Falls is festive. Kids ramble up and down the streambed, while the adults bask on the rocks or follow the youngsters around with cameras. Because the walk in is quite easy, Zealand Falls Hut is a great place for a family adventure.

Historical Detour

"Thank God they cannot cut down the clouds!" Thoreau said of the loggers—even before the arrival of the railroads and the advent of woodpulp papermaking triggered destructive lumbering in the late nineteenth century. Along with Franconia Brook to the west, Zealand Valley epitomizes the cycle of devastation and regeneration. C. Francis Belcher's *Logging Railroads of the White Mountains* provides an authoritative account of the dramatic saga of the Zealand forests.

As late as 1887, Moses Sweetser's *The White Mountains: Handbook for Travellers* averred that the upper watershed of the East Branch of the Pemigewasset "is still in a condition of primeval wildness, and has not been invaded by clearings, roads, or trails." Actually his information was slightly out of date. J.E. Henry had begun construction of the Zealand Valley Railroad up to the notch in 1884, logging as he went. In these early days Henry was not clear-cutting. He concentrated on the larger spruce trees in what was then a conifer forest. Henry's base was the village of Zealand, which was located just west of today's campground. At that time Zealand was a sizable community complete with a rail yard, a depot, a mill, homes, shops, and a school. Today, not a trace remains.

In 1886, a major fire consumed 12,000 acres of forest in the Zealand area, including virgin tracts well up into notch. Reportedly the fire was ignited by sparks from one of Henry's engines. In an 1891 speech the state fire commissioner described the effects:

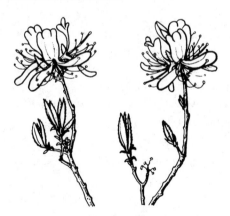

Rhodora

> If there is any sight entirely disheartening, it is that of these
> fire denuded tracts, from which everything has been swept
> clean, down to the underlying rocks. . . . For seven miles up
> the valley, the fire swept resistless across it from crestline to
> crestline. . . . (Belcher, 1980)

Yet the logging continued, pushing farther up the notch. By the early
1890s logging trains ran 11 miles into the former wilderness, crossing the
North Fork a short distance above Thoreau Falls. A large railroad yard was
located where the placid beaver marshes now stand, just north of Zealand
Pond. A writer in 1892 viewed the operations and called the Zealand Valley
a "vast scene of waste and desolation."

That same year Henry moved his company to Lincoln (see chapter 14),
and by 1897 the Zealand railroad ceased operations. In 1903 the debris of
slash from Henry's logging operations kindled a second intense fire that
burned another 10,000 acres and transformed Zealand Notch into a "deso-
late ash wasteland."

Many feared that the notch—or "Death Valley," as one writer called
it—would never again be able to support plant or animal life. But as
Thoreau had observed many years earlier: "How swift Nature is to repair
the damage that man does!" A landmark date in the restoration of the forest
is 1915, when the entire Zealand River watershed was purchased by the
White Mountain National Forest.

By 1922 the *AMC White Mountain Guide* was still referring to "bare,
fire-scarred walls of Zealand Notch," but it also reported that the old
railbed was choked with young cherry trees. In 1926 Harrington found
alders, poplars, and birch growing back, as well. In 1933 the Zealand Falls
Hut opened to the public. The "Zealand wilds" had been devastated and
then reborn.

A similar story can be told of the forests around the North Fork, near
Thoreau Falls—though without the fires. In 1907 the interior region was
still all virgin forest, but by 1922 the lumberjacks were at work on the last
major stands of old-growth timber below Thoreau Falls. Hikers called this
"the Desolation region." And now—well, see for yourself.

Thoreau supplied the tale with a fitting moral, which has become the
motto of the Wilderness Society:

> In wildness is the preservation of the world. . . .

Rocky Gorge

THE SACO WATERSHED

◆

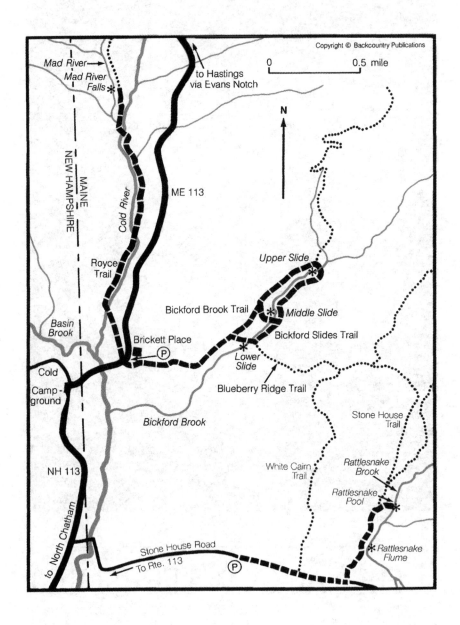

Copyright © Backcountry Publications

0   0.5 mile

Mad River →
Mad River
Falls *

to Hastings
via Evans Notch

N

MAINE
NEW HAMPSHIRE

Cold River

ME 113

Royce
Trail

Upper Slide *

Bickford Brook Trail

* Middle Slide

Bickford Slides Trail

Brickett Place
(P)

Basin
Brook

Lower
Slide *

Blueberry Ridge Trail

Cold
Camp-
ground

Bickford Brook

Stone House
Trail

NH 113

White Cairn
Trail

Rattlesnake
Brook

Rattlesnake
Pool *

to North Chatham

Stone House Road

To Rte. 113
(P)

* Rattlesnake
Flume

CHAPTER 17

WATERFALLS FROM BRICKETT PLACE

◆

Mad River Falls
Bickford Slides
Rattlesnake Brook

Location: Southern end of Evans Notch, Route 113 between Chatham, New Hampshire, and Gilead, Maine

Maps: AMC #5 Carter Range–Evans Notch Map (F-12/13); DeLorme Trail Map (C-15)

◆

High in Evans Notch, under the defiant cliffs of East Royce Mountain, the Cold River springs to life. For 3 miles the slender watercourse cuts through tangled forests, dropping more than 800 feet to the broad valley that bears its name. Because of the rugged headlands to the north, the Cold River valley never developed into a major artery for commerce or tourism. To this day it remains an oasis of tranquillity, unspoiled by crowds or commercialism.

At the tip of the Cold River valley, where Route 113 crosses the New Hampshire–Maine state line and begins ascending Evans Notch, there is a well-preserved redbrick farmhouse called Brickett Place. Starting at Brickett Place, the Bickford Brook Trail climbs Speckled Mountain (2906 feet) to the east of Evans Notch, while the Royce Trail mounts the abrupt ridges of Royce Mountain (3116 feet) on the western wall of the notch. Only 300 vertical feet up each of these two trails you will reach a lovely waterfall: to the east, the shady ravine of Bickford Slides; to the north, the golden basin of Mad River Falls. Like the valley below, these waterfalls are balms for the spirit: serene, picturesque, and secluded. The valley contains many other riverine landmarks: Chandler Gorge, Eagle Cascades, Emerald Pool, Brickett Falls, Hermit Falls, Rattlesnake Brook, and Kees Falls. Mad River

Falls and Bickford Slides are the stars of this collection, so we'll leave you to find your way to these other smaller beauties. However, a quick description of Rattlesnake Brook is certainly in order.

Just a quarter mile south of Brickett Place the Forest Service maintains the Cold River Campground and the adjacent Basin Campground, together totaling thirty-five sites. Set beside a reservoir in a deep valley lobe, the Basin Campground is especially lovely. (Swimmers be warned: The reservoir is said to have leeches.) These campsites provide an excellent base for exploring the eastern front of the White Mountains. Probably the most popular local hike is the circuit of spectacular Baldface Mountain, which starts on the west side of NH 113, 1.9 miles south of the Forest Service campgrounds.

MAD RIVER FALLS

Hiking Data

Distance: Parking area to falls, 1.6 miles
Altitude gain: 300 feet (to altitude 900 feet)
Difficulty: Moderate

The Mad River (not to be confused with the one in Waterville Valley) drains the eastern slope of West Royce Mountain and joins the Cold River about 1.5 miles above Brickett Place. The hike in to Mad River Falls simply accompanies the Cold River up to its junction with the Mad River and then climbs to the falls. Faded blue blazes mark the way.

Access
A small white trail sign across Route 113 from Brickett Place locates the start of the Royce Trail. Ample parking space can be found behind Brickett Place.

The Trail
For the first quarter mile the trail follows a level logging road over to the Cold River. Where the logging road enters a clearing and veers left, the trail heads straight down to the river and hops rocks across to the west bank. This may be overgrown with grass and easy to miss. After heavy rains all the river crossings on the Royce Trail may require wading through moderately strong currents.

Apart from some irregular footing, the hike up the Cold River is quite easy and rather delightful. One treat for hikers is a wall of low cliffs on the

BRUCE AND DOREEN BOLNICK

Mad River Falls

east bank of the river where frost wedging has exposed clear fold patterns in the gray paragneiss bedrock that underlies the district. Beyond the cliffs the trail returns to the east bank and soon passes four pools separated by small slides and cascades, where the north-south line of the channel catches the warm midday sun. A scooped pothole in the bed of the third pool up is nearly irresistible for a quick swim—if you don't mind the cold water or the tiny trout that nibble at intruding toes.

Continuing north, the Royce Trail crosses a rock-strewn side stream and fords back to the west bank, passing more pools and small cascades. Promptly after this last zigzag across the Cold River the trail crosses the Mad River, feeding in from the west. Shortly, the path begins climbing up a long, steep ridge. Summit-bound hikers have a hard slog ahead, but waterfall seekers have to climb only 0.1 mile before reaching a small sign that marks the short spur path to Mad River Falls.

The spur path leads to an overlook at the edge of a precipitous basin. Fifty feet underfoot an amber pool sparkles with darting rays of sunlight that penetrate the high forest canopy overhead to cast a golden hue over the scene. At the far corner of the basin the waterfall slips in fine strands down channels of fractured bedrock flanked by tall sentinel cliffs. The rustling of the forest boughs muffles the gentle rush of the falls. From top to bottom Mad River Falls descends 100 feet over a receding series of drops and slides. In low water the falls are an ornament for the basin, like spun-glass artwork in a golden cathedral. After a storm, however, the falls roar headlong over the steep ledges and sweep across the basin floor. At such times the normally gentle stream earns its imposing name.

For a close-up view of the pool, the falls, and the fractured rock formations, you will have to climb into the basin. The word "climb" is used deliberately here because the descent is steep and tricky, with dirty footing. A few well-placed tree roots render the passage manageable, however, even for people who are not prone to accept foolish dares. Down in the bowl you will discover that you are not looking at a waterfall scene at all; rather, you are *in* a waterfall scene. It is the difference between watching a play and being in the cast. You are surrounded by the landscape and the music of Mad River Falls.

Of course if you are unsure of your scrambling abilities, you should heed the old cliché: Better safe than sorry. Enjoy the view from the overlook and then backtrack down to play in the pools along the Cold River. Or head back to Brickett Place for Act II.

BICKFORD SLIDES

Hiking Data

Distance: From parking area to the first slide, 0.7 mile; to the upper slide,
1.1 miles

Altitude gain: 300 feet (to altitude 900 feet) to first slide; 500 feet to upper slide
(altitude 1100 feet)

Difficulty: Easy to the lower slides, rougher above

Two long buttress ridges fall toward Brickett Place from the summit ridge of
Speckled Mountain. The buttresses terminate at high knobs called Sugarloaf
Mountain and Blueberry Mountain. In the deep ravine between the two
knobs, Bickford Brook has bared a series of bedrock ledges known as the
Bickford Slides: Lower, Middle, and Upper. The brook has a very modest
current for much of the season, but even when the water is low, the slides are
lovely.

Access

Park behind Brickett Place, where a Forest Service sign to the right of the
white garage marks the start of the Bickford Brook Trail.

The Trail

The trail enters the woods—a second-growth mix of scrubby trees—and
immediately climbs 200 feet to join a well-graded Forest Service track. This
grassy track then winds around the lower slope of Sugarloaf Mountain and
climbs at a very moderate grade into Bickford Brook ravine. Here the forest
changes to mature northern hardwoods that are dazzling during foliage
season. Looking around, you will find it hard to imagine that only seventy
years ago the AMC guide described these slopes as "steep pasture."

At mile 0.6 the Blueberry Ridge Trail forks off to the right (east) toward
the Lower Slides, To see the whole set of slides you can hike a loop that
consists of the two trails meeting here plus a rough Chatham Trail Association path up Bickford Brook. You can either turn at this first junction and
then climb along the brook from the Lower Slides, or you can continue up
the service road another 0.4 mile and then descend the brook from the
Upper Slides. On the latter course watch carefully for a small sign saying
CTA PATH, UPPER SLIDES on a tree to the right shortly after the track narrows.
The route described below follows the first of these options.

Turn onto the Blueberry Ridge Trail, which descends directly to Bickford Brook. Beyond the brook the trail climbs steeply up Blueberry Ridge, which, as the name suggests, bursts with blueberries in early August. This trail connects to the Stone House Trail just below the summit and so could be used to reach Rattlesnake Brook. At Bickford Brook one sign points to the Lower Slide just below and another sign steers you to the left up the Bickford Slides Trail (not to be confused with the Bickford Brook Trail, which you were on a few moments earlier).

The Lower Slide begins with a 45-foot-long chute through a small flume overhung with slender oak, maple, hemlock, and beech trees. Below this flume, the brook flows across a small terrace and slips 25 feet down a steep wall of gneiss to an unusual trough pool in a very narrow gorge. Invisible from the trail above, this glistening pool is about 15 feet long but only 2 to 4 feet wide. Its sheer, smooth walls are sprinkled with clinging mosses and wildflowers. The ledge at the head of the trench can be reached most readily by walking down through the woods above the far (eastern) wall of the ravine to an obvious ramp that angles back into the gorge.

This first set of slides is entirely unlike the others higher up the brook. To see for yourself follow the Bickford Slides Trail (yellow blazes) up the ravine. For the few rods the path is moderate and well trodden, but it soon becomes rough and steep. After 0.25 mile of ascending through excellent mushroom and wildflower habitat (watch for purple-flowering raspberries), the trail climbs a small ridge and descends to the Middle Slide.

Here you enter a shady glen at the foot of a transparent pool that mirrors the soft green radiance of the mosses on surrounding rocks and the dome of spreading hardwood boughs overhead. Forty feet above the pool Bickford Brook passes through a gate of dark-gray cliffs and slides down a mossy bank of ledge, the slope of which is broken by small terraces cradling shallow pools. An eroded footpath circles to the left of the pool, skirts a deep cave under a precarious crag of fractured rock, and climbs alongside the cascades to return to the main Bickford Brook Trail. Another path exits up the opposite (east) wall.

Beyond the Middle Slide the path is narrow and overgrown as it parallels a shallow gorge that the brook is busy chiseling. After a long 0.1 mile you will approach the rim of another deep basin at Upper Bickford Slide. Here the gentle brook slips over a headwall carpeted with thick moss and gurgles down to a shimmering pool cupped in a narrow ravine. The path circles the rim of the slide basin, crosses to the west side of Bickford Brook just above the Upper Slide, and angles over to the main Bickford Brook

Trail, only 100 yards away. You don't need a compass and map to figure out that down is the way back to Brickett Place.

RATTLESNAKE BROOK

Hiking Data

Distance: From parking area to Rattlesnake Flume, 0.7; to Rattlesnake Pool, 1.1 miles

Altitude gain: 100 feet (to altitude 1300 feet)

Difficulty: Easy

It is tempting to discuss the origin of this brook's name by stating outright that the area is infested with rattlesnakes. Although that would be an outright lie, it would have the attractive side effect of discouraging many visitors, leaving this small natural wonder to be enjoyed by the select few who know better. This being a guidebook, however, we do have some obligation to report the truth, and to uncover a few secret places. In the interests of compromise, note that although there are no rattlesnakes that we know of in the area, the mosquitoes are as bad as any in the White Mountains and seem to last long after other areas are free of them.

Access

To reach Rattlesnake Brook, head south on Route 113 from Brickett Place and take the left turn onto Stone House Road 0.7 mile beyond the campgrounds. Crossing a small bridge, turn right and follow this rough dirt road to a metal gate across it, where you park and continue on foot. This is private property, so please stay on established Forest Service or CTA trails.

The Trail

Follow the road beyond the gate, passing several fields and the White Cairn Trail. At 0.5 mile you reach a building, after which a faded CTA sign points you to the Stone House Trail and Blueberry Ridge. This trail climbs slightly before reaching a side trail to a bridge over the Rattlesnake Flume at 0.7 mile.

Rattlesnake Flume comes as a surprise: a small fissure seemingly out of place in the otherwise well-graded hillside, through which flow the clear waters of Rattlesnake Brook. This cleft in the granite is only about 4 feet wide and at most 10 feet deep, but its 200-foot length contains several perfect pools, and at the top the stream enters as a single spout of water issuing from under a boulder lying atop the head of the flume. A bridge spans the center of this seam in the bedrock, while side paths access the length of the gorge, including a 25-foot-long and 6-foot-deep sandy pool at the lower end of the gorge, a perfect way to escape the mosquitoes.

But don't spend too much time swimming in this pool: Better waters await ahead. The Stone House Trail continues past the flume, climbing slightly and crossing a tributary, immediately reaching a right turn marked by a small sign hidden behind a hemlock tree at 1.0 mile. On the left, a sign points ahead to Blueberry Mountain. Take the trail to the right, and after 0.1 mile you reach the top of a small cascade into Rattlesnake Pool. The brook cuts through a small mossy U-shaped notch forming a steep stairlike gully into the end of a kidney-shaped, deep aquamarine pothole pool, formed by a bedrock dam at its lower end. The normally objective AMC guide refers to the pool as "exquisite," a characteristic understatement. Despite the lack of good smooth rocks to lie on and the hemlocks shading the pool's environs, swimming is almost inevitable.

Historical Detour

A primitive trail through the northern pass to the Androscoggin valley was established by the Pequawket Indians, who inhabited the Cold River valley before the arrival of the Europeans. For the most part, though, colonial history bypassed the Cold River valley. It was the Saco River that served as a primary artery of exploration and migration. Like today's tourists, early adventurers were more interested in reaching the heart of the mountains than in exploring the frontal range. During the French and Indian War, famous battles were fought to the south of the Cold River valley. In 1762 nearby Fryeburg became the first town chartered in the White Mountain region, and the following year it was the first town to be settled—beating Plymouth (New Hampshire) by one year on each score. Fryeburg soon became the foremost gateway to the White Mountains, but the Cold River valley slept under its blanket of wilderness forests.

A few early settlers did travel up the Cold River and across the old Indian trail to Gilead and Bethel. The first settlers to cut homesteads from the great forests of the upper valley itself arrived in 1781, fourteen years after Chatham was chartered. That same year Captain John Evans was put in charge of protecting settlers in the region following an Indian raid on Bethel (see chapter 27). Evans Notch now honors his name.

John Brickett arrived in 1803. He settled in a log cabin on the Cold River, cleared farmland for corn and potatoes, and burned hardwood logs to make potash, which, among other things was used for fertilizer and soap making. The farmhouse now called Brickett Place was built in 1812. Brickett used bricks, which he fired himself, to avoid having to make long trips to the nearest planing mill down on the Saco River. His family lived in this house for generations; in fact, direct descendants still live in the neighborhood.

According to local folklore, John Brickett played a unique role in preserving the serenity of the Cold River valley. When the Portland & Ogdensburg Railroad line up the Saco River valley was being planned, the company was daunted by the prospect of building a track through Crawford Notch. As an alternative the railroad considered routing the line over Evans Notch to the Androscoggin valley. Legend has it that Brickett was hired to survey the route. Unhappy at the prospect of having trains thundering past his front door, he measured the slope of the notch from the floor of valley to the top of Royce Mountain! The gradient he reported was too steep for the railroad, so the engineers turned their attention back to Crawford Notch. Characteristically, the only railroad ever to penetrate the Cold River valley was a quiet one: the Underground Railroad for runaway slaves in the 1840s and 1850s.

Victory over the great iron horse may have nothing to do with it, but the Brickett family earned a permanent spot on the map: Two miles to the south, off the Mount Meader Trail, you can find Brickett Falls. Despite its handsome rock wall, Brickett Falls did not make the final cut for this book because in dry weather it has only a trickle of water.

By World War I, when the White Mountain National Forest acquired Brickett Place and the surrounding properties, the old brick farmhouse had fallen into disuse and disrepair. It was renovated during the Depression by Civilian Conservation Corps workers who also built the highway through Evans Notch. Brickett Place was used as a ranger station for a number of years, and after around 1960 it was leased by a scout troop from Lexington, Massachusetts. The house is now a registered National Historic Building and an information center.

There is no room left for the Bickford story, which is just as well since no one seems to know it!

CHAPTER 18

ROADSIDE FALLS OF THE EASTERN KANCAMAGUS

◆

Lower Falls
Rocky Gorge (Upper Falls)
Sabbaday Falls

Location: Kancamagus Highway in the vicinity of Passaconaway, west of
Conway. *Note:* No gas stations between Conway and Lincoln!
Maps: AMC #3 Crawford Notch–Sandwich Range Map (I/J-8/9); DeLorme
Trail Map (J-9/10/11)

◆

Three fascinating waterfalls lie within an easy stroll of the Kancamagus
Highway as it winds along the route of an old logging railroad through the
valley of the Swift River. Starting from Conway, the first two falls—Lower
Falls and Rocky Gorge (also called Upper Falls)—carry the powerful waters
of the Swift River itself. These falls are the largest drops in 12 miles of rapids
formed by the Swift, which tumbles nearly 700 vertical feet from the flatlands
of Passaconaway (Albany Intervale) to the Saco valley. Along this stretch of
road one can stop at almost any parkable shoulder and descend the rugged
river bank to see fine rapids. One rapid, called the Gorge, located about 2.5
miles below Lower Falls, is notorious among spring whitewater paddlers.

The third falls, Sabbaday, interrupts Sabbaday Brook as it descends the
steep eastern slopes of Mount Tripyramid to join the Swift just west of
Passaconaway. Though less powerful than the first two, Sabbaday Falls has
long been a favorite of tourists and artists. Over a hundred years ago the
New Hampshire state geologist, Professor J.H. Huntington, described the
falls as "a picture of beauty, which, once fixed in the mind, is a joy forever."

Another nearby trail, not described in detail here, leads up Mount
Chocorua past Champney and Pitcher Falls. This is a longer hike (1.6 miles

each way), and the falls have little water except in the spring or after periods of heavy rain, at which times they are very beautiful.

LOWER FALLS

Hiking Data
Distance: Roadside
Altitude gain: Zero (altitude 1000 feet)
Difficulty: Easy

If it's a warm day, bring along a swimsuit and a bottle of sunscreen when you visit the Lower Falls Recreation Area on the Kancamagus Highway, just over 7 miles from its terminus at Conway. This spot is the closest thing to Coney Island that you will find in the White Mountains, complete with parking-lot jams, changing rooms, picnic tables, and (small) sandy beaches. There are fast currents and foaming basins for thrill seekers as well as quiet eddy pools above and below the falls for tamer souls and small children.

If you don't like crowds, you may have to visit Lower Falls when the weather is less inviting. Even in the chilly days of early spring, though, you may have a lot of company. When the currents are high and fast from snowmelt and spring rain, the Swift River becomes a mecca for whitewater paddlers and curious spectators. Along a river famous for smashing boats, Lower Falls and Rocky Gorge are the two spots that even expert kayakers usually prefer to portage.

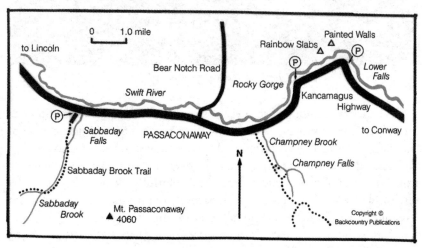

Lower Falls (along Kancamagus Highway)

Whatever the timing of your visit, Lower Falls is a compelling sight. Here the collected waters of the entire Swift River basin surge through a maze of channels, slides, chutes, curtains, and spouts arrayed across a broad band of polished ledges and boulders. Though the river drops only 10 feet, you have a front-row view of panoramic cataracts and colorful rock gardens, framed by birch and conifer. The view ranges from lovely to thrilling, depending on the level of the river, which rises and falls quickly after heavy rains.

Across the river, Moat Mountain rises more than 2000 feet above the valley floor. This mountain contains a large remnant plug of volcanic rock thousands of feet thick, evidence of an 80-million-year epoch of volcanism that began as the North American crustal plate pulled back from a primeval collision with Europe or Africa. The entire White Mountain region was once blanketed by a similar deposit of ash and magma. In most places the soft volcanic rock has weathered away completely over the past 100 million years. Here the volcanic remnant was preserved when a large caldera sank into an underlying body of magma, like a cork falling into a bottle. The magma then cooled to form a protective ring of granite. Just upstream from the parking area, some of this granite is on display in a huge amphitheater of colorful ledges known as the Painted Walls.

ROCKY GORGE (UPPER FALLS)

Hiking Data
Distance: Parking area to falls, 0.1 mile
Altitude gain: Zero
Difficulty: Easy

Rocky Gorge is located 9 miles from Conway and just over 3 miles east of the Bear Notch Road. At this point the Swift River flows north, but it curves sharply around to flow south at nearby Lower Falls. A sharp turnabout also distinguishes the character of the two waterfalls. Whereas Lower Falls consists of a broad cataract, at Upper Falls the river surges through a narrow gorge.

Each of these two waterfalls has a vertical drop of just over 10 feet, but Upper Falls is more dramatic. Indeed, to early writers Rocky Gorge was "the" Swift River Falls. Moses Sweetser's popular nineteenth-century guidebook described the formation in typically graphic terms:

> The river plunges downward . . . through a series of boiling eddies, and is narrowed into a straight passage between regular and massive granite walls about twenty feet high and several rods long. The stream roars down through this contracted gorge, and overflows during high water.

A short path leads down from the parking lot to the falls across open ledges edged with wildflowers, such as goldenrod, blue aster, and pearly everlasting. The walkway crosses the bleached granite shoulder of the river channel to a footbridge that provides a bird's-eye view of the mesmerizing waterfall, the steep, scoured granite walls of the gorge, and the turbulent currents racing through the channel below. The bridge also provides access to the far bank, where you can explore the woods up- and downstream, walk to nearby Falls Pond, and escape the transient crowds that congregate at the gorge.

Though swimming is prohibited in the gorge itself, excellent pools have been chiseled into the broad, sunny ledges along the river's edge above the falls. Depending on the water level, you should be able to find channels out of the main current that are safe enough for even (supervised) tots. Swimming is also permitted below the gorge, but access there is more difficult, the currents are stronger, and the steep walls block the sun.

If you do go into the water above the falls, be triply careful not to take any chance of getting caught in the main current and dragged into the powerful waterfall. A 1949 *Reader's Digest* article tells the miraculous story of a young woman who foolishly tried to wade across the river just above Rocky Gorge and was swept away by the current. Hours later she was found—alive—in an air pocket under the waterfall, dangling headfirst by an ankle that had wedged in the rock!

Like Lower Falls, Rocky Gorge has been developed as a National Forest Recreation Area, with a large parking lot, picnic tables, and pumped drinking water to go along with the splendid scenery.

SABBADAY FALLS

Hiking Data
Distance: Parking area to falls, 0.3 mile
Altitude gain: 100 feet (to altitude 1400 feet)
Difficulty: Easy

Sabbaday Falls has been a prime scenic attraction ever since the Passaconaway area began welcoming tourists after the Civil War. To reach the falls, watch for a large Forest Service sign announcing the Sabbaday Falls Picnic Area on the south side of the Kancamagus Highway, 3.4 miles west of Bear Notch Road, and 3.9 miles east of the Livermore Trail and Lily Pond.

From the picnic area a gently graded gravel path leads south to Sabbaday Falls. The path is broad and well marked, with information signs posted along the way. Among them, one warns that NO SWIMMING is permitted at Sabbaday Falls or within 500 feet above or below the falls. The prohibition applies to "entering or being in the water," under threat of fines,

The basin at the top of Sabbaday Falls

imprisonment, or both. Clearly Sabbaday Falls is reserved for spectators, not bathers.

Sabbaday Falls consists of three separate drops combined in an enchanting display of natural architecture. The waters of Sabbaday Brook pour through a smooth channel chiseled in the ledge and then cascade into a bubbling emerald basin, molded smooth and undercut by the swirling currents. From this basin the waters slide down a shallow chute and tumble

Velvet-leaf Blueberry

as a broad, glistening curtain over a 25-foot-high wall of broken granite. At the base of the drop lies a deep pool where the water "boils and roars and is churned into a foam" (Beals, 1916) before turning at a right angle to surge through a beautiful flume.

The flume itself is a chasm about 10 feet across. On the far side perpendicular cliffs rise 50 feet, wet with spray and ornaments of dripping moss. This flume is the result of a dike of volcanic basalt that penetrated vertical cracks in the tough granite bedrock, only to be worn down by erosion. A distinct vein of dark basalt can be seen embedded in the ledge at the mouth of the chasm.

The flume is the first part of Sabbaday Falls that you see when you approach from the picnic area. Stepping from the trail to the edge of the clear pool below the flume, you can examine a perfectly formed pothole that has been gouged out of the flat ledge by swirling waterborne sand and stones. The pothole is known as "the devil's wash basin." Above the pool the trail mounts a set of steps onto a walkway along the rim of the flume to the rest of the waterfall. The walkway is guarded by a sturdy log rail. Beyond the falls the path loops back to the Sabbaday Brook Trail. To the left the trail climbs to the summit ridge on Mount Tripyramid, 4.6 miles from the trailhead. To the right the trail returns to the parking area.

The waterfall was named Sabbaday because a party of settlers who were trying to cut a road to Waterville abandoned their arduous labor nearby the brook one Sabbath day as winter was approaching. In his 1887 guidebook, Moses Sweetser tried to introduce the name "Church's Falls on Sabbaday Brook," in honor of Frederick E. Church, a famous landscape painter. This noble effort failed to pass the test of time.

The hike to Sabbaday Falls is very popular, so expect company if you visit during tourist season.

Historical Detour

Look where the braves are gathered
Like the clouds before a flood!
And Kancamagus' tomahawk
Is all athirst for blood!

—Mary Wheeler, "Warsong of Kancamagus"

To Indians who lived along the Saco River, the valley of the Swift River was a favored hunting ground teeming with deer, bear, beaver, and otter. They called the river Chataguay. Today the highway and the mountains to the south stand as monuments to the Indians, and their story adds a fascinating dimension to this waterfall trip. The historical information presented here is drawn primarily from *Passaconway in the White Mountains,* by Charles Edward Beals Jr. (1916).

The source of the Swift River is located on Mount Kancamagus, which Professor Huntington named for the last *bashaba,* or great chief, of the Pennacook people. Before the Pilgrims arrived the Pennacook confederation of small New England tribes had been unified by Kancamagus's legendary grandfather, Passaconaway, for defense against raiding Mohawks. It is said that Passaconaway possessed magical powers. Early colonists recorded hearing stories that "he can make water burn, the rocks move, the trees dance." This magic was ineffectual, though, against the white man and his feared "iron pipe." So Passaconaway fervently preached peace and kept his people out of the early Indian wars against the colonists.

According to Pilgrim accounts, Passaconaway was already about sixty years old when he visited the Plymouth plantation in 1623. Yet he remained chief of the Pennacook until 1669, and lived until 1682—long enough to see his land taken, his tribe pauperized, many of his braves shipped as slaves to the Caribbean, and his people dispirited by rum and commercial exploitation. Today both the intervale between Sabbaday Falls and Rocky Gorge, and the 4060-foot mountain looming to the south honor the name of Passaconaway, "Son of the Bear."

Kancamagus succeeded his uncle Wonalancet as *bashaba* in 1684 and sought revenge for the humiliations suffered by his people. In 1689 he led a bloody attack on Dover but was pursued into Maine and forced to entreat for peace in 1691. Not long thereafter the Pennacook emigrated to Quebec, leaving behind only scattered bands.

One such band was headed by Chocorua. Chocorua lived in peace with early settlers of the Swift River valley until around 1761 when, according to legend, his son was accidentally poisoned while in the care of Cornelius Campbell, a local farmer. Enraged, Chocorua massacred Campbell's family and was pursued to the summit of the mountain that bears his name today. There he died after issuing a chilling "curse upon ye, white man!"

When the town of Albany was chartered in 1766, the intervale was still wilderness forest uninhabited by white men. The first intrepid settlers who moved into the intervale after the Revolutionary War found their lives beset with tragedies that were attributed to Chocorua's curse: illness, sick cattle, floods, hurricane winds, wild animal attacks, and winter storms. By 1815 the intervale had been abandoned. In 1821 Professor Dana, of Dartmouth, found that the history of illness in the intervale had been caused by "muriate of lime" in the waters, not by an Indian curse. The valley was resettled shortly thereafter and became a popular summer resort after the Civil War.

As elsewhere in the White Mountains, loggers followed the Indians and settlers into the virgin forests of the Swift River valley. A railroad through Bear Notch and a second that ran south from the Sawyer River brought loggers to the area around Sabbaday Brook beginning in 1877. The most destructive logging occurred after the Swift River Railroad was run 20 miles up the valley from Conway in 1906—the route now followed by the highway. With conservationist momentum building, the loggers resorted to cut-and-run tactics "so that not even a bush could be seen" on the slopes of Mount Paugus above Passaconaway. In 1912 forest fires and floods swept the valley. From this devastation has emerged the lovely national forest that visitors enjoy today.

CHAPTER 19

JACKSON FALLS AND DIANA'S BATHS

◆

Location: Jackson village
Maps: AMC #5 Carter Range–Evans Notch (H-10); DeLorme Trail Map (F-12)

Hiking Data
Distance: Roadside
Altitude gain: Zero (altitude 900 feet)
Difficulty: Easy

◆

The village of Jackson has been called a plaza in the city of mountains. Many plazas have a pond or fountain where folks can cool off and kids can play. But none can match Jackson, with its acres of waterfall playground on the colorful ledges of the Wildcat River.

By the same token, purists may grumble about devoting a chapter of a book on *mountain* waterfalls to a *downtown* waterfall. Let them grumble, while the rest of us enjoy the finest waterfall in the North Conway–Jackson area. Then again, Jackson Falls alone does not make for a very full waterfall trip—unless you are an ardent sunbather who can spend the whole day baking on sunny ledges. So, to fill out the trip and to add a woodsy dimension to the chapter we include an excursion to a very pretty waterfall close by at Diana's Baths.

A few words should be added about two duds that keen observers might notice on maps of the North Conway–Jackson area. The first is Goodrich Falls, which is located below the Ellis River bridge on NH 16, 1.6 miles south of Jackson. Goodrich Falls was once quite a spectacle, but, alas, an 80-foot drop of the powerful Ellis River was too good to remain undisturbed. More than a century ago the waterfall was dammed, first for a mill and later for electricity. Today the dull blank wall of a concrete dam overshadows a remnant of this once-glorious waterfall. There is no public trail to the falls and no view from the road.

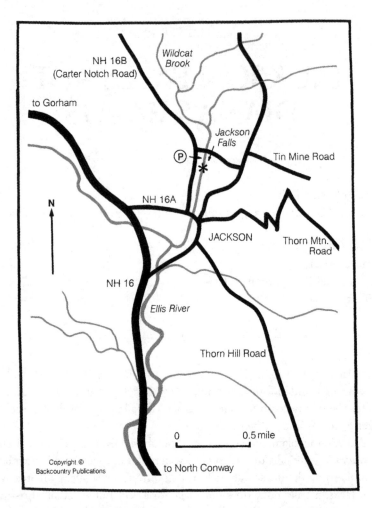

The second is Artist Falls in North Conway. Despite its fetching name, this was never much of a spectacle. The name dates to the nineteenth century, when North Conway was a flourishing art center. Artist Falls was a favorite subject for painters who preferred a short walk to a teensy waterfall over a long walk to something worthwhile. Evidently it is easier to embellish a painting than to tote art supplies over mountain trails.

If you spot Goodrich Falls or Artist Falls on a map, head for Jackson Falls.

Access

The village of Jackson lies just off NH 16 about 10 miles south of Pinkham Notch and less than 3 miles north of US 302. Two ends of NH 16A are 0.5

mile apart, and lead east into Jackson from NH 16. Take the northernmost of the these for 0.4 mile to a left turn onto Carter Notch road, just before crossing the Wildcat River, which, in 1988, was designated as one of the nation's Wild and Scenic Rivers. Carter Notch Road penetrates more than 5 miles up the picturesque river valley, but to reach the waterfall—which can be seen from Jackson village—simply drive up the first hill and park at the dirt pullout. The distance is 0.4 mile.

The Falls

Jackson Falls is not so much "a waterfall" as a maze of cataracts and pools spread across an enormous ledge of beautiful pink granite (technically, it is porphyritic quartz syenite). In some spots the ledge is smooth and polished, while elsewhere it is more fractured and scattered with broken boulders. The ledge is so large that if pulled flat and smoothed over, it could easily accommodate landing aircraft. So there is plenty of room for exploring.

The crown of the ledge is a fairly level platform the size of a football field. Along this platform the river drops only a few feet at a time, though some of its pools are large enough to be envied by most hotels and many municipalities. The riverbed is also graced with pothole tubs, slides, and small showers. It has an open southern exposure that soaks up the sun and warms the water, at least in comparison to most other mountain streams.

The top platform ends at a hillside where the ledge banks down sharply—though not too sharply for careful scrambling. Here the river shoots down long cascades, selecting from a multitude of bedrock channels depending on the volume of water. Two slender cascades race lengthwise down sloping corners that cut laterally across the wide riverbed, like huge, tilted stairs climbing down from the woods on the east bank.

On our first visit to Jackson Falls we were accompanied by three Boy Scouts coming home from a camping trip. In view of the long drive ahead, we made it quite clear to the Scouts that we were stopping to investigate the falls and *not* to swim. But once the kids were out on the sunny ledges scampering around the cascades and pools, no warnings could keep them from accidentally getting—oops!—soaking wet, at which point they entreated us successfully to let them go for a swim. The anecdote serves as a warning: Jackson Falls is so much fun that restraint and discipline may suffer. (Be sure that everyone understands the hazards of wet, slick rocks; it isn't fun to slip and break an arm or a leg.)

DIANA'S BATHS

Location: Access is from West Side Road in North Conway, near Cathedral
Ledge.
Maps: AMC #5 Carter Range–Evans Notch Map (I-10); DeLorme Trail
Map (H-12)

Hiking Data
Distance: parking area to falls, 0.5 mile
Altitude gain: 100 feet (to altitude 700 feet)
Difficulty: Easy

Diana's Baths is described in many tourist guidebooks as a fascinating
collection of potholes and ledges on Lucy Brook, near North Conway. The
brook is also adorned with a long sash of pretty cascades and a very beautiful
small waterfall.

Access
Finding the trail is the hardest part of the trip to Diana's Baths. The trailhead
is only 5 miles south of Jackson as the crow flies, but earthbound vehicles are
confined to a circuitous route that doubles that distance. Taking NH 16
south from Jackson, turn right (west) on US 302. After 2 miles the highway
crosses the Saco River, and 0.25 mile later West Side Road branches off to the
left at a very acute angle. Turn onto this road, which winds along the Saco
back downstream past Humphrey Ledge. On your right (west) less than 0.5
mile after passing the Bartlett-Conway town line, and 4.2 miles south of route
302, you will see two fenced meadows and a white farmhouse posed in the
foreground of a superb view of Cathedral and Whitehorse Ledges, with a
gravel road between the meadows. Pull off onto the gravel shoulder of the
main road. No sign marks the trailhead on the main road, but a small hiking
sign at the far end of the gravel road confirms that you are at Moat Mountain
Trail, which leads to Diana's Baths.

An alternative route from Jackson is less scenic and 1 mile longer but
great for shoppers. Take US 302 into North Conway. After shopping, turn
onto the road to Echo Lake State Park, at the north end of town. Across the
Saco River, keep right at the first fork. A half-mile later turn right onto
West Side Road. The two fenced meadows and the gravel road for trailhead
parking are on the left after 0.7 mile.

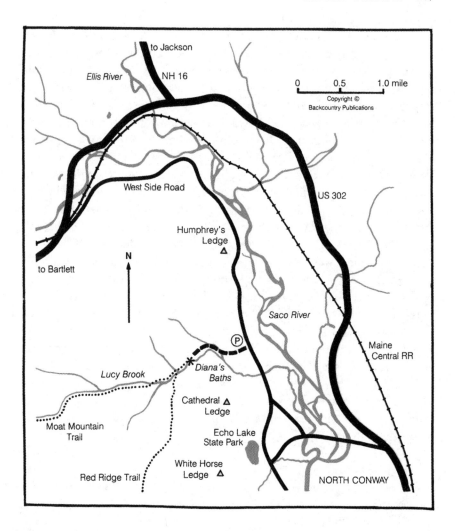

The Trail

From the end of the gravel road, the Moat Mountain Trail enters the woods and follows a wide, smooth forest road through young deciduous woods interspersed with handsome specimens of mature ash, hemlock, and pine. The trail spans a small side stream, passes a stand of tall red pines alongside Lucy Brook, and then enters a clearing (posted: NO CAMPING). At the edge of the clearing, beside the brook, you can find the remains of an old water-powered grist mill, overgrown with brambles. Above the mill site, Lucy Brook cascades down more than 200 yards of granite terraces.

To reach the cascades, take any one of the short side paths to the left after the clearing. Once you reach Lucy Brook, it is easy to explore up and down the ledges or on the paths through the woods alongside. (The main trail continues to North Moat Mountain and a long traverse of the Moat summit ridge.) Starting at the bottom of the cascades, you come first to a sloping waterslide 15 feet high, then to an abrupt 8-foot fall, and then to a feathery waterspout gushing from a chute etched in the bedrock.

Next comes the main attraction. It was described in 1881 by Samuel Adams Drake as "a solid mass of granite, more than a hundred feet across the bed of the stream, and twenty feet high," with crystal streams slipping down the face "into basins they have hollowed out. It is these curious, circular stone cavities, out of which the freshest and cleanest water constantly pours, that give to the cascade the name of Diana's Baths." According to legend the ledges were inhabited by goblins who bedeviled the Pequawket Indians of the Saco River valley. Heeding the Indians' prayers, a mountain god swept the goblins away in a flood. From this legend the cascade was originally called "the Home of the Water Fairies."

Above the broad granite wall at Diana's Baths, the incline of the molded ledge and the cascades both become more gentle, but they are still great fun to explore. Above the main falls, however, you will also see signs posted: NO SWIMMING: PUBLIC WATER SUPPLY. The Forest Service assures us that the public water supply intake pipes are located above the falls. Therefore, swimming is indeed permitted in the sparkling pools at Diana's Baths, *below* the waterfall.

Historical Detour

The waters of Jackson Falls and Diana's Baths feed into the major thoroughfares of early White Mountain history: the Ellis and Saco Rivers. Darby Field followed these rivers on his pioneering expedition to "the top of the white hill" in 1642. He was guided by Indians from the Pequawket village (what is now Conway), though only two braves set aside superstition and accompanied him to the summit. Nearly thirty years later John Josselyn used the same river highway to explore the mountains. His account, published in 1672, was the first to use the name White Mountains. He also described the Indian settlements in detail and recorded the Indian legends. The first man to use the name Mount Washington, Jeremy Belknap, followed the same rivers on his expedition in 1784.

Later, at the end of the French and Indian War, these rivers became major thoroughfares for settlement. Fryeberg, Maine, drew the first White

Diana's Baths

Mountain settlers in 1763. Only two years later Conway was incorporated; the grantee, Daniel Foster, became the first settler at North Conway in 1766. Soon the former Indian meadowlands were flooded with new arrivals.

It took twelve more years before settlement penetrated the Ellis River valley. Sturdy Benjamin Copp moved his family to the junction of the Wildcat and Ellis Rivers in 1778. Although trout and moose were abundant in-season, the Copp family suffered terrible hardships living alone in the dense forest wilderness until 1790, when five more families moved to what was then called New Madbury. (The town's name was changed to Adams in 1800, to honor John Adams, and then to Jackson in 1829, as a statement of support for Andrew Jackson over John Quincy Adams.)

One new settler was Captain Joseph Pinkham, whose ten-year-old son Daniel grew to become a pioneer of what is today called Pinkham Notch (see chapter 20). Although it was early April when the Pinkhams moved to Jackson, the valleys were still blanketed with 5 feet of snow. This made it very difficult to pull the hand sled on which all their stocks and supplies were drawn. As an experiment the children hitched the family's one hog to the sled. "Though less fleeting than the horse, and less powerful than the ox, he did us good and sufficient service," Daniel later wrote. The crude log house his father had built the previous autumn—with no chimney, no stove, no floor, and no windows—was half buried in snow when the family arrived.

Belted Kingfisher

After ushering explorers and settlers into the mountain region, these river valleys later became highways of development. The first road through the mountains followed the Saco into Crawford Notch in 1785, creating a trade route that stimulated development of the north country. The road also spawned the first small inns for teamsters. The earliest tourist hotels also took root in the upper Saco valley, beginning around 1812. By 1825—decades before the grand hotels were established at the major notches—North Conway had five lodges and regular stage coach service. Guidebook writers gushed about the beauty of the mountain views, the towering ledges, and the nearby cascades. Landscape artists were soon drawn to the village "like bees to the sweetest flowers."

Jackson developed more slowly as a tourist center. The first hotel (Jackson Falls House) was not built until 1858. Thereafter the popularity of the "enchanted valley" grew quickly. Jackson has also been slow to follow the lead of North Conway in terms of commercial development. Rather than becoming a plaza of factory outlets and tourist shops, the village remains a quiet plaza in the city of mountains.

CHAPTER 20

SHORT WALKS AT PINKHAM NOTCH

◆

Glen Ellis Falls
Crystal Cascade
Thompson Falls

Location: Pinkham Notch is the height-of-land on NH 16 between Gorham and Jackson, on the eastern flank of the Presidentials
Map: AMC #1 Presidential Range Map (F/G-9/10)

◆

Almost everything in nature, which can be supposed of inspiring ideas of the sublime and beautiful, is here realized. Aged mountains, stupendous elevations, rolling clouds, impending rocks, verdant woods, crystal streams, the gentle rill, and the roaring torrent, all conspire to amaze, to soothe and to enrapture.

—Jeremy Belknap, 1792 (as quoted in Anderson, 1930)

In describing his 1784 expedition to the mountains that local Indians called Agiochook, the Rev. Dr. Jeremy Belknap did not name the "roaring torrent" that so impressed him. Clearly, though, the "sublime and beautiful" scenery was in Pinkham Notch, where Belknap's party established camp between Glen Ellis Falls and Crystal Cascade (to use the modern appellations). Dr. Belknap was not a moonstruck prose poet but a careful historian who renounced the "temptation to romance" in recounting his expedition. The quotation above reveals that scholarly objectivity proved no match for the romantic allure of the notch's mountains, woods, and watercourses.

Today, despite its picture-book familiarity and its traffic, Pinkham

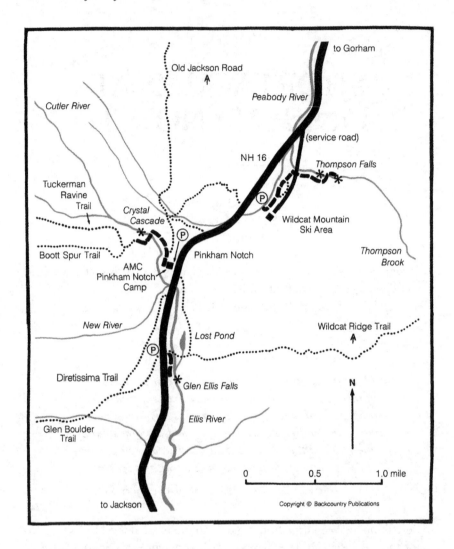

Notch still conspires to amaze, to soothe, and to enrapture visitors. Among the most popular attractions in the notch are two roaring torrents: Glen Ellis Falls and Crystal Cascade. Glen Ellis Falls is queen of the region's waterfalls in terms of power, form, and setting, while Crystal Cascade is unexcelled in graceful beauty. The third waterfall of the chapter, nearby Thompson Falls, is not in the same league with its famous neighbors in terms of splendor or popularity. In fact, it isn't even in the same watershed, since it lies on the Peabody River side of the notch. What Thompson Falls offers is a taste of seclusion, excellent views across to Mount Washington, and a quarter of a mile of tumbling cascades.

Each hike is easy and accessible, so all three falls can be seen in a day without difficulty. Accommodations are available at the AMC guest lodge at Pinkham Notch Camp. (For reservations, call 1-603-466-2727, or write to Reservations, Pinkham Notch Camp, Gorham, NH 03581.)

GLEN ELLIS FALLS

Hiking Data
Distance: Parking area to falls, 0.2 mile
Altitude gain: Minus100 feet (altitude 1850 feet)
Difficulty: Easy

The Ellis River is formed by the confluence of the New River and the Cutler River, both of which gather the waters of the great glacial cirques on the eastern wall of Mount Washington: Huntington Ravine, Tuckerman Ravine, and the Gulf of Slides. From its point of origin the Ellis River skirts the ragged cliffs of Wildcat Ridge and then races through a narrow chute that discharges over the precipitous headwall of Glen Ellis. As if being poured from a giant pitcher, the seething spout of whitewater plunges 64 feet into the deep basin. For its appearance the waterfall was called Pitcher Falls until 1852, when the name Glen Ellis Falls was suggested by Henry Ripley (whose name was tagged to an even loftier waterfall; see chapter 24).

At the bottom of the Glen Ellis basin, swirling currents have hollowed out a dark green pool that is bound on three sides by high, tree-capped crags. Piled at the pool's outlet are large boulders that centuries of frost have wedged from the cliffs. To Moses Sweetser, editor of the best-known nineteenth-century guidebook to the region, Glen Ellis Falls was "probably the finest in the White Mountains." This assessment is widely shared.

Access
The well-marked turn-off to Glen Ellis Falls is 0.7 mile south of Pinkham Notch on the west side of NH 16. The same parking area also serves the Glen Boulder Trail up Mount Washington (via Slide Peak and Boott Spur) and the Wildcat Ridge Trail to the east. A sign at the parking lot explains that the Forest Service acquired the area around the falls in 1915 after the surrounding forests had been devastated by fire.

The Trail

To reach the falls, pass through the pedestrian tunnel to the east side of the highway and turn right onto the smooth gravel path along the bank of the Ellis River. Very shortly you will reach a small cataract above a glistening pool, with a backdrop of 20-foot cliffs. Some writers have given the name Upper Glen Ellis Falls to this first cascade. Immediately below the pool large, angular, rust-hued boulders channel the rushing waters to the lip of the main waterfall. An overlook at this point (with sturdy masonry protection) provides a bird's-eye view of the river's seething plunge. There is also an information sign here summarizing the geological history of the glen.

The footpath then descends to the foot of the gorge by way of a long, winding flight of regular stone steps. Just before the descent bottoms out, a short spur of steps on the left climbs to a second overlook midway up the falls. The view here can be mesmerizing: You can easily imagine being suspended above the swirling currents of the pool, watching the falls surge past. Continuing to the bottom of the stone staircase, you will reach a third viewing point beside the outlet of the basin pool. This vantage provides an unexcelled view of Glen Ellis Falls and the rugged cliffs of the glen. You also have access to the spray-dampened slabs alongside the pool—a favorite spot for snapshots.

On one trip to Glen Ellis Falls we watched a grandfatherly visitor, evidently quite out of condition, accompany his family down the long flight of steps to the base of the falls. Approaching the last corner he grumbled, "This had better be worth it!" But the moment the waterfall came into view, one of the children cried out, "Awesome!" The others simply nodded in quiet consent.

The glen opens to the south, inviting the sun to paint subdued rainbows in the fine spray from the falls. When the river thunders with spring snowmelt, however, the spray is so heavy that the area is doused with mist, rendering photography all but impossible. It is said that the spray reveals ghostly forms of two young lovers holding hands. According to an Indian legend, a local chief promised his beautiful daughter to a warrior, but the maiden fell in love with a brave from a neighboring tribe. A bow-and-arrow contest was arranged to settle her fate. When the warrior won the contest, the maiden fled with her lover, and the two leaped to their deaths, hand in hand, over the brink of the falls.

Most visitors go no farther than the terminus of the maintained trail at the base of the falls. After all, that's the main attraction. A short distance farther down the gorge, however, you can find a delightful sideshow of cata-

Glen Ellis Falls

racts, pools, and sunny ledges to explore. An informal path runs though the woods alongside the river. Not far downstream a table ledge provides the safest crossing to the east bank of the river, where more paths run through the woods.

Even if you are not in top condition for climbing stairs, do pay Glen Ellis Falls a visit. Just take it easy on the stairs and rest as often as you wish.

CRYSTAL CASCADE

Hiking Data
Distance: Parking area to falls, 0.3 mile
Altitude gain: 200 feet (altitude 2200 feet)
Difficulty: Easy

To reach Crystal Cascade, park at the AMC Pinkham Notch Camp, and get onto the path that passes to the left of the Trading Post (where you can obtain maps, books, snacks, minor supplies, and information). This is start of the Tuckerman Ravine Trail, the most popular trail up Mount Washington. Keep to the right on the main trail when the Old Jackson Road forks off to the right a few dozen yards from the trailhead. After a few hundred more yards of very easy walking the trail bridges the Cutler River above a pretty cascade. If you look upstream from the bridge, you can see the river tumbling out of a deep ravine that narrows to a dark gorge. Crystal Cascade is at the head of this gorge.

Continue up the trail past the bridge. The path gets considerably steeper now, but you have only 100 yards to go before reaching a side path to a set of steps leading up to the rim of the gorge. Directly across from this vantage point the Cutler River—named for the Rev. Dr. Manasseh Cutler, a botanist whom Belknap accompanied in 1784—emerges from a canopy of thick forest to tumble down a steep bank of dark rock in a series of lively leaps. To Thomas Starr King (1859) the cascade's sprightly descent gave the impression of "graceful and perpetual youth." The cascade is 80 feet high, in two drops. First, a broad curtain of dancing whitewater falls 60 feet to a

Bluebead Lily

small ledge, followed by another 20-foot plunge. On both sides are dark cliffs, hemmed with moist green boughs of spruce, fir, birch, and mountain ash. At the bottom of the narrow gorge the river churns through an abrupt right-angle turn.

The geology at Crystal Cascade is quite unlike that of any other waterfall in the area. Its dark rockbed is a remnant volcanic vent that intruded into the surrounding field of schist and quartzite during relatively recent geological times. Another small volcanic vent is exposed at the footbridge below the cascade; Billings, et al. (1979), explain that the formation is distinguished "by angular fragments of dark rock embedded in a dark-greenish base."

In some respects, it is a misfortune for Crystal Cascade to be located on the Tuckerman Ravine Trail. Visitors make a special stop to admire Glen Ellis Falls, but Crystal Cascade is often rewarded with little more than a passing glance by hikers en route to or from the summit of Mount Washington. Evidently many visitors to the mountain palace are not distracted by dazzling jewels when they have an audience with the king!

Crystal Cascade did not always play second fiddle to the summit. Before Tuckerman Ravine Trail was established the footpath from the notch stopped at the cascade. Carriage rides to see Crystal Cascade and Glen Ellis Falls were favorite excursions for the well-heeled guests who lodged up the road at the elegant Glen House. Samuel Drake (1881) devoted three doting pages to describing Crystal Cascade, and Julius Ward (1890) picked it over Glen Ellis as "perhaps the most beautiful of the White Mountain falls."

Beautiful though it is, Crystal Cascade suffers another ill effect from being located on the Tuckerman Ravine Trail: Heavy foot traffic has led the Forest Service to post notices for hikers to stay on the trail. This means that exploratory side trips are expressly discouraged. Consequently, there is not much to do at Crystal Cascade except enjoy the view. Unless, of course, you join other hikers and head up to Tuckerman Ravine, where you will find some of the most inspiring scenery in the region. The ravine, a superb glacial cirque that is famous for its spring skiing, lies 3 miles of steady climbing farther along. During the spring and after heavy rains, its precipitous headwall is laced with white ribbons of cascading waters, which early guidebooks called the Fall of a Thousand Streams. Alternatively, a right turn onto the Huntington Ravine Trail, 1 hard mile beyond Crystal Cascade, leads past numerous small cascades en route to one of the steepest headwall trails in the White Mountains. This headwall itself is graced with an awe-inspiring cascade down the left gulley. This is called Pinnacle Gully Cascades. The summit of Mount Washington is the ultimate side trip, 4 miles and 4000 vertical feet above Crystal Cascade.

THOMPSON FALLS

Hiking Data
Distance: Parking area to falls, 0.7 mile
Altitude gain: 100 feet (altitude 2000 feet)
Difficulty: Easy

Unlike its esteemed neighbors on the south side of Pinkham Notch, Thompson Falls doesn't appear at the top of anyone's list of the most beautiful waterfalls in the White Mountains. Most guidebooks overlook it altogether. Books that do mention Thompson Falls are usually referring to a less interesting waterfall of the same name that is located behind White Horse Ledge in North Conway.

While exaggerating the mileage, Moses Sweetser's reliable old *White Mountains: Handbook for Travellers* (1887) points readers in the right direction. Sweetser describes Thompson Falls as

> a chain of cascades ½ M. long, sweeping down through pretty forest scenery, and furnishing rich ground for pleasant rambles. The view of Mount Washington and its E. ravines, from the head of the main fall, is one of the best in the mountains. . . .

Access
The falls are on Thompson Brook, which flows off Wildcat Mountain into the Peabody River just north of the Wildcat Ski Area. The hike begins at the main Wildcat parking lot, 0.8 mile north of the AMC Pinkham Notch Camp and 2 miles south of the Mount Washington Auto Road.

The Trail
Cross the footbridge over the narrow Peabody River directly behind the Wildcat Base Lodge and look for the "Way of the Wildcat" Nature Trail leading to your left. This self-guided trail parallels the river for 0.25 mile and then loops back to the lodge. The path to Thompson Falls diverges from the nature trail at the far end of this loop.

The Thompson Falls Trail proceeds on level ground through cool forests for 0.25 mile before crossing a paved service road that leads to the Wildcat C parking lot. From this point the trail ascends gently for another 0.25 mile, crosses a small rise, and descends into a lovely glen, which encloses a large,

The lowest cascade of Thompson Falls

shady pool. At the head of the glen a 12-foot-high ribbon of water spills across the mouth of a giant clam-shaped ledge and splashes off the lower "lip" of the clam into the pool. The pool is an especially inviting place to swim, but the water is bitterly cold. We have noticed that children can tolerate the cold water on a dare, but most sensible people will settle for a quick footbath.

The quality of the path indicates that most visitors proceed no farther than the glen, perhaps under the impression they have seen Thompson Falls. Actually this is just the last of a long string of cascades. To explore the rest of the waterfall, follow faded yellow blazes on the rough path to the right of the giant clam falls and cross the ledges to the north side of the stream. The path then stays on the north bank, passing a succession of charming waterfalls, mossy pothole basins, and crystal-clear cascades sliding down open ledges. The uppermost ledge provides the best views across the Peabody valley to Mount Washington. Be sure to bring binoculars along on this hike!

In addition to the waterfall and the views, the hike also offers a handsome mix of trees, a host of wildflowers in the late spring, and an easy escape from the Pinkham Notch crowds. This is not the same wild forest that Sweetser found so endearing, since the area was logged clean prior to World War I. But even having lost its wilderness spirit, the forest retains a sense of solitude and charm.

Thompson Falls and Thompson Brook are both named in honor of Colonel J.M. Thompson, the first proprietor of Glen House, which opened in 1853. The Glen House became one of the grandest of the White Mountain inns, with a dining room for two hundred guests, a parlor a hundred feet long, and a stable of more than a hundred horses. Glen House coaches, drawn by eight white horses, would transport guests in style to and from the train depot at Gorham. Thompson was also a trail builder. In addition to trails to nearby waterfalls, he cut the first bridle path up Mount Washington—the predecessor of today's Mount Washington Auto Road.

Tragically, Thompson drowned in the swollen Peabody River during a severe storm in 1869. The original Glen House burned down in 1884. An even more luxurious replacement was reduced to ashes in 1893, and a third, more modest, Glen House burned down in 1967.

Historical Detour

At the time of Belknap's expedition in 1784, Pinkham Notch was simply known as the "eastern pass." A rude trail, called the Shelburne Road, had been blazed through the pass by a Captain Evans, who served as Belknap's guide. More than forty years later the state contracted Daniel Pinkham, son of Jackson's pioneer settler (see chapter 19), to improve the path through the notch so it could accommodate wagon traffic between Conway and Gorham. In return for this service Pinkham received a grant of land extending a quarter mile on each side of the road, from Glen Ellis Falls to just above Glen House. In short, he was granted the notch that now bears his name.

Pinkham's Grant was never incorporated as a town, and the only early development in the vicinity—the Glen House site, cleared in 1853—was located just outside the grant boundary. The Appalachian Mountain Club began developing hiking trails in the notch shortly after the club's founding in 1876, but the district was essentially undeveloped when the AMC acquired its Pinkham Notch property in 1915. The first structures to be built, in 1920, were two log cabins. The road then was just a gravel track that closed each winter. Under the guiding hand of Joe Dodge, who took on the job of hut master in 1922, the Pinkham Notch Camp developed into the center of AMC operations and activities in the White Mountains.

Let your visit to the waterfalls of Pinkham Notch serve as a tribute to the Appalachian Mountain Club for its dedication to enhancing the accessibility of New England's natural treasures while protecting the region's great beauty.

CHAPTER 21

NANCY CASCADES

◆

Location: Nancy Pond Trail, off US 302 below Crawford Notch
Maps: AMC #3 Crawford Notch–Sandwich Range (H-8); DeLorme Trail
Map (G-9)

Hiking Data

Distance: Parking area to cascades, 2.4 miles
Altitude gain: 1500 feet (to altitude 2400 feet)
Difficulty: Moderate

◆

From the serene waters of Nancy Pond, high in the mountains above Notchland, Nancy Brook flows for less than 2.5 miles to the Saco River, 2100 feet below. The brook begins its short run to the valley floor by meandering quietly through a broad, moss-carpeted headland of virgin spruce forest. The meandering ends abruptly at the head of a deep ravine where the brook tumbles down 400 feet of steep ledges, forming the long line of lacy waterfalls called Nancy Cascades.

Although Nancy Brook was christened in the earliest years of the republic, the lofty cascades on the mountain headwall seem to have been unknown until after the Civil War. When Benjamin Willey described Nancy Brook in 1856—"the eye is never weary in gazing upon the cascades and deep transparent basins"—he was referring only to the bottom mile. Between US 302 and the Saco River, Nancy Brook races through a small gorge that encloses a set of minor cascades. In Willey's time a carriage road crossed this gorge on a wooden span called Nancy's Bridge. So these minor cascades were familiar, while the brook's upper reaches were merely "unknown heights in the dark forest above."

Only since 1960 has a maintained trail reached Nancy Cascades. More accurately, a trail was established by the AMC in 1938 but destroyed within months by the Great Hurricane which struck New England that autumn. In 1960 crews from the Pasquaney Camp at Newfound Lake restored and

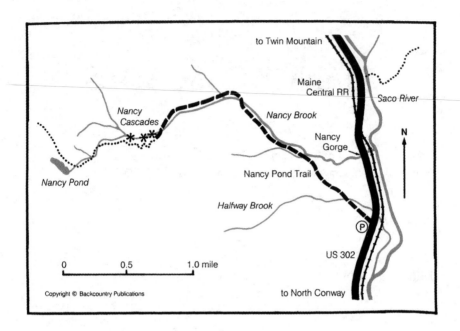

extended the Nancy Pond Trail. Perhaps because the trail does not reach any summits, and perhaps because the hike to Nancy Cascades is a solid climb, there are not usually many hikers here. The sparsity of visitors makes this major cascade all the more attractive.

Access

The Nancy Pond Trail begins from a gravel roadside parking area on the west side of US 302, 1 mile below the Notchland Inn and 3 miles north of the Sawyer Rock Picnic Area. The small trailhead sign at the entrance to the forest path is easily visible from the road. Directly across the highway there is a larger dirt parking area. A path from this lot leads down to the Saco River at a point called Rowan's Rapids, which is popular with spring whitewater paddlers. The beautiful pool here is deliciously refreshing on a hot summer's day. In fact, you can find numerous swimming holes along the Saco on a hot day just by watching for concentrations of parked cars along the highway.

The Trail

To bypass private property, the trail starts 0.75 mile south of Nancy Brook and therefore begins by angling northwest back to the brook. After starting out on a wide forest road, the trail quickly turns left into the woods and climbs a small rise to a second logging road. This road climbs gradually for about 0.4 mile through handsome beech forest before crossing Halfway Brook, where we once saw two toddlers squealing with delight in a small pool—under the watchful eyes of their parents. Less than 1 mile from the highway an ugly red-painted cairn marks your entrance into the national forest. From here to the shallow col between Mounts Nancy and Anderson the trail traverses the Nancy Brook Scenic Area, a 460-acre protected zone established in 1964.

The trail parallels Nancy Brook on a ridge well above the south bank before crossing to the north bank at mile 1.6. To this point and a short distance beyond, the trail is easy to follow, well graded, and clearly blazed. Much of the route is on old logging roads and a forest road that once served a fire tower on Mount Bemis, which flanks Nancy Brook to the north. During the early part of this century, logging roads penetrated most of the area. AMC guidebooks before World War II described the range as having been heavily lumbered from both east and west, "leaving in many places a mere fringe of trees along the crest of the ridge." The stand of virgin spruce beside Nancy Pond is one spot they missed, though it was extensively damaged by the 1938 hurricane. This valley forest was also severely damaged by the 1998 ice storm—at times it seems that half the trees in the forest were bent or broken under the weight of the ice.

Immediately past the Nancy Brook crossing, the trail turns left off the old Mount Bemis service road onto another logging road that ascends along the north bank. After passing the remains of an old mill, the trail becomes narrower, rougher, and steeper as the beech forest gives way to birch and then to conifers. A number of slides cut across the path, contributing to the rough footing. Here you may notice that the water has a distinct teakish tint and that a brown foam accumulates in eddy pools along the brook. Both are natural effects of acids generated by the decay of organic matter in the stagnant water in and around Nancy Pond. The foam is caused when the acids weaken surface tension and allow turbulence from the cascades to form small bubbles.

After 0.5 mile of steady climbing, the trail crosses back to the south bank and soon thereafter approaches the shimmering white curtain of Nancy Cascades. From this bottom cascade (at mile 2.4) the trail switchbacks up the steep headwall of the ravine to the top of the cascades (mile 2.8). The last 0.6 mile to Nancy Pond passes through an enchanting conifer forest and a wild highland marsh. Backpackers can continue over the height-of-land and down into Carrigain Notch in the Pemigewasset Wilderness.

The Cascades

Stepping down from the trail to the base of the first cascade, you come to the edge of the large, rippling pool. Across the pool a tapered curtain of whitewater ribbons leaps down a steep bank of weathered gray gneiss (pronounced "nice") that is eight stories high and 30 feet wide. With either a few brisk strokes across the pool, or a careful barefoot scramble around the perimeter, you can clamber onto the base of the ledge and play under the waterfall. You have to be tough to go in the water, however, because the glen is well shaded, and cooled by a draft that rides down the cascade. Kids can be lured into the cold water by the prospect of having their picture taken. Most visitors, though, will be content just to soak in the spectacle from a dry perch on the boulders at the foot of the pool.

What you see from the base pool is only the first in a long line of impressive cascades. A detailed account of an early exploration of Nancy Brook, *Appalachia* (1883), described four distinct cascades totaling over 300 feet of vertical drop. Modern topographic maps indicate that the drop is closer to 400 feet.

Climbing one long switchback farther up the trail, you will reach a platform with a stunning view of the middle cascades. From heights above, the water rushes down a nearly continuous series of chutes and slides to a brown pool on a small shelf below—which forms the crest of the bottom cascade. After a few more steep switchbacks you will come to the brink of the top cascade and another spectacular view. From a secure aerie you can watch the brook tumble headlong down a steep corridor of ledge, framed by feathery boughs of mountain ash. Out beyond, you can trace the winding ravine back down to the Saco River valley and across to the Montalban Ridge, the long southern leg of Mount Washington. The spot is truly idyllic, as is Nancy Pond farther up the trail.

Although some hikers bushwhacked up the cascades before the present trail was established, the scrambling opportunities are poor on the sheer ledges. Not only is the rock steep and treacherous, but a thick copse of spruce and fir trees blocks the passage up the falls. By far the best spots for exploring the streambed are above and below the headwall.

The gray gneiss bedrock that is exposed at Nancy Cascades is one of the oldest rock forms in the region. This tough metamorphic rock began as silt at the bottom of a shallow sea more than 500 million years ago. After being compressed by millions of years of overlying sediments, the rock was contorted and subsumed by movements of the earth's crustal plates. The resulting pressure and heat recrystallized the ancient sediments (and also destroyed

ROBERT KOZLOW

Nancy Cascades at Crawford Notch

any fossil records in the formation). Later intrusions of magma produced the attractive granites that are found in much of the region, but here—and in the Presidential Range to the north—all of the overlying rock has eroded away to expose the ancient metamorphic foundation.

Historical Detour

Nancy Cascades, Nancy Brook, Nancy Pond, Mount Nancy, Nancy's Bridge. If you suspect that there is a Nancy story behind all these names, you're right. It is one of the most widely known tales in White Mountain history and one of the few that is a romance, albeit a tragic one.

The story begins with a Colonel Joseph Whipple, who was the first settler to pass north through the White Mountain Notch (Crawford Notch, today) after the passage was discovered in 1771. As the pioneer settler in the town of Jefferson, Whipple gained control of vast tracts of land over which he exercised autocratic, though benign, authority. As one example of his noblesse oblige, he refused to sell any of his grain to starving farmers from Bartlett in order to conserve supplies for his dependent neighbors in Jefferson. His noncommercial exploits included piloting Jeremy Belknap's 1784 exploration of what was later named Mount Washington and escaping from Indians who had been sent by the English to capture him during the Revolutionary War.

Nancy Barton (the surname is uncertain), a servant girl at Whipple's manor, fell in love with one of the colonel's farmhands. The two lovers arranged, so Nancy thought, to accompany Whipple to Portsmouth on his annual trading trip in the late fall of 1778, there to be married. But after Nancy entrusted two years of savings to her lover, he and the colonel set out for the coast while she was off in Lancaster. Nancy was frantic when she heard about their departure and assumed that the two men had left her behind mistakenly. Resolving to catch up with the party and be reunited with her lover, Nancy tied together a small bundle of clothes and set off toward the White Mountain Notch in deep snow and a bitter northwest wind.

Though poorly clad for the wintry storm, Nancy managed to tramp over twenty miles down into the notch, only to arrive at Colonel Whipple's campsite a bit too late. The party had moved on, though the embers of the campfire were still alive. After warming herself briefly by the dying embers Nancy pushed on in desperation, having eaten nothing since leaving Jefferson. When she crossed the Saco River, her clothes got wet. Exhausted and cold, Nancy collapsed in the snow, where a search party from Jefferson found her, frozen, the next day.

Her lover, it is said, went mad after hearing of her death and died only months later. Some say, as well, that the lover's wails can still be heard when the winds sweep across the place where Nancy died.

In memory of the tragic tale of this love-struck young woman, Nancy Brook took its place in the geography of New Hampshire decades ahead of Mount Washington or Crawford Notch and a century before the cascades were first described. It might be noted, too, that nothing of any significance today bears the name Whipple.

CHAPTER 22

ARETHUSA FALLS

◆

Location: Western wall of Crawford Notch, just inside the southern boundary of the state park

Maps: AMC #3 Crawford Notch–Sandwich Range Map (H-8); DeLorme Trail Map (F-9)

Hiking Data

Distance: Parking area to Bemis Brook Falls and Coliseum Falls, 0.5 mile; to Arethusa Falls, 1.3 miles

Altitude gain: 750 feet to Arethusa Falls (altitude 2000 feet)

Difficulty: Easy to Bemis Brook Falls and Coliseum Falls; moderate to Arethusa Falls

◆

In early editions of the *AMC White Mountain Guide,* Arethusa Falls was described as being "about 140 ft. high." More recent editions have the falls stretching to "over 200 ft. high." An average of these two estimates comes close to what was reported in 1875 by M.F. Sweetser and Professor J.H. Huntington, who named the falls and *measured* its height as 176 feet. Even their figure is not clear-cut, however, since the measurement depends on exactly where the observers spotted the top and the bottom of the falls. All agree, though, that Arethusa Falls is the highest single drop in New Hampshire as well as one of the most spectacular—especially when Bemis Brook is running high.

Along with a grand main attraction, this trip also features a delightful sideshow of delicate miniatures. Bemis Brook Falls and Coliseum Falls are about as small as waterfalls come, yet they are also about as pretty as they come. In fact, if you are traveling with young children you might choose to visit Bemis Brook and Coliseum Falls and skip Arethusa Falls altogether. A short excursion to the two small waterfalls would be an excellent way to spark a child's interest in the woods and streams.

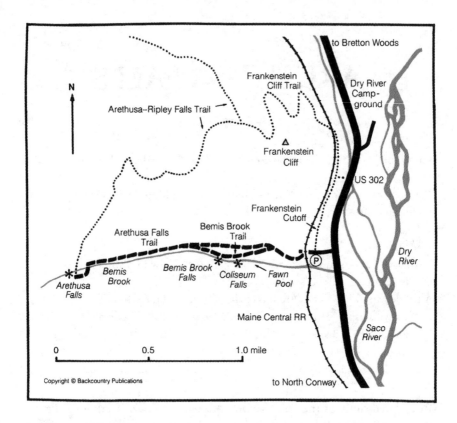

Access

Driving up US 302 from Conway or Pinkham Notch, turn left onto the paved side road just past the sign marking the entrance into Crawford Notch State Park. If you are coming down the notch from the north, the turn is on your right about 0.5 mile beyond the Dry River Campground. (Campers staying at Dry River can easily reach Arethusa Falls in the early morning or late afternoon, when it is much less crowded.) Park at the end of the short side road, below the railroad tracks. The white house above the tracks is privately owned, so keep out of the yard.

The Trail

Alongside the Forest Service information board at the parking area, an obvious trail can be seen leading into the woods. This is not the trail to take unless you want to reach the falls by hiking *up* the Frankenstein Cliff Trail on a 4.5-mile loop. The loop trip is quite beautiful, but most people prefer hiking *down* the imposing cliffs after visiting the falls.

Frankenstein Cliff, named for an eighteenth-century landscape artist, is the home of a peregrine falcon family. These swift avian predators can be recognized by their size (about that of a crow); their long, pointed wings; and their long, narrow tail. The cliffs are also a favorite haunt for another interesting species: winter ice climbers. In midwinter ice climbers may also be found picking their way up the blue-green mask of ice at Arethusa Falls itself.

The Arethusa Falls Trail enters the woods above the railroad tracks, to the left of the private yard and a small ice-cream stand run by the residents of the house by the parking lot. Two adjacent Forest Service signs provide contradictory distances to the falls: either 1.2 miles or 1.5 miles. The trail shortly makes a right turn, ascends a small ridge, and then begins a steady climb along the north wall of the Bemis Brook ravine. The path is well blazed and easy to follow after the initial turns have been negotiated, but irregular rocks and a maze of spruce roots farther along make for rough footing, with the brook out of sight below. When the trail does touch the brook, you will find small cascades and pools set in the smooth, flat slabs of exposed bedrock. These are excellent spots for a rest and a snack.

About 1.2 miles from the parking lot the trail crosses to the south bank of Bemis Brook on a small and somewhat rickety footbridge. Clambering up the roots and rocks beyond the crossing, you will begin to detect the

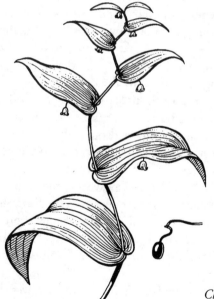

Clasping-leaved Twisted Stalk

rumble of the waterfalls. In only 0.1 mile a sheet of shimmering silver appears as a backdrop to a tall spruce tree, and the trail emerges into a granite basin at the foot of the falls.

The hike up to Arethusa Falls is lengthened only slightly by taking the detour along Bemis Brook Trail, which forks off to the left 0.2 mile from the parking lot. This pretty side trail crosses over to the brook and follows its rise past charming Fawn Pool, Coliseum Falls, and Bemis Brook Falls, before climbing steeply to rejoin the main trail at about 0.7 mile.

From Arethusa Falls you can either retrace your steps back to the parking lot or continue into the woods on the north side of the basin onto the Arethusa–Ripley Falls Trail. The latter connects with Ripley Falls (2.1 miles north), after climbing over an intervening ridge, and descends to Willey House Station (see chapter 24). By turning right onto the Frankenstein Cliff Trail after 1 mile, however, you can loop back to your car. After crossing the crest of the cliff, this trail descends steeply to US 302, where the Frankenstein Cutoff returns to the Arethusa parking lot. Sensible caution should be exercised on top of the cliff: one of the few waterfall-related fatalities in recent years occurred when a man slipped off the top of the falls. (Note also that hiking on the railroad tracks is strictly prohibited.)

Coliseum and Bemis Brook Falls

Coliseum Falls is located about 75 yards above Fawn Pool on the Bemis Brook Trail. Between the pool and the falls the brook slides in transparent sheets down a gently sloping ledge of brown, weathered granite. You can approach the falls by the trail or by exploring up the streambed. Since the brook faces east here, the open ledges benefit from the morning sun, making Coliseum Falls an inviting place to enjoy the brook.

The falls consist of two short drops separated by a broad, flat slab. At each drop the rock is fractured horizontally and eroded in layers to form a series of short, regular steps. The lower drop, only 4 feet in height, has etched a wide horseshoe into the rock, ringing the curtain of water with layered platforms like the tiers of a miniature coliseum.

Above Coliseum Falls the trail angles away from the brook and climbs a bit before regaining the stream at an overlook atop a small crag beside Bemis Brook Falls. This picturesque waterfall consists of four short drops separated by terraces that are adorned with clear, shallow pools. Although not a very apt term for a waterfall, the word "delicious" comes to mind when I think of this tantalizing scene.

At Bemis Brook Falls the ravine is steeper and narrower than at Coliseum Falls, so it's not a good playground for little kids. But big kids can scramble down to the brook and explore the pools and the falls.

Arethusa Falls

Emerging from the woods at Arethusa Falls, you will be standing in a cool downdraft among angular boulders at the bottom of a small bedrock basin. Three sides of the basin are lined with spruce and birch. The fourth side, to the left, is a towering wall of pink-gray Osceola granite, draped with a wide veil of lacy rivulets. Depending on the water conditions, the falls can appear as an elaborate fountain tumbling playfully from ledge to ledge or as a thundering curtain surging over the wall in a single drop and filling the basin with chilly spray.

At the base of the falls the stream skips down slabs of scalloped bedrock, turns, and then slides off into the woods below. There is no pool of any significance right at the falls. If you want to swim, there are good (but shaded) spots downstream, including one unusual tub pool lined with benches of horizontal rock strata.

Arethusa Falls is not made for scramblers any more than for swimmers. The bottom of the wall may look inviting to climb, but the rocks here are too steep and slippery to be safe. One young man who succumbed to the temptation in 1983 slipped and fell, resulting in severe head injuries. Less tragic, but equally to the point, the one and only dent in my camera was incurred while I was "testing" the rocks for this description! On a subsequent trip we saw three people slip on the rocks in a span of fifteen minutes. Fortunately no one was hurt. On the whole, though, scrambling is best confined to explorations farther downstream. One last word of warning: Unguarded snacks may become chipmunk food!

Seen from below, Arethusa Falls does not appear as high as it is reputed to be, regardless of which estimate you accept. One way to appreciate its true size is to hike to the top by the badly eroded side path in the woods to the left. But the top of the waterfall is a very dangerous place, and farther upstream there is not much to see. In July 1995 a visitor exploring the top of the falls fell to his death. So in deference to the poor condition of the ascent path, it is best just to enjoy the superb view of the falls from below, and leave the problem of gauging its height to the experts.

Historical Detour

According to Moses Sweetser's 1887 *The White Mountains: Handbook for Travellers:*

> Arethusa Falls were discovered by Professor Tuckerman many years ago, but not visited by a dozen people since, and are well nigh forgotten. They were visited and measured by the Editor and Professor Huntington in September, 1875, and then (being nameless) received the provisional name of Arethusa Falls, in allusion to Shelley's lines. . . .

The professor here was Edward Tuckerman, a distinguished botanist after whom the great ravine on Mount Washington is named, and the allusion to Shelley refers to the poem "Arethusa," written by Percy Bysshe Shelley in 1820. The poem relates a story, from Greek mythology, of a beautiful nymph named Arethusa, a companion of Artemis. In a vain attempt to escape the amorous advances of the river god Alpheus, Arethusa was transformed into a fountain on the island of Ortygia. As described by Shelley:

> Arethusa arose
> From her couch of snows
> In the Acroceraunian mountains,—
> From cloud and from crag,
> With many a jag,
> Shepherding her bright fountains.
> She leapt down the rocks,
> With her rainbow locks,
> Streaming among the streams;
> Her steps paved with green
> The downward ravine
> Which slopes to the westward gleams;
> And gliding and springing,
> She went, ever singing,
> In Murmurs as soft as sleep.
> the Earth seemed to love her,
> and Heaven smiled above her,
> and she lingered towards the deep. . . .

It is probably no coincidence that this very poem had been quoted by Thomas Starr King in his popular book on the "White Hills," published in 1859. King, however, used the poem to describe Silver Cascades, just up Crawford Notch, and he mentioned the waterfalls on Bemis Brook not at all.

Arethusa Falls is not mentioned in Lucy Crawford's *History of the White Mountains* either. This is curious because for five decades Lucy's father-in-law, Abel Crawford—"the old Patriarch" of the Notch—resided at Mount

ROBERT KOZLOW

Arethusa Falls

Crawford House, only 3 miles south of the falls. Later, it was her brother-in-law, Nathaniel Davis, who forfeited Mount Crawford House and virtually all the real estate up to the head of Crawford Notch to Dr. Samuel Bemis, after whom the nearby brook and falls are named.

Bemis was a Boston dentist, an inveterate fisherman, and a pioneer tourist, if there can be such a creature. After visiting the notch every year from 1827 to 1840, he moved into the neighborhood permanently after foreclosing on a loan to Davis, who was the innkeeper at Mount Crawford House (and the pioneer of the Davis Path up Mount Washington). Despite having come by the inn as a financier, Bemis was widely beloved as a host, nature enthusiast, and local explorer. As a nature photographer, he was one of the first Americans to import a daguerreotype camera from Europe, where it had been invented in 1839. For his home Bemis built the stone house called Notchland, now the Notchland Inn.

Considering that Dr. Bemis and Abel Crawford were both living nearby when Professor Tuckerman discovered Arethusa Falls—indeed, Tuckerman stayed at Mount Crawford House—it is a mystery how the professor's tremendous discovery could have been "well-nigh forgotten" by the time the falls were christened!

Less of a mystery is how the surrounding virgin forests disappeared. In the late 1880s the whole area came under the control of timber interests. Just a mile south of Bemis Brook, Jones & Company established a large sawmill that grew into a substantial town called Carrigain. Beginning in 1892 a logging railroad into the Dry River basin was built through the very spot where you park your car to visit Arethusa Falls. Consequently, the highest waterfall in the White Mountains was still largely unknown to tourists when the state started acquiring property for the Crawford Notch State Park in 1912.

Finally, in the 1930s, the property around Arethusa Falls was acquired by the state, and thus preserved for Arethusa and her suitor:

> At sunrise they leap
> From their cradles steep
> In the cave of the shelving hill;
> At noontide they flow
> Through the woods below
> And the meadows of asphodel. . . .

CHAPTER 23

DRY RIVER FALLS

◆————————◆

Location: Deep in the Presidential–Dry River Wilderness, reached from US 302 in Crawford Notch

Maps: AMC #3 Crawford Notch–Sandwich Range Map (G-8); DeLorme Trail Map (E-10)

Hiking Data

Distance: Parking area to falls, 5.4 miles

Altitude gain: 1600 feet (to altitude 2800 feet)

Difficulty: Moderate, but long

————————————◆————————————

Picture in your mind a walk along the Dry River into Oakes Gulf. Not very exciting? Unlike "Death Valley" or "Grand Canyon," the name "Dry River" doesn't exactly stoke the imagination. Neither does the view along US 302 by the trailhead. Passing through the southern reaches of Crawford Notch State Park, your attention will probably be drawn westward to the crags of Frankenstein Cliff, not to the wall of hardwoods on the east side of the road where the Dry River joins the Saco. Back in 1887 the Dry River basin didn't excite Moses Sweetser either: "There is but little of interest in this long glen . . . because the bottom and sides are so clothed with large trees as to hide the adjacent mountains."

Now think about hiking along the perilous Mount Washington River into the vast forests of the Presidential Wilderness to a thundering waterfall. Does that sound better? Welcome to Dry River Falls.

The Dry River—which was also called the Mount Washington River for many years—drains an enormous basin formed by the southern Presidential ridge to the west, Mount Washington to the north, and the long Montalban Ridge to the east. At the head of the basin is Oakes Gulf, the most remote of the great glacial cirques of the Presidential Range. The name "Dry" describes the river's bony appearance in Crawford Notch, which belies the formidable character of the watercourse.

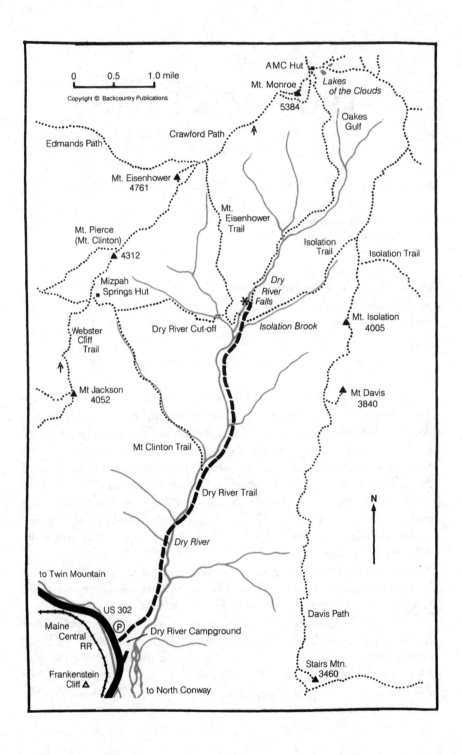

0   0.5   1.0 mile

Copyright © Backcountry Publications

AMC Hut

Mt. Monroe
5384

Lakes of the Clouds

Crawford Path

Oakes Gulf

Edmands Path

Mt. Eisenhower
4761

Mt. Eisenhower Trail

Mt. Pierce
(Mt. Clinton)
4312

Isolation Trail

Isolation Trail

Mizpah
Springs Hut

Dry River Falls

Dry River Cut-off

Isolation Brook

Mt. Isolation
4005

Webster
Cliff
Trail

Mt Jackson
4052

Mt Davis
3840

Mt Clinton Trail

Dry River Trail

N

Dry River

to Twin Mountain

US 302

Davis Path

Maine
Central
RR

P

Dry River Campground

Frankenstein
Cliff

Stairs Mtn.
3460

to North Conway

The Dry River is actually longer than the Saco above the point of confluence, suggesting to some that the true source of the Saco lies up Oakes Gulf. Rain and snowmelt from the huge basin of the Dry River are funneled through a narrow constriction between the southern shoulder of Mount Webster and the northern flank of Stairs Mountain. This topography causes the water level to fluctuate dramatically in response to changes in the weather. These volatile moods make the Dry River a killer, as can be seen in the grim record of fatalities on Mount Washington posted at the AMC Trading Post in Pinkham Notch. At times the dull Dry River becomes the brash Mount Washington River: a Dr. Jekyll and Mr. Hyde of mountain streams. Fortunately the trail has been constructed to provide access to Dry River Falls from Crawford Notch without requiring visitors to risk fording the river during its violent Mr. Hyde phases—when the waterfall is especially impressive.

In 1974 the Dry River basin was incorporated into the 20,000-acre Presidential Range–Dry River Wilderness Area to protect its wild, natural beauty.

Access
In Crawford Notch, park on the gravel shoulder on either side of US 302, 2.6 miles south of the Willey House Site, or 0.2 mile north of the Dry River Campground. Watch for an inconspicuous trailhead sign on the east side of the road opposite Frankenstein Cliff.

The Trail
The hike to Dry River Falls from Crawford Notch is not particularly difficult, but it involves an 11-mile round-trip. So this is one waterfall that is best suited for people who love to hike. Because the Dry River Trail follows an old logging railroad route much of the way to the falls, long stretches are smooth and well graded. This is certainly true of the first leg, a fast and easy 1-mile hike through a fine hardwood forest.

Where an old rail trestle once spanned the river, the trail turns to the left and surmounts a minor ridge. Just before this detour you can step down to the river from the trail and find a modest set of pools near the site of a former shelter. When the area was designated as wilderness, most tent shelters were removed, and the remaining shelters will soon be dismantled. Camping is now restricted to small groups applying low-impact backcountry camping techniques at sites at least 200 feet from the trail, or at designated sites marked by inconspicuous brown tent signs.

Dry River Falls

After climbing over the first ridge, the roller-coaster trail tackles a second, larger ridge. The path climbs steeply and then contours across the brow of the ravine wall, 200 feet above the river. Curving around the far end of this high platform, the trail passes the first and best panorama of the hike. Through a window framed in red spruce boughs you look across waves of overlapping ridges that sweep down from the mountaintops, like ribs protecting the heart of the wilderness. Here and there bristly spikes of white pine penetrate the matted canopy of tree crowns. Down the middle of the panorama winds the deep cleft of the Dry River.

The trail rapidly descends to cross the Dry River by the suspension bridge at mile 1.7 (according to the AMC trail guide; it seems farther, though). On the east bank now, the trail's ups and downs continue, though much more gently. As you pass into a transitional forest richly endowed with white birch trees, you can see that the ups are coming out ahead. In early summer the forest wildflowers are abundant here, while later in the summer you will find a splendid mushroom show along the trail.

After pulling temporarily away from the river, the trail returns to a smooth stretch of the old railbed where you can find numerous opportunities for a riverside rest. Soon thereafter the Mount Clinton Trail branches off to the left (mile 3) to ford the Dry River and climb toward Mizpah Hut. At times the ford here may be impassable or unsafe. Remember: The Dry

River is not just tricky; it has killed hikers trying to cross in high water.

The Dry River Trail continues along the east bank, ascending slowly but steadily for over 1 mile before making a sharp right turn. The trail then climbs eroded switchbacks to a junction with the Isolation Trail, just across Isolation Brook, at mile 5. Again, stay on the Dry River Trail, which contours around a narrow shoulder of land through an enchanting boreal forest. Its legions of spindly spruce and fir trees are bedecked with gray-green mosses and scaly lichens. A tenth of a mile on you will pass a clearing where the trees have been trimmed to provide a view up Oakes Gulf. This gulf is named for William Oakes, a pioneer of White Mountain botany and one of the first people to explore the basin's steep headwalls and thick forests. Oakes also wrote what is regarded as the first popular guidebook to the region, *White Mountain Scenery,* which was published in 1848 only five days before his untimely death. (He drowned in Boston Harbor after falling overboard from a ferry.)

The Mount Eisenhower Trail comes in from the left at mile 5.2. This trail, too, fords the Dry River and may be impassable in high water. Beyond this last junction, the Dry River Trail becomes rough and narrow. It also badly needs a trim. Even when it is not raining, you may need rain gear to protect your clothes from foliage wet from earlier showers or heavy dew. Very soon a low, steady rumble can be heard in the ravine to the left. As the sound intensifies, watch for a very small hand-lettered sign tacked onto a birch tree, indicating that you have reached the short spur path down to Dry River Falls.

Beyond the falls, the Dry River Trail continues climbing into Oakes Gulf, mounts the steep headwall beneath the sheer cliffs of Mount Monroe, and terminates at Lakes of the Clouds Hut. Altogether, a hike from US 302 to the Lakes hut (or vice versa) is just under 10 rugged miles. The Dry River must be crossed 0.25 mile above the falls. The current is less formidable here than farther downstream, but caution is still advisable.

Rather than trekking in from US 302, you can also reach Dry River Falls from Mizpah Hut, a mere 2.7 miles away. The elevation change is no different, 1300 feet, except that you descend first. From the hut, follow the Mount Clinton Trail for 0.5 mile and turn onto the Dry River Cutoff, which descends eastward to the Mount Eisenhower Trail. There, turn right and descend to the Dry River, while hoping the river is low enough to be forded safely. Both going and returning! Once across the river the trail mounts the east bank and terminates at the Dry River Trail. The falls are less than 0.25 mile to the left. Alternatively, the falls may be accessed from the AMC Lakes-of-the-Clouds Hut by following the Dry River trail 4.4 miles down Oakes Gulf, a rough descent of 2450 feet.

The Falls

We hiked in to Dry River Falls one chilly (55 degrees), misty, drizzly day in mid-August after three nights of thunderstorms had ended a parching heat wave. Despite the preceding drought, these thunderstorms were enough to feed the Dry River to a fury. Dry River Falls mimicked the previous evening's thunder so loudly that we had to shout to be heard. From the waterfall heavy clouds of spray drifted down the ravine on powerful drafts, like ghosts of the Indian spirits that are said to haunt the gulf.

At Dry River Falls, the river's powerful current plunges more than 50 feet in three irregular steps down steeply inclined ledges of gray gneiss. The spur path from the main trail climbs down to the midsection of the primary drop, a turbulent plume of whitewater dashing 35 feet to a deep pool at the base of a narrow glen. The formation has been likened to Glen Ellis Falls (Chapter 20) on a smaller scale. But unlike Glen Ellis, the sides of this sheer ravine are shrouded with spruce, birch, and fir. The ambiance is quite wild, as befits a waterfall at the foot of Mount Isolation.

You can easily descend to the pool at the base of the glen or climb a trodden footpath to the top of a jagged crag on the shoulder of the head-wall. This high perch provides a dizzying (and unprotected) bird's-eye view of the main falls and the winding ravine below, as well as a close-up view of the upper cascades. A quick scramble up the smoothed slabs above the crag takes you to a superb pothole pool fed by cascades 5 feet high. Although the

Eastern Hemlock

waterfall itself is at its most spectacular when the river runs strong, the pool on the top deck is most inviting in sunny weather when the currents are less powerful and the water is not quite so cold.

A small knob just above the upper pool bears the scars of backpackers who evidently knew nothing about low-impact camping. The site is an excellent example of where and how *not* to camp in the wilderness.

Historical Detour

> *The Indians believed in vast treasures of precious stones . . . suspended from big cliffs in the mountains. Darby Field the first colonist to climb Mount Washington, in 1642, to the day of his death talked of dazzling diamonds and emeralds that blazed and flashed in the mountains. . . .*
>
> —Ernest Bisbee, 1938

The legend of the Great Carbuncle—variously reported as a lode of diamonds, emeralds, rubies, or gold—was a favorite fireside tale of the early White Mountain settlers. It is said that local Indians observed the treasure on many occasions, and some had climbed the great mountain Agiochook seeking the Carbuncle, never to return.

Nathaniel Hawthorne heard the legend from Ethan Allen Crawford, on a visit to the mountains in 1832. Hawthorne's moralistic short story, "The Great Carbuncle," was very popular when published in 1835. Crawford, as a boy, had actually encountered a party of trampers who claimed to have found the treasure high on the steep headwall of the Dry River basin. They had been unable to reach the carbuncle without assistance, in part because they believed that the treasure was guarded by Indian spirits. Under the guidance of Abel Crawford (Ethan's father), the fortune seekers headed back up the Dry River—accompanied this time by a minister who went along to ward off evil spirits. They set out anticipating "how rich they should be in coming home laden with gold" (Morse, 1978). But nothing was found, and the treasure was never seen again.

In truth, the earliest explorers, including Darby Field, hoped to find precious minerals in the White Mountains. Field even brought home a load of "diamonds" from his pioneering climb, only to find that the stones were merely quartz. Based on Field's report of seeing crystals, the White Mountains were often called the Crystal Hills.

The lower reaches of the Dry River basin—still called Cutt's Grant—were purchased from the state in 1810 by two Mainers, Thomas Cutt, of Saco, and Richard Conant, of Portland. They paid $340 for a grant of 7,680 acres of dense, unexplored forestland extending 6 miles up the river and 1 mile to each side. This land remained in the hands of the original families until it was acquired by the federal government in 1932 as part of the White Mountain National Forest.

Before the federal government got there, though, the vast stretches of virgin timber attracted the attention of the loggers who operated a large mill only a few miles down the notch. (See chapter 22.) Francis Belcher (1980) relates that the landowners leased out timber rights to the Saco Valley Railroad in 1891. They restricted the lease to a period of not more than fifteen years, stipulated that no trees less than 8 inches in diameter could be cut, and limited the lease to only a single round of cutting. Needless to say, this was remarkably conservative forestry at the time.

A logging railroad was constructed up the Dry River valley to within 0.75 mile of the falls. It remained in operation only five years. As Belcher explains,

> This area was actually one of the most inaccessible of all the White Mountain locations to be logged by railroad. . . . The maintenance costs of this lumber railroad line alone kept its owners on the narrow edge between failure and success at all times.

The topography of the Dry River basin forced the railway route to cross the river thirteen times, putting the ill-fated line at the mercy of the river's violent moods. By 1898 the track was dismantled, the lumberjacks were gone, and the forest had begun to recover from its limited encounter with the ax and saw. Perhaps the Indian spirits were hard at work once again, protecting their mountain treasures.

CHAPTER 24

RIPLEY FALLS

◆

Location: Willey House Station, in Crawford Notch
Maps: AMC #3 Crawford Notch–Sandwich Range Map (H-8); DeLorme Trail
Map (F-9)

Hiking Data
Distance: Parking area to falls, 0.6 mile
Altitude gain: 400 feet (to altitude 1800 feet); 700 feet to Sparkling Cascade
(altitude 2100 feet)
Difficulty: Easy

◆

> *A more wild and beautiful waterfall than any*
> *hitherto seen on the western side of the mountains,*
> *was discovered on Mount Willey in September, 1858, by*
> *Mr. Ripley of North Conway, and Mr. Porter of New*
> *York. . . . Exploring the stream nearly a mile higher,*
> *other falls were discovered, each one deserving especial*
> *notice, and one or two of most rare beauty.*

When Thomas Starr King wrote this announcement in 1859 he reported that
Ripley and Porter had chosen the name "Sylvan-Glade Cataract" for the wild
and beautiful waterfall. They christened the rare beauty above as "Sparkling
Cascade." Both falls graced the channel of what was then known as Cow
Brook. King suggested that the lower falls be renamed in honor of Mr. Ripley,
and he expressed hope that the brook could be renamed as a memorial to a
tragic avalanche that had occurred nearby. These proposals took root, so
today we can visit Ripley Falls on Avalanche Brook, rather than the Sylvan-
Glade Cataract on Cow Brook.

Sparkling Cascade, meanwhile, effectively has vanished from view.
Guidebooks in the early 1900s referred vaguely to "upper falls" on Avalanche
Brook, and by 1940 trail descriptions had Ripley Falls standing alone. As

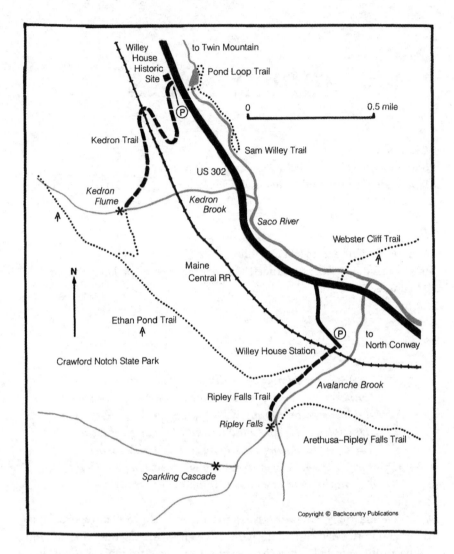

recently as the early 1950s hikers could follow an old logging road up Avalanche Brook beyond Ripley Falls, but that route has since been reclaimed by the forest. (A park ranger we spoke to in 1988 knew of no upper falls, by any name.) To be sure, the upper falls—the merits of which King greatly exaggerated—never vanished from the mountainside. If a trail were ever restored, Sparkling Cascade might reappear on the roster of White Mountain waterfalls. Until then, however, the popular trip to Ripley Falls rests easily on its own laurels.

To complement the short hike to Ripley Falls, you might consider the nearby climb to Kedron Flume. The side trip to this interesting but unspectacular cascade is described briefly below.

Access
The Arethusa–Ripley Falls Trail heads to both Arethusa and Ripley Falls, as the name suggests (chapter 22 described a more direct route to Arethusa Falls). The trailhead is located at the end of a short side road off US 302 at the old Willey House station. A sign for Ripley Falls marks the turn, 1 mile south of the tourist information center at the Willey House Site and 1.8 miles north of the Dry River Campground. If you see cars parked at the corner, don't conclude that the lot up the road has overflowed; these cars probably belong to hikers climbing the spectacular Webster Cliff Trail across the highway.

The Trail
Starting behind the information sign at the top of the parking area, the trail crosses the railroad track and climbs through a stand of white birch. At the outset the Ethan Pond Trail coincides with the Arethusa–Ripley Falls Trail, so Appalachian Trail signs and white paint blazes mark the way. After only 0.1 mile the two trails diverge. The Ethan Pond Trail (and the white blazes) continues up the ridge, while the route to Ripley Falls, clearly posted, forks to the left and contours along the wall of the ravine. In rainy weather the trail crosses a few slippery spots that require caution, since the drop on the left is fairly steep. After climbing gradually for less than 0.5 mile, the trail abruptly turns left (watch the blue blazes) and descends to a narrow basin at the foot of Ripley Falls.

Here the trail crosses to the south bank of Avalanche Brook and ascends by switchbacks to the woods just above the falls. This section of trail is narrow and eroded, with exposed conifer roots that are slippery when wet. The smooth ledges at the top of the falls should be avoided when wet, since this is not a place where you would want to slip. In dry conditions, however, the ledges upstream from the head of Ripley Falls are fun to explore. From the top of the falls the trail itself turns generally south, climbs 800 feet to a ridge behind Frankenstein Cliff (mile 1.7), and traverses to Arethusa Falls (mile 2.7).

For the side trip to Kedron Flume, drive 1 mile north on US 302 to the Willey House Site. At the picnic area south of the gift shop you will find a sign marking the base of the Kedron Flume Trail, 0.7 mile away. After one long switchback the trail crosses the old Maine Central Railroad tracks. Above this you continue to gain elevation on shorter switchbacks and then contour toward the south. Shortly after the trail enters a zone of spruce and crosses a set of angular boulders, you reach Kedron Brook at the foot of the flume. Beyond this point the trail climbs steadily to intercept the Ethan Pond Trail, which connects to the Willey Range Trail and the summits on the west wall of Crawford Notch. The Ethan Pond Trail could also be used to descend to Ripley Falls, allowing you to connect both falls in a single hike.

The Falls

At Ripley Falls, Avalanche Brook slips over a steeply inclined ledge 100 feet high. Compared to Arethusa Falls, its neighbor to the south, Ripley Falls is less precipitous and not quite as high. This makes it less dramatic but no less beautiful. "Apples versus oranges," is how we heard it explained to inquiring tourists at one information booth, "and Ripley Falls is much easier to reach."

From the boulder-strewn basin at the foot of the falls you will see a long rippled ribbon of silvery water leaping and sliding down a steep bed of orange-gray granite. On overcast days the gray tones prevail, casting a cool and pensive mood over the waterfall basin. Summer days accentuate the orange tones, displaying the falls in a warm, playful light that contrasts sharply with the bright green of the surrounding forest. This contrast highlights the outline of the granite bed, which is remarkably similar in shape to the state of New Hampshire!

A small, waist-deep pool lies at the foot of the cascade, enclosed on the right by a vertical rock wall 20 feet high. With the falls facing east, the basin catches the summer sun from late morning through midday. A spell of sunny weather can warm the bright amber water to temperatures more tepid than usual for a mountain pool—near 60 degrees Fahrenheit. (In contrast, the water was only 36 degrees one chilly afternoon during foliage season.)

You can reach better swimming holes, however, by following the trail to the top of the falls. Just upstream you will find a series of small, delightful cascades and sunny, shallow pools scooped in the handsome bedrock. In his original description of Ripley Falls, King regarded these cascades as an integral part of the "singularly grand" formation.

The upper ledges are also the best place for exploring, especially considering that the steep granite wall of the waterfall itself is not a safe place on which to climb around. But above the main falls you can scramble quite a way up the smooth granite ledges with little difficulty. If you are lucky, you might hear the lively piccolo trill of a winter wren from the thick brush above the streambed. There is a flavor of wildness about the place—a flavor that visitors should take care to preserve. Although exploring upstream can be great fun, it bears repeating that the ledges just above the brink of the falls can be slippery and dangerous and should be avoided in wet weather or high water.

One brook north of Ripley Falls at Kedron Flume, Kedron Brook has hewn a shallow trench into a sloping granite ledge above the trail. Below the trail, the brook slips down a long chain of precipitous waterfalls. Unfortunately the brook tends to run low, so both the flume and the waterfall below are often unimpressive.

At the Ripley Falls turnoff from US 302, a road sign states that the hike to the falls takes only twenty minutes. An early AMC guide was more helpful in suggesting that it could take more than four hours "to visit and enjoy all the falls." Adding Kedron Flume to the itinerary, you can spend the best part of a full day enjoying the waterfalls in the vicinity.

Historical Detour

Two intriguing historical questions are posed by the place names Ripley Falls and Avalanche Brook. First, who was Mr. Ripley? And second, what avalanche?

Henry Wheelock Ripley was a friend and traveling companion to both Abel Crawford and Thomas Starr King. (Remember that King was the one who suggested naming the falls for Ripley.) Evidently addicted to the tonic of mountain air from an early age, Henry Ripley tramped the White Mountain trails for over fifty years, beginning at age seven. He is reported to have climbed Mount Washington eighty-five times (Hixson, 1980). In addition, it was Ripley who prepared the second edition of Lucy Crawford's *History of the White Mountains* for publication in 1883.

As recounted by his friend King, Ripley and Porter discovered the falls on Cow Brook after "an old fisherman" at Crawford House told of encountering some wonderful unknown cascades in that vicinity. Moses Sweetser, however, later wrote that Abel Crawford discovered the falls "while out on snowshoes, trapping sable," and that Ripley and Porter merely revisited and christened the falls in 1858. If these accounts seem contradictory, it might be noted that Abel Crawford was himself an old fisherman. Perhaps the Sylvan-Glade Cataract should have been renamed Crawford Falls instead.

The avalanche that King had in mind when proposing to rename Cow Brook was the 1826 Willey disaster—the most tragic catastrophe in the history of the White Mountains. It is also probably the most familiar story

Ripley Falls

of the mountains, recounted time and again in book and ballad. The first detailed account, and still by far the best, appeared in Reverend Benjamin Willey's fascinating book, *Incidents in White Mountain History* (1856). Reverend Willey was motivated to write the book by the fact that he had been asked innumerable times to give his firsthand account of the story of his brother's doom.

In the autumn of 1825, Samuel Willey Jr., son of one of Bartlett's early settlers, moved with his wife and five children into a small house deep in the trough of Crawford Notch. The house had been built before the turn of the century but was occupied only intermittently. During winter of 1826–27 Willey began providing shelter and hospitality to teamsters working their way through the notch. Sometimes the winter winds were so severe, they say, that a man required help just to keep his hair on. The following spring the Willeys expanded their modest facility to provide better service for travelers.

After a June rain triggered small slides near his house, Willey grew apprehensive about his chosen location. He considered moving but decided that the risk of recurrence for such a rare event was slight, and so he chose to stay. That summer, the topsoil was dried to an unusual depth by extremely hot and arid weather that lasted until after mid-August. Then came the rains. Light showers were followed by an extraordinary downpour on the night of August 29 that severely flooded both the Saco and the Ammonoosuc and destroyed the turnpike.

The next morning, as the rivers subsided, Ethan Allen Crawford accompanied a traveler through the flood debris and down the storm-strewn notch from the north. Arriving at Willey House, they found the buildings undamaged, though totally surrounded by the massive tongues of an enormous landslide. As the only living creatures to be found were the family dog and two oxen, the men assumed the Willey family had escaped southward before the avalanche. Crawford returned home, while the traveler spent a night in the vacant house. He proceeded to Bartlett the next morning and learned that the Willey family had not been seen.

A search party was quickly dispatched to the scene of the devastating slide. From the swarms of flies the searchers—including Benjamin Willey himself—quickly found the bodies of Samuel Willey's wife and one hired hand. With some digging they also uncovered the bodies of Samuel Willey, two of his children, and another farmhand. The three other Willey children were never found.

Some say that when the family fled the house, presumably seeking high ground to escape the terrifying flood, their Bible was left open to the Eighteenth Psalm:

> In my distress I called upon the Lord. . . . Then the earth shook and trembled; the foundations also of the hills moved and were shaken, because he was wroth. . . . He made darkness his secret place; his pavilion around him were dark waters and thick clouds of the skies. . . . Then the channels of waters were seen, and the

foundations of the world were discovered at thy rebuke, O
Lord. . . . He sent from above, he took me, he drew me out of
many waters. . . .

—King James Version

The Willey house was reoccupied within a few years, and today the
Crawford Notch visitor's center is located at the very site of the disaster,
1 mile north of the trailhead for Ripley Falls.

Cold Brook Fall

THE ANDROSCOGGIN
WATERSHED

ROBERT KOZLOW

CHAPTER 25

WATERFALLS OF GRAFTON NOTCH

◆

Step Falls
Screw Auger Falls

Location: On ME 26, north of Newry, Maine
Map: AMC #6 North Country–Mahoosuc Map (B/C–13/14)

◆

Grafton Notch, at the northeastern tip of the Mahoosuc Range, is a splendid gallery of glacial earth art. Like other dramatic U-shaped valleys in the White Mountain region—such as Crawford Notch and Franconia Notch—this narrow mountain pass was molded and scoured by the grinding advances of the continental ice cap. Later, in retreat, the ice cap ornamented exposed surfaces of granite with the abrasive force of its gritty meltwaters. In the vicinity of Grafton Notch the glaciers left behind one stunning ornament on the Bear River at Screw Auger Falls and a fascinating swath of sculpted granite on Wight Brook at Step Falls.

Although Step Falls and Screw Auger Falls highlight the waterfall trip to Grafton Notch, they are not the only waterfall exhibits in the gallery. Two neighboring formations, Mother Walker Falls and Cascade Brook, are also described briefly below.

Grafton Notch is a scenic delight in its own right, quite apart from its waterfalls. Precipitous cliffs rise 800 to 1000 feet on each side of Route 26, which traces the path of the glaciers through a gap between Baldpate Mountain on the east and Old Spec Mountain on the west. North of the height-of-land, the Swift Cambridge River flows to Umbagog Lake, a natural jewel at the head of the Androscoggin River. The Bear River runs south through the notch to join the Androscoggin at Newry. Thus Grafton Notch has the distinction of dividing two watersheds that serve the same river!

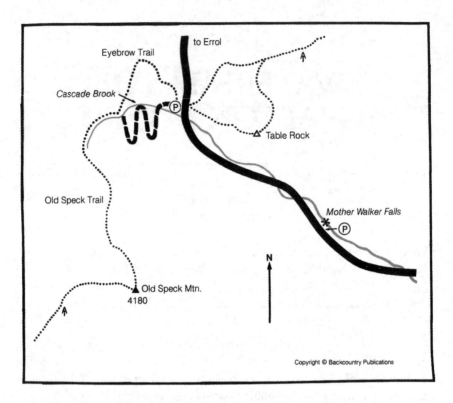

Grafton Notch State Park can be reached from Newry, Maine, or from Errol, New Hampshire. The nearest camping facility is at Umbagog Lake, just across the state line in New Hampshire.

Step Falls

Hiking Data
Distance: Parking area to top of falls, 0.6 mile
Altitude gain: 300 feet (to altitude 1200 feet)
Difficulty: Easy

If you are driving north from Newry, your first stop will be at Step Falls. This waterfall consists of an extensive series of cataracts and pools laced across a long bank of ledge on Wight Brook, which feeds into the Bear River about 1.5 mile below Screw Auger Falls. On approaching the notch you can see a set of cliffs, called Lightning Ledge, high on the mountain flank north of the road. Below these cliffs the ravine of Wight Brook can be discerned as a

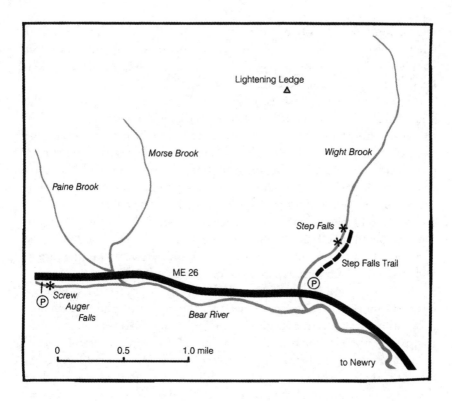

Lightening Ledge ▲

Morse Brook

Wight Brook

Paine Brook

Step Falls ✳

Step Falls Trail

ME 26

Screw
Auger
Falls

Bear River

0   0.5   1.0 mile

to Newry

shallow groove in the Bear River escarpment, lined with dark conifer crowns.

Step Falls is located on a 24-acre preserve owned and managed by The Nature Conservancy, a quietly effective environmental organization that protects sensitive ecosystems and precious natural treasures through direct action: It buys the land, or it buys easements restricting future development.

Access
Just before ME 26 crosses Wight Brook, 8 miles north of US 2, a track on the right (north) runs to the Step Falls parking area. The turnoff is marked by a sign for Wight Brook and a small sign that simply says PRESERVE. To confirm that you have taken the correct turn, look for a trail heading into a grove of spruce and balsam fir at the end of the parking area.

The Trail
You only have to walk a few yards along the trail to reach a large sign identifying the nature preserve. There is also a guest registration box here,

with a limited stack of information brochures supplied by the Maine Chapter of The Nature Conservancy. According to the brochure, the water volume in Wight Brook averages 6 cubic feet per second but can swell nearly ninetyfold during the spring!

The path to Step Falls is easy to follow as it ascends gradually through the shady forest. The only minor complication is that the path temporarily splits; the left-hand fork edges the rocky brook, while the main path stays on the bank and heads directly to the falls. Higher up, a web of side paths should present no problem: They eventually all lead to the same place. The forest changes to northern hardwoods as the path approaches the brook, where it emerges onto a pile of large boulders. Scramble onto the boulders for an introductory view of falls. From this vantage point, at the foot of the waterfall, you can see more than 100 yards of inclined ledges capped by an attractive cascade that fans over a granite bulge. But this is only the bottom half of the formation, and the most beautiful part is out of view above the bulge.

The path continues for 0.25 mile and nearly 200 vertical feet beside a chain of cataracts, passing sensational pools, smooth waterslides, small pothole bathtubs, and terrific scrambling ledges. In one radiant pool, the deep, transparent waters glimmer with a cool tint of lemon-lime. At another spot, a finger of current curls through a corkscrew slide into a bubbling trough tub. Best of all, the broad ledges face south and draw in the full warmth of the sun. Even the bedrock is fascinating. A blend of Devonian-period granites, the rock is interlaced with quartz bands and studded with mineral crystals, including garnet, mica, and tourmaline. The climb up Step Falls is also rewarded with fine views down the ravine and across the Bear River valley.

About halfway up the Step Falls trail you will notice a large pipe crossing the footpath. This pipe feeds water from a small dam above the falls (on private property) to a microhydroplant that generates electricity without marring the beauty of the falls.

The upper boundary of the preserve is just past a stand of red pine trees at the top of the falls, where a logging road approaches the brook. Avoid this logging road on your descent because it is private property and not part of the preserve.

SCREW AUGER FALLS

Hiking Data
Distance: Roadside
Altitude gain: Zero (altitude 1100 feet)
Difficulty: Easy

You can drag the family away from Step Falls by promising them another fascinating waterfall just up the road. The Screw Auger Falls parking lot is located on the south side of ME 26, at 1 mile above the southern boundary of Grafton Notch State Park. There is now a $1 per person fee in the state park, payable on the honor system at any of the parking lots. At the parking area, a line of picnic tables traces a sweeping bend in the Bear River, under the shade of a well-mixed roadside forest (bring a tree guide to practice identifications). To the west, the blunt pyramid of Old Speck Mountain, cloaked in forest green, looms above the valley floor.

Downstream from the picnic area, the Bear River slips quietly across a broad, sunny terrace of granite ledge and then plunges 20 feet into the wildly contorted Screw Auger Gorge. Overall the river descends about 50 feet from the picnic area to the foot of the gorge, but what makes Screw Auger Falls extraordinary is its setting, not its size. The gorge is adorned with remnant arcs of giant potholes, scooped alcove shelves, and sharply undercut grottoes that usher the river through the slender defile.

This fancifully twisted granite masonry was crafted only ten to fifteen thousand years ago. As the ice cap slowly retreated, it blocked drainage to the north and created a temporary lake above the notch. For centuries— until further melting of the ice cap uncorked the reservoir—a torrent of highly erosive glacial outwash was discharged southward to scour the Bear River bedrock. These swirling currents carved out the Screw Auger Gorge.

The approach to the gorge from the east end of the parking lot is an easy stroll of only a few dozen yards. A well-maintained gravel footpath skirts the broad upper terrace and crosses to the rim of the gorge, where sturdy handrails provide secure views of Screw Auger Falls and the marvelous rock formations. With minor difficulty it is possible to scramble down the side of the steep ravine below the gorge for a bottom-up view of the contorted chasm walls. In low water you can wade right up the river into the mouth of the formation, assuming the role of Jonah opposite nature's granite whale.

The best place for water play, however, is above the gorge, where the broad, sun-baked ledges furnish shallow pools with gentle waterfall curtains 4 to 8 feet high. These crystal-clear pools are safe enough for young children to splash and wade and lovely enough for everyone to enjoy. After nature labored so long and hard to carve the fountains, how can anyone resist?

Neighboring Falls

The next stop is Mother Walker Falls. A short distance above Screw Auger Falls the road curves to the right, climbs straight toward the ramparts of Table Rock, and then dips slightly as it passes a paved pullout beside a chain-link fence on the right (northeast). A small sign announces that this is the parking area for Mother Walker Falls. Steps lead down to a walkway along the rim of a deep, wild ravine, strewn with granite blocks. From some vantage points you may see rapids, but nothing much resembles a waterfall, and there is no obvious path down to the river.

There is indeed a waterfall here, however. It consists of a narrow 9-foot spout that pours into a small horseshoe-shaped pool. The interesting part is that the waterfall is located inside a cave formed by an enormous flake that has split off from the bluff on the far side of the ravine. For this reason Mother Walker Falls can be difficult to find, and it is a bit disconcerting to contemplate that other huge chunks of rock will someday crash into the ravine. Not to spoil the thrill of the hunt, only two clues will be given here: (1) a rough path enters the ravine from upstream; and (2) don't go during earthquakes or heavy thunder.

Canada Mayflower

A second waterfall bonus, Cascade Brook, sounds more promising than it turns out to be. The brook is identified by name in descriptions of the Old Speck Trail—formerly the Cascade Brook Trail—but it was not deemed important enough to appear on either the USGS topographic map or the AMC map of the notch.

The starting point for the Old Speck Trail is a large parking lot near the height-of-land, 1.5 miles above Mother Walker Falls. In this lot we once found two severely vandalized automobiles that had been left overnight by midweek hikers on the Appalachian Trail (of which the Old Speck Trail is a link). Regrettably, it is wise to check with local police before leaving a vehicle at a remote site like this for extended periods of time. *Do not leave valuables in your vehicle.* Follow the white blazes, keeping left at the Eyebrow Trail fork. Two long switchbacks mount the wall of the notch, returning to the brook each time at feathery cascades on steep, irregular ledges. Above the cascades the trail continues to the summit of Old Speck Mountain, which, at 4180 feet, is Maine's third highest peak.

Surprisingly, the most dramatic waterfall in Grafton Notch is none of the above. Once, after a week of rain, we observed a spectacular 80-foot cascade plunging down the corner of a sheer bank of cliffs 0.1 mile south of the Old Speck Trail—with more water plumes leaping from higher ledges above. A rough, unmarked footpath led up a tongue of rockslide rubble to the base of this unnamed waterfall. It turns out that this dazzling cataract reverts to nothing more than wet rock for much of the season. After heavy rains, though, watch for the intermittent beauty above the forest floor on the west side of the notch just below the trails parking lot. If you can't see it from the roadside about 50 yards north of the trails parking lot, it probably isn't there.

Historical Detour

Traveling Route 26 between Newry and Errol, one sees little more than mountains and forests. This sums up much of the history of Grafton: mountains, forests, and a road. The best account of Grafton's history is a paper by Charles Fobes (1951), from which much of the following information is drawn.

Pioneer James Brown passed through Grafton Notch in 1830, when a blazed path was the only sign of development. Settling above the notch, Brown hewed a timber business out of the vast tracts of northern forest. He started by harvesting the towering white pines, and then proceeded to the spruce and fir. By 1838 Brown had built a mill and dammed the Swift

BRUCE AND DOREEN BOLNICK

Screw Auger Falls

Cambridge River to control the water flow for the purpose of driving logs down to the Androscoggin River via Umbagog Lake. The community that grew up around the mill was incorporated as the town of Grafton in 1852. Small farms flourished and schools were built, but Grafton was a lumber town from start to finish. In the 1850s a competing sawmill was built right at the top of Screw Auger Falls. By one account, part of the spiraling gorge was blasted away by the lumbermen.

The town's population climbed to 110 in 1880, when demand for softwood pulp fueled a period of relative prosperity. It is said that Mother Walker Falls is named for one of the last homesteaders to arrive during the town's period of growth. After the best forest resources had been cut, the community began to shrink. By 1919, when its charter was repealed, the town of Grafton reported only one elderly inhabitant.

James Brown died in 1881, just as his company's timber operations were peaking. At about the same time another Brown was forming a timber company based in Berlin, New Hampshire William Wentworth ("W.W.") Brown, formerly a shipbuilder from Down East, began aggressively acquiring forestlands and logging rights in the area. (A decade earlier, yet another family of Browns built a logging railroad out of Whitefield.) By the turn of the century the Brown Company of Berlin controlled most of the north-country timber on both sides of the New Hampshire–Maine state line. In 1919 the company acquired the forestlands in Grafton that had first been logged by James Brown. To this day much of Grafton remains in the hands of the Brown Company's modern embodiment, the James River Corporation.

Unlike many other timber companies, which desecrated the White Mountain forests around the turn of the century, the Brown Company was a forerunner of modern forest resource management (Holbrook, 1961). Influenced by Austin Cary, an innovative forester, the company began as early as 1895 to plan in terms of long-range tree harvests. This meant selective cutting and careful fire prevention. One indication: The observation tower on top of Old Speck Mountain was built for spotting forest fires long before the state park was created.

In addition to supporting 150 years of timber operations, Grafton has long been a lure for tourists. In his guide to the White Mountains (1887), Moses Sweetser became unusually tongue-tied writing about the notch. He described the scenery as being "of a high order of majesty and impressiveness." At that time Screw Auger Falls and Mother Walker Falls were among the prime attractions of western Maine. (Sweetser made no mention of Step Falls.) During the summer, stagecoaches served Grafton Notch three days per week from the railway station in Bethel. There was even a hotel in town—Captain Brown's.

CHAPTER 26

MORIAH BROOK

———————◆———————

Location: Reached from the Wild River Road, west of Route 113 via Hastings, Maine

Maps: AMC #5 Carter Range-Evans Notch (F-11/12); DeLorme WMNF Trail Map (C-14)

Hiking Data

Distance: Parking area to Moriah Gorge, 1.4 miles; to Upper Cascades, 3.4 miles

Altitude gain: 500 feet to the Gorge (altitude 1500 feet); 800 feet to Upper Cascades (altitude 1800 feet)

Difficulty: Moderate

———————————◆———————————

At the back of this book you will find a master list of more than one hundred waterfalls. These are the generals and ranking officers of the army of White Mountain waterfalls. Missing, though, are the troops: the innumerable small cascades scattered along watercourses throughout the region. No names distinguish their identity, and no signs trumpet their presence. Yet it is the miniature falls that truly personify the spirit of the region's mountain streams. Unlike the other trips described in the book, this one highlights some of the waterfall foot soldiers.

On the "back" side of the Carter Range, nature echoes the great ravines of the eastern slopes of Mount Washington. One such echo is the ravine of Moriah Brook. Scooped between the brawny shoulders of Middle Carter Mountain and Mount Moriah, the ravine slopes more than 4 miles eastward to merge with the vast woodlands of the Wild River valley (formally Bean's Purchase; population: zero). Along its 3300-foot descent to the Wild River, Moriah Brook never drops in a single step much higher than a basketball hoop. Nonetheless, the brook bears a fascinating collection of small cascades, fine pothole pools, and an impressive gorge.

The Moriah Brook Trail provides access to these cascades from the Wild

River Campground, which is located in the heart of Bean's Purchase. The campground has only eleven units, and no services or supplies are available nearer than Bethel or Gorham. Other than backpacking in from beyond the valley perimeter, the only access route to the campground is a 5-mile-long dirt road along the Wild River from ME 113, south of Gilead.

A larger (twenty-four unit) and less remote campground is located at Hastings, just across ME 113 from the Wild River turnoff. Hastings is the name of a vanished logging village that once occupied the site. Enormous quantities of Wild River timber were transported to large mills at Hastings by a logging railroad that penetrated a dozen miles up the valley. Today the Wild River Road follows the old railbed, and the Moriah Brook Trail climbs one of its spur lines.

The Trail

Driving into the Wild River Campground you will find the hikers' parking area on the far side of the last bridge before the camping area. The hike starts on the Wild River Trail, which follows a new path along the river before joining the old railroad route. After 0.3 mile of easy walking, watch for a sign on the right marking the Moriah Brook Trail. This trail immediately descends to the Wild River and crosses on a wonderful suspension footbridge, which sways like a high cradle to the river's lullaby. As you enjoy the view from the bridge, watch for belted kingfishers swooping along the edge of the river.

On the west bank the Moriah Brook Trail turns left and heads upstream, merging temporarily with the Highwater Trail. The path passes through a dark grove of hemlocks and then enters a bright stand of white birch, where it curves to the right (northeast) and enters the wide mouth of the Moriah Brook ravine.

The Highwater Trail departs to the left at mile 0.7 from the parking area, while the Moriah Brook Trail continues in a beeline up a well-graded railbed, now scarred with gullies. After one large washout, the footing becomes rougher as the trail climbs a small rise and swings to the left. Here you have your first view of Moriah Brook, in a deep ravine below the trail. What you see is the outlet from Moriah Gorge, but the access points, described below, are still ahead. At mile 1.7 the trail reaches and crosses the brook just above the gorge. If you are hiking only to the first set of cascades, this is the end of the line.

Otherwise, cross to the south bank where the trail regains the easy gradient of the old railbed. Shortly, you enter a zone of white birch trees. In the undergrowth young spruce and fir trees—the forest of the future—

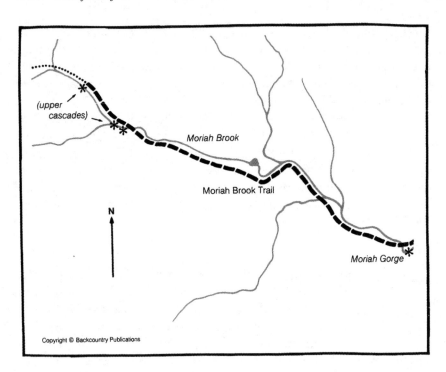

(upper
cascades)

Moriah Brook

Moriah Brook Trail

N

Moriah Gorge

Copyright © Backcountry Publications

patiently await their day in the sun. The path soon pulls away from the brook, passes a large beaver marsh, fords some small side streams, and then climbs back to Moriah Brook at mile 3.1, crossing again to the north bank. This middle stretch of trail is in rather bad condition, with muddy washouts and encroaching brush.

For the next 0.3 mile the trail climbs more steeply and enters boreal forest just before reaching a knob of gray ledge that is bisected by a tumbling side stream. This very attractive landmark is a good terminus for the waterfall hike. The trail beyond climbs steadily to a col on the summit ridge between Mount Moriah and Imp Mountain. Other small cascades can be found higher up the brook, but the prettiest cascades lie off the side of the trail on the climb up to the gray knob. So have a snack, and then turn to the enjoyable task of exploring the cascades.

The Gorge and the Cascades

Moriah Gorge is a rugged chasm over 100 yards long and yet barely 5 feet across at the neck. Constricted by high, sheer walls of the gorge, Moriah Brook accelerates down a series of abrupt steps separated by terraced pools.

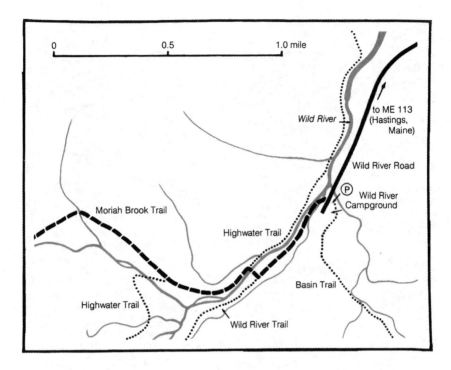

The lower shelves of the gorge are completely flooded by large pools, which preclude safe passage by anything other than trout, bugs, and small birds. The upper part of the gorge, however, provides more secure ground for scrambling, with good views of the formation. The prudent boundary for exploring is dictated by the level of the brook and common-sense caution. You won't want to risk being swept down the gorge by the swift currents.

You can climb down to the gorge two ways. First, from the point above the gorge where the trail crosses Moriah Brook you can scramble and wade down along the sloping ledges beside the top cataracts. This can be done in a relative safety if the brook is not too high and if you are careful about slippery footing. Alternatively, you can descend by a steep, dirty side path that turns off the trail about 50 feet below the brook crossing.

Either approach brings you to the top of a large rectangular block of ledge 12 feet above a slender trench pool. At the head of this pool, a surging cascade spurts from a narrow side channel, ricochets off the opposite wall, and rushes down through the trench to the next cascade. And the next. And the next. And the next.

Although the gorge is a remarkable formation, the best water playgrounds

Moriah Brook

are the upper cascades. Only a few choice examples will be described here.

About 200 yards beyond the brook crossing at mile 3.1, the trail skirts the streambed beside a wonderful pool carved into a polished bank of banded gray gneiss. Quartz bands in the rock give the pool the appearance of an elegant designer spa. Below the designer pool, as we would call it, the brook tumbles down 30 feet of rapids through a portal of low bedrock walls, with horizontal fractures that resemble rough masonry. At the foot of the rapid is another fine pool.

But don't stop at the first set of pretty pools you see! Not far above the designer pool, the trail crosses a mud patch where a short log bridge has been placed to help with footing. Just beyond this mud patch watch for signs of foot traffic through the undergrowth in the direction of the brook, which here is hidden by the forest. Making your way to the brook, you will find an extraordinary pool beneath a set of sloping waterchutes spread across a 6-foot-high bedrock dike. A side stream entering on the far side of the channel spills over a similar collection of small chutes. Wedged between the brook and the side stream, the ledge has sprouted a water garden of wildflowers, shrubs, and young trees. For later reference, let's call this spot the "Water Garden Cascades."

About 0.1 mile below the gray knob at the end of the hike, the trail passes another beautiful formation that might well be called the Triplet Cascade. From the trail only the near channel is visible, but when you climb out onto the open slabs of the streambed, you find three silver ribbons of water pouring through separate notches etched side by side in a broad wall of red-gray ledge. The largest of the triplets is about 10 feet high. Look for small, exquisite pothole tubs under the cascades. They are just the right size for a refreshingly chilly wilderness bath under the warm gaze of the noon-day sun.

Historical Detour

> *It is a child of the mountains; at times fierce,*
> *impetuous and shadowy, as the storms that howl*
> *around the bald heads of its parents, and bearing*
> *down everything in its path; then again, when*
> *subdued by long summer calms, murmuring gently*
> *in consonance with the breezy rustle of the trees. . . .*
> *An hour's time may swell it into a headlong torrent; an*
> *hour may reduce it to a brook that a child*
> *might ford without fear.*
>
> —Benjamin Willey, 1856

Willey's moody "child of the mountains" was the Wild River. The unpredictable volatility of this river was appreciated even by the earliest settlers who arrived in Gilead, Maine, around 1780. For over a century thereafter human activity made no permanent mark in the deep backcountry of the Wild River valley.

The eastern section of the Wild River valley, in Maine, was part of an 1807 grant to Josiah Batchelder of Boston. Although portions of the

Mountain Alder or Green Alder

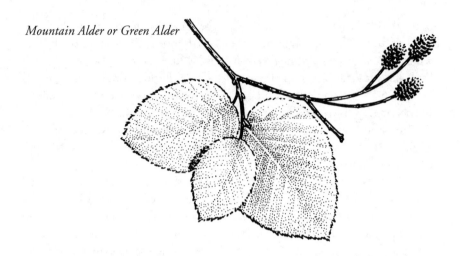

Batchelder grant up through Evans Notch were logged, the Wild River valley itself was still pristine wilderness in 1832 when Alpheus Bean bought the bulk of the remaining property from the state of New Hampshire. He paid $1033 for 33,000 acres. Even after Bean's purchase, the Wild River woodlands were disturbed only by occasional forays for hunting and fishing and intermittent logging for local use. The only inhabitant of the watershed before 1850 was a solitary fugitive slave who temporarily occupied a crude shack in the intervale at the mouth of Evans Brook. The fertile soil of this intervale, as well as its proximity to Gilead, lured the first Wild River homesteaders in 1852.

That same year the Atlantic & St. Lawrence Railroad was completed to Gorham, opening the region's timber resources to the voracious urban centers along the coast. A Saco lumber dealer, Joseph Hobson, acquired Bean's Purchase and began driving logs down the Wild River to the Gilead railhead. In 1860 he built a retaining dam near the present site of the Wild River Campground, to release water during the spring log drives. That same autumn, though, the dam was destroyed when the river's wild fury was unleashed by a heavy storm. Faced with the prospect of battling the unpredictable floods, Hobson's choice was to pull out. Round One to the river. Its prize was a thirty-year reprieve.

During the 1880s, Major Gideon Hastings developed major timber operations up Evans Brook, and the village of Hastings began to flourish. The only camps up the Wild River valley at this time were for hunting. One

Wild River visitor in 1885 was a youngster on his first hunting trip, whose name later became a symbol for outdoor sporting supplies: L.L. Bean.

In 1890, a second Hobson took up the challenge of taming the Wild River. This time it was Samuel Hobson, who bought Bean's Purchase for $100,000. After forming the Wild River Lumber Company in association with two timber barons from Island Pond, Vermont, he began building a logging railroad into the wilderness in 1891. The river responded with a huge freshet during a December thaw, destroying the new railroad bridges as well as other company structures.

This time the river's rage did not discourage the intruders. The bridges were rebuilt, and the railroad soon penetrated all the way to the end of the valley. One spur ran 2 miles into the Moriah Brook ravine to a camp just up the side stream above the "Water Garden Cascades." Moriah Gorge was spanned by a long trestle. After the ravine was logged clean, nearly 5000 acres of brush and slash along Moriah Brook went up in flames. In addition to fire, the Wild River Lumber Company was also plagued by spectacular train accidents, including one on the Moriah Brook spur. For a fascinating account of the wreck, complete with old photos, find a copy of D.B. Wight's *The Wild River Wilderness* (1971), on which much of the history recounted here is based.

In 1898 the lumber operations and the entire village of Hastings were sold to the Hastings Lumber Company. Under the new management disasters became commonplace. The first, in 1899, was a legendary train wreck in which an engine boiler exploded, shredding the locomotive and killing three men. Two years later the river brought down destructive floods, which were all the more severe due to loss of forest cover in the watershed. In the spring of 1903 devastating freshets recurred. That same May a severe fire burned out even the railroad ties. After this, the logging operations in the Wild River valley shut down completely. The "child of the mountains" had won Round Two, but not before incurring scars that have not yet healed completely.

The Wild River Road replaced the old railroad track in 1905. Between 1912 and 1918 the US Forest Service acquired the entire watershed as part of the new White Mountain National Forest. The virgin wilderness that the state had sold for $1000 plus change in 1832 was returned to public ownership as a ravaged landscape for $205,000—a single lifetime later.

The story, of course, has a happy ending. See for yourself when you visit the cascades of Moriah Brook.

CHAPTER 27

GIANT FALLS

◆

Location: Off the North Road in Shelburne
Maps: AMC #6 North Country–Mahoosuc Range Map (D-11/12); DeLorme
   Trail Map: A-15 (waterfall is off the map)

Hiking Data
Distance: Parking area to top of falls, 1.9 miles
Altitude gain: To top of falls, 1100 feet (altitude 1900 feet)
Difficulty: Moderate

◆

In his reverent chronicle of nature's annual cycle, *Seasons at Eagle Pond*, Donald Hall calls springtime "the least of our seasons" in northern New England. His claim that spring, the mud season, "has built no constituency" is a common sentiment. Mud season is the time when proprietors shutter their inns and take a holiday, and the time when local townsfolk are most tempted by dreams of Caribbean islands. Only whitewater paddlers seem to welcome with good cheer the soggy months of melting snows and chilly rains.

Spring serves another devoted constituency, however: the waterfall buffs. The same conditions that thrill kayakers also transform the region's waterfalls into spectacles that summer visitors can hardly imagine. Many waterfalls and cascades are as different, spring from summer, as a gale from a breeze. Giant Falls, at the southern end of the Mahoosuc Range, is one of the region's finest spring specials. It is also one of the loftiest waterfalls in the White Mountains.

Giant Falls lies on Peabody Brook 800 vertical feet below the marshy outlet of Dream Lake, which occupies a shallow highland basin between Bald Cap Peak (2795 feet) and Mount Bald Camp (3065 feet). Most of the year the marshes of Dream Lake release a steady dribble of water, but in spring the runoff becomes a flood.

Over on the eastern side of the Bald Cap ridge, a sister waterfall called

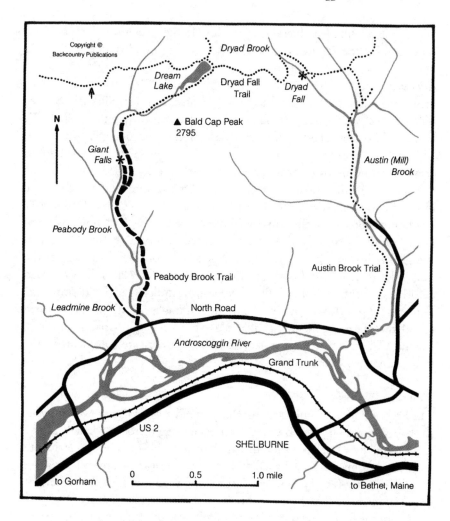

Dryad Fall is even higher and dryer than the Giant of Peabody Brook. In full flush during spring runoff, Dryad Fall is a towering silver column 400 feet high— or so they say. On our visits in early July, mid-August, and mid-September, however, Dryad Fall was hardly more than a steady trickle!

Both waterfalls can be reached in a single day trip by hiking across the flat-topped divide at Dream Lake. Keep in mind, however, that these waterfalls peak when the trails are at their mucky worst. In the depths of mud season the divide over to Dryad Fall becomes virtually impassable, (though the Fall can be approached from the east from Austin Brook Trail), and all of the trails are highly vulnerable to erosion. In the interests of conservation, wait until the footing dries up a bit before attempting this hike.

Access

From the junction in Gorham where NH 16 turns south for Pinkham Notch, follow US 2 east through Shelburne. After passing through a lovely birch forest and skirting a lake formed by a dam on the Androscoggin River, you will reach a left turn onto North Road, 3.4 miles from Gorham. North Road crosses the Androscoggin atop the narrow dam, where you have a memorable view upriver to the northern Presidentials. After passing over the dam, the North Road turns sharply to the east and soon dips to cross a bridge over Leadmine Brook—continue up the North Road another 0.25 mile. A pair of houses on the north side of the road—one with cobbled walls and one with shingled walls—mark the base of the Peabody Brook Trail by a sign for the trail and a small pull off. Parking is also available in a few places along the road before and after the trailhead. Please respect the understandable desire of the residents for peace and privacy. Overnight parking is not allowed. It is worth noting that the hike past Giant Falls used to be a leg of the Appalachian Trail, but the AT had to be relocated because its heavy use created problems for the local property owners.

The Trail

The Peabody Brook Trail starts out along an old grassy logging road between the two landmark houses. Bear right where the logging road forks at 0.1 mile, as indicated by a small brown trail sign. Pay no attention to the conspicuous red-diamond markers on the left fork; these are not meant for hikers, as we discovered when leading a group of grumbling Scouts on a fruitless excursion to see Giant Falls. The proper route is marked with blue blazes.

From the fork the trail fords Peabody Brook and turns upstream, entering a small reserve owned by the Society for the Protection of New Hampshire Forests. After 0.5 mile of gentle climbing through a grove of hemlocks the trail follows a logging road to the right (clearly marked), while another logging road forks off to the left and fords the brook. Shortly thereafter the trail turns left (mile 0.8 from the North Road). This turn, too, is clearly posted. After 0.1 mile of level walking through open hardwood forest you begin to ascend more earnestly past a wall of interesting crags. Another 0.25 mile of moderate climbing brings you to the spur path to the foot of Giant Falls. The 0.4-mile-long spur path becomes rough, narrow, and badly eroded as it descends into the ravine.

To reach the top of Giant Falls, continue up the main trail, which slabs up the steep eastern wall of the ravine. Watch for an inviting rock bench with an excellent view across the Androscoggin valley to Mount Moriah and the northern Presidentials. After approximately 0.5 mile of moderate climbing, the trail levels off and approaches the brookside. From this point you can easily scramble down to the crest of the falls.

If Giant Falls is your sole destination, you can terminate the hike here. But there is more to see higher up the trail. Dream Lake is worth a visit just to see whether it lives up to its intriguing name. The upper trail climbs steadily along Peabody Brook for 0.4 mile, passing a nearly continuous succession of cascades that are very attractive in high water. When the brook divides, the trail crosses the main branch and turns right to climb a final 0.3 mile to the flat headland basin, where the brook is crossed one last time. The trail then makes a wide circle around the basin to reach the far end of Dream Lake and the Mahoosuc Trail (3.1 miles from the North Road). Unhappily, in high water the last mile of the trail can be extraordinarily wet and mucky. Part of the trail is a virtual streambed, part is a gooey marsh, and a few spots do a good imitation of quicksand. This is great territory for moose, bullfrogs, and white-throated sparrows, but not for hikers.

Your first view of Dream Lake comes almost immediately after you reach the headland basin. At this point, though, you see only a shallow marsh at the tip of the lake. The dreamiest views are around to the far (east) side. That is also where you find the Dryad Fall Trail (clearly marked). The trail descends eastward, following yellow blazes. After crossing tiny Dryad Brook, the trail turns to the southeast and descends along an old logging road parallel to the brook. After about a third of a mile, an obvious side path runs south from the main trail for 100 feet to the crest of the towering bluff of Dryad Fall.

The Dryad Brook Trail formerly descended directly alongside the falls, but the route was very steep and slippery and became badly eroded. Thus, the trail below the crest of the Fall has been rerouted to follow the logging road for another third of a mile, joining the Austin Brook Trail approximately 2.4 miles from its trailhead off the North Road.

The full loop up the Peabody Brook Trail, down the Dryad Fall Trail and out the Austin Brook Trail is slightly over 9 miles long, including a 2.2-mile trek back up the North Road to the base of the Peabody Brook Trail. It is possible to cut this distance down to under 6 miles if you can leave a car—or a mountain bike—at a pull-out where Mill Brook Road crosses Austin (Mill) Brook, 1.7 miles north of the North Road. Mill Brook

Road is a passable gravel logging road that angles off the North Road 0.5 miles east of the Austin Brook Trail parking area, and a few yards west of the intersection between North Road and Meadow Road (which crosses the Androscoggin from Shelburne village). If you drive up Mill Brook Road, be sure to stay left at two different forks. And be sure to park well off the road to leave room for any logging trucks that might rumble by.

The Falls

The Giant at Giant Falls appears in the form of a precipitous wall of ledge several hundred feet high, where a wide swath of tough mica schist cuts across the path of Peabody Brook. When nourished by melting snows or soaking rains, the brook rushes down from Dream Lake, surges through a narrow sluice on the cornice at the top of the wall, and dashes playfully down the dark-gray facade of ledge in silvery ribbons of braided lace.

The very size of Giant Falls makes it hard to command a full view. The waterfall is a flirt, constantly hiding vital parts behind a veil of treetops or a steep outcrop of ledge. So, like the blind men investigating the elephant, we perceive only part of the waterfall from each point of contact. The initial contact is back along the North Road. From the edge of a pasture just west of the trailhead you can see a preview of the distant ribbon of falls adorning the tapered ravine of Peabody Brook.

A second vantage point is at the base of the falls. Following the spur path down into the ravine from the main trail, you will reach the brook at a very minor cascade. On one trip a friend ran ahead to see the falls—and found only this tiny cascade at the end of the path. He turned back, keenly disappointed. The trick is that you must scramble another 150 yards upstream to reach the main attraction. The path here ranges in quality from indistinct to nonexistent. Footing is tricky since the ravine is steep and the brookside is strewn with tumbled-down boulders and slippery leaves. Fortunately, though, the high cover of hardwood trees keeps the basin floor relatively free of tangled scrub. The forest also creates a healthy environment for spring wildflowers, including fine crops of trillium and hobblebush.

There is nothing fancy about the design of Giant Falls: The plane of the stream and the adjacent woods simply tilt up steeply. The brook has hardly dented the bank of tough ledge, so no pool of any significance has been crafted at the foot of the falls, and no gorge has been carved into the mountainside to frame the scene. From the woods alongside the falls or from the angular boulders in the streambed, you obtain intimate close-up

Giant Falls in low water

ROBERT KOZLOW

views of the animated currents, but you can only catch a glimpse of the Giant's upper body.

To reach the top of the falls, you have to return to the main trail and scramble down from above, as described earlier. The view from the top is the highlight of the trip. In addition to watching the current pour endlessly over the brink, you have an excellent view across the Androscoggin River valley. The fresh-scented conifer forest here is beautiful, too. It includes a stand of distinctive red pines. Far less common in the mountains than its majestic cousin, the white pine, the red pine is characterized by ruddy bark and tufts of extra-long double needles that flip up proudly at the tip of each bough. Above the falls the streambed is handsomely carved because at this elevation the brook dashes across lime-silicate rock that is more easily eroded than the headwall schist. Consequently, the higher cascades can be very pretty, though dwarfed by the Giant in scale.

Historical Detour

Shelburne was chartered in 1769. One year later settlers began arriving to cultivate the fertile alluvial soils of the Androscoggin River valley. The biggest story in Shelburne's history was the Indian attack of 1781. Benjamin Willey (1856) provides a stirring narrative of this "outrage," drawing on an account written by one of the Indian's captives, a Revolutionary War veteran named Nathaniel Segar. By 1781 the French and Indian War was already a receding memory. Most surviving Indians had fled, defeated, to Canada, and frequent visits by these Indians to the colonial settlements were not considered a threat. On August 3, 1781, however, a band of six Indians went on a marauding spree along the Androscoggin River.

The Indians set upon Segar and two companions working in a field in Bethel, took the men captive, and plundered a house nearby. After killing a settler in Gilead, they led their captives to Shelburne, "now on the very outposts of the scattered frontier settlements." The group crossed the Androscoggin River to raid the house of Hope Austin, who just that April had battled five-foot snowdrifts to settle in Shelburne with his wife and three children. (Presumably, "Austin Brook" bears the family's name.) Finding Mr. Austin away, the Indians left his wife and children unharmed and proceeded to "the last house on the frontier," that of Captain Jonathan Rindge, another recent arrival. There they plundered the house, killed Peter Poor, an early settler, and seized a black farmhand named Plato.

Then the Indians turned north into "the unbroken wilderness." They compelled Segar to write on a piece of bark a warning that all the captives would be killed if they were pursued. Fearing further attacks on their homes, some of the remaining settlers spent the night atop a steep mountain near Austin's homestead. Not far in the distance they could hear "the whoopings and shoutings" of the renegade band. From the geography, the Indians might well have been camped at Dream Lake.

After being driven to Canada, abused and half starved, the unfortunate captives were ransomed to British officers. Under Indian guard they were transported by canoe to Montreal, where they were interrogated and then imprisoned in a rat-infested jail for sixteen months. Segar later returned to the Androscoggin valley. In his own words, he lived to see the valley "rise from a howling wilderness into fruitful fields" (Willey, 1856).

Later in Shelburne's history, Giant Falls became a popular scenic attraction. This is not surprising, considering that the old north road was well traveled even in the early nineteenth century, when a lead mine was discovered nearby. In 1859 Thomas Starr King exclaimed that "the rock and cascade pictures in the forests of Baldcap well reward the rambles of an hour or two." An article in an early issue of *Appalachia* (Volume II) described a path to Giant Falls that was cut in 1878, but King's description suggests that a route was known much earlier. The old AMC account describes Giant Falls as "truly magnificent cascades . . . after a heavy rain." And in the spring.

CHAPTER 28

WATERFALLS OF THE GREAT GULF

◆

Weetamoo Falls
Sphinx Cascades

Location: In the Great Gulf Wilderness
Maps: AMC #1 Presidential Range Map (F-9); DeLorme Trail Map (C-10)

Hiking Data
Distance: Parking area to falls, 5.7 miles
Altitude gain: 2400 feet (to altitude 3700 feet)
Difficulty: Strenuous

◆

Though Weetamoo Falls is considered by many to be the loveliest waterfall in the Great Gulf, the star attraction on this trip is the Great Gulf Trail itself. This rugged trail follows the West Branch of the Peabody River into the heart of the Great Gulf Wilderness, passing a succession of unnamed surging cascades, deep pools, and powerful rapids en route to Weetamoo Falls. As the trail penetrates farther into the Gulf, the currents diminish in strength, but the cascades grow more numerous and the mountain views more grand.

Like its cavernous neighbors to the south, Tuckerman and Huntington Ravines, the Great Gulf was carved by local mountain glaciers before the great continental ice sheets arrived. The Gulf forms a huge dogleg basin with steep walls that drop more than 1500 feet from the shoulder of Mount Washington. Weetamoo Falls is the first major waterfall formed by the West Branch of the Peabody as it drains this huge basin—and therefore the last waterfall reached by hikers climbing upstream.

Most visitors to the Gulf's inner sanctum are backpackers hiking a long circuit up to the Presidential ridge. Serious trampers, though, can reach

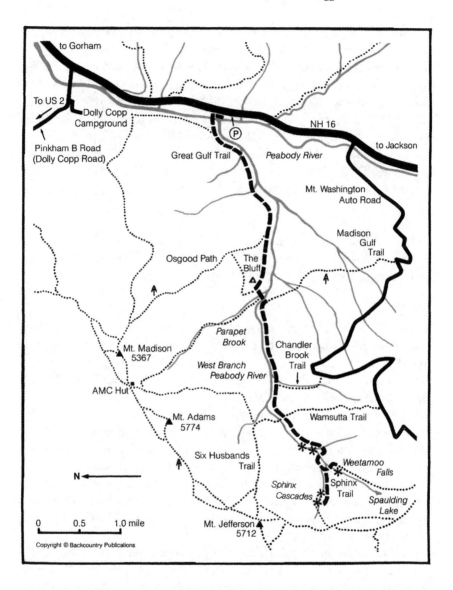

Weetamoo Falls as an invigorating day trip. The hike is most inviting during midsummer when the days are long, the blackflies are on the wane, the more familiar trails are beset with crowds, and the Gulf's cold pools and cool conifer forests are especially refreshing.

If you are not enthusiastic about a strenuous hike, you can still enjoy the beautiful river scenery closer to the trailhead. Your trip can be as short as a 0.1-mile stroll to the footbridge spanning the Peabody River or as severe as the 7.8-mile ascent of Mount Washington.

Darby Field, the first colonist to explore Agiochook (Mount Washington) in 1642, reported observing an extraordinary ravine to the north of the summit cone—an "almost unfathomable abyss," in the words of Benjamin Willey (1856). Not long after the first hiking trail was blazed to the summit of Mount Washington in 1819, Ethan Allen Crawford led a party astray in the clouds and wandered to "the edge of a great gulf." His simple description gradually displaced the earlier name, Gulf of Mexico. Not until 1881 was a path cut into the Gulf itself.

Access
A large Forest Service sign announces the present Great Gulf trailhead parking lot on the west side of NH 16, roughly halfway between the Mount Washington Auto Road and Dolly Copp Campground.

Trail
From the north end of the parking lot, the Great Gulf Trail crosses a long suspension footbridge over the Peabody River and then proceeds the entire length of the West Branch past Weetamoo Falls to Spaulding Lake. From the lake the trails ascends the towering headwall to the Gulfside Trail, 0.6 mile below the summit of Mount Washington.

For the first 2 miles the hike is quite gentle. At intersections with a cross-country ski trail from Dolly Copp Campground hikers should stay on the well-trodden footpath. At several points you can descend easily to the river and find large pools, sunny ledges, and thundering rapids. Here are some of the most beautiful swimming holes in the region. But swimmers should bear in mind that even in midsummer this stretch of the Peabody is swept by strong currents, and the water stays very cold. This river has claimed at least two lives.

At 1.7 miles the Osgood Trail diverges right to head up Mount Madison, while the Great Gulf Trail stays by the river and enters the Wilderness Area. Note that special camping restrictions apply in the Wilderness Area. Camping groups must not exceed ten people, and campsites should be located at least 200 feet from a trail or a watercourse except at designated sites. Also, no camping is permitted beyond the Sphinx Trail junction. You will pass spots along the trail where backpackers have obviously pitched tents, but using these sites is a violation of both the Forest Service rules and the spirit of wilderness camping.

ROBERT KOZLOW

Weetamoo Falls

About 0.3 mile into the Wilderness Area the trail passes a rocky set of rapids known as Boulder Falls. Notable only in high water, this inconsequential waterfall spills over a small overhanging face formed by a pair of huge boulders into a diminuitive pool. To find Boulder Falls, keep an eye out for evidence of an island in the river and the fairly obvious boulders. In low water, the falls disappear entirely, as the water finds shorter and less interesting routes down the riverbed.

About 0.6 mile into the Wilderness Area the trail veers away from the river and ascends to a prominent clearing called the Bluff. After 2.7 miles of hiking through the forest, beautiful though it may be, reaching the Bluff will feel like emerging from a tunnel into daylight. Surrounded by the tallest mountains in the Northeast, the Bluff provides a spectacular panoramic view. Rough, eroded paths descend from the Bluff to Parapet Brook deep in the ravine below, but there is no need to add to the erosion. Where the Osgood Cutoff Trail continues up the bluff, the Gulf Trail drops left to the brook immediately past the Bluff and crosses on a swaying suspension bridge. Here (mile 2.8) the Great Gulf Trail merges briefly with the Madison Gulf Trail. Soon, another footbridge crosses the West Branch of the Peabody above a darling set of small cascades. The Madison Gulf Trail branches off to the left, leaving the Great Gulf Trail to pursue the river into the Gulf.

The path now becomes rougher and steeper, and the river is diminished in size—though not in beauty. Indeed, you continue encountering splendid pools and cascades, which are beset with great boulders and framed with dark forest. River formations that would be notable landmarks on other trails are simply nameless bends in the stream here.

The Chandler Brook Trail branches off from the Great Gulf Trail after a mile of hard hiking. Beyond this junction the main path climbs a steep shoulder and passes through a handsome stand of young balsam firs before reaching the intersection with the Wamsutta Trail and the Six Husbands Trail (mile 4.5). With luck you may spot the yellow cap of a black-backed woodpecker exploring the slide-damaged conifers.

The path then becomes rougher still. After mounting a slippery slab, you will skirt a churning cascade that winds down a long, weathered ledge in a graceful arc into a glittering pool. Almost immediately, you reach another fine waterfall: A bulging curtain of water is split by a narrow crag into a steep chute on one side and a 15-foot vertical drop on the other. From the trail only the left half of the lower falls can be seen, so you must scramble to the pool below to get a full view, with Mount Jefferson towering overhead. These waterfalls are as worthy of attention as Weetamoo itself, leading one to wonder how they have so far remained unnamed. We will resist the natural urge to name them on the grounds that an unnamed waterfall in a wil-

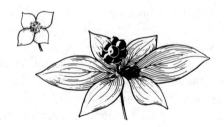

Bunchberry

derness has a certain poetry, a whiff of personal discovery for each passerby, that we could not match.

After passing yet another waterfall—a broad white sheet spilling over fractured brown ledge—the path flattens out, crosses the streambed, and enters a marsh scattered with storm-strewn trees. The footing through the marsh is tricky. At mile 5.5 the Sphinx Trail cuts off to the right, after which the Great Gulf Trail crosses the river one last time. Only a short climb remains to Weetamoo Falls.

For those with time and energy, the trail beyond Weetamoo Falls ascends a long rockslide overgrown with dense scrub fir. The drudgery of climbing the scree is rewarded by the unforgettable pleasure of seeing Spaulding Lake (mile 6.4), a tranquil gem encircled by the awesome mountain wall.

The lake is named after John Spaulding, an avid White Mountain explorer whose trip into the Great Gulf in 1853 was one of the earliest on record. (The first recorded trip was in 1829, by Dr. J.W. Robbins, a botanist after whom no local landmarks are named.) In a book published two years after his exploration of the gulf, Spaulding described the set of cascades and falls he had found as "at least worth a trip from the Atlantic from all who would look with proud satisfaction upon nature in her sublimest mood."

The Falls

No trail sign signals that you have reached Weetamoo Falls; the spot is marked only by the enchanting geometry of the waterfall and the foot pool. From the trail you see a vivid white curtain of water dancing laterally down the steps of a sloping ledge of ancient schist. The final tumbling step of the cascade sends ripples shimmering toward you across the clear pool. In subdued tones, the gray-green waters reflect the rocks and mosses that line the pool as well as the fir and the mountain birch that frame the scene. Just below, the river offers an encore in the form of another miniature waterfall, with its own sparkling pool.

Weetamoo Falls is not a place for scrambling on the ledge rock or sporting in the pool. The water is bitter cold, and the dense encroaching forest precludes exploration. A bit of rock hopping is possible at the foot of the pool, but the cascades back down the trail are much better suited for recreation. At Weetamoo Falls you will have to settle for wilderness scenery of great beauty.

Sphinx Cascades

If you are inhumanly strong, or just masochistic, you may be tempted by the promise of an unbroken string of remote cascades above Weetamoo Falls. Return down the Great Gulf Trail to its junction with the Sphinx Trail. This trail ascends alongside Sphinx Brook, at first just a mossy stairway of jumbled boulders and rivulets of water. Starting on the south side, the trail soon crosses to the north bank and at 0.1 mile recrosses. Looking ahead, you can see a hint of spray. The path climbs a steep rocky prow between a mossy glen on the left and a set of perfect slides and cascades on the right. A second cascade follows on the heels of the first. Then immediately you reach a third cascade where the river rushes through a V-shaped notch into a golden swimhole. The trail crosses to the north bank once more in a rather scary traverse above the top of this waterfall. Although the trail moves farther away from the stream from this point, you continue to spot pretty falls and inviting pools until the trail actually merges with the streambed, now a trickle of water under scree. This stream/trail emerges at the base of a 20-foot-high wall over which four seperate miniature cascades run down, glistening silver in the afternoon sun. At the far end of this wall, the waterfalls end, and a sign welcomes you to the Alpine Zone. This side trip along the Sphinx Cascades takes you 0.6 miles and 700 vertical feet to these top falls and is graced with spectacular views over the Great Gulf to compliment the cascades. Given that you had already hiked in 5.5 miles to reach the base, this excursion is only recommended for the masochist. Much to my surprise, in checking out these falls, I met one such hiker, who swore that the trip was "absolutely worth it."

Historical Detour

> *Child of the forest! Strong and free*
> *Slight-robed, with loosely flowing hair.*

So John Greenleaf Whittier described Weetamoo in his narrative poem, "The Bridal of Pennacook." In this poem Weetamoo is presented as a lovely daughter of the great chief Passaconaway (see chapter 18) and a romantic heroine who sacrificed her life in duty to her cold-hearted husband, Winnepurkit, sachem of Saugus.

More scholarly sources reveal that there was in fact an Indian queen by the name of Weetamoo and that Passaconaway did indeed marry off an ill-fated daughter to the sachem of Saugus, but Whittier was exercising artistic license in matching names. Perhaps he favored Weetamoo's lyrical name over Wanunchus, the bride's true name. He also found Winnepurkit more poetic than Montowampate, the sachem's actual name.

The historical Weetamoo was a far more important figure than the bride of Pennacook, though her story is less romantic. She was a female chieftain of the Wampanoag tribe of what is now eastern Rhode Island and southeastern Massachusetts. Her first husband (of six, according to tradition) was Wamsutta, son of Massasoit, the great friend of the early Pilgrims. Wamsutta succeeded Massasoit as chief in 1662 but soon died. His brother Metacomet, who became known as King Philip, later led the Indians in a war with the colonists. In percentage of population killed, King Philip's War was the bloodiest in American history.

As one of King Philip's most ardent supporters, Weetamoo was pursued by the colonists' militia. She drowned crossing a river while fleeing on August 6, 1676, six days before King Philip himself was killed. Both Indian leaders suffered the fate of those guilty of treason—their heads were cut off and displayed on poles.

Both Weetamoos, the historical and the poetic, died by drowning. Whittier's queen met her fate when her canoe was swept over Amoskeag Falls on the Merrimack River (in what is now Manchester, New Hampshire):

> Down the white rapids like a sear leaf whirled,
> On the sharp rocks and piled-up ices hurled.
> Empty and broken, circled the canoe
> In the vexed pool below—but where was Weetamoo?

CHAPTER 29

WATERFALLS OFF DOLLY COPP ROAD

◆

Triple Falls
Coosauk and Hitchcock Falls

Location: Dolly Copp Road (officially, the Pinkham B Road), which is a rough shortcut route from NH 16 (at Dolly Copp Campground) to US 2 in Randolph
Maps: AMC #1 Presidential Range Map (E-9/10); DeLorme Trail Map (A-11/12)

◆

Dolly Copp Campground is by far the largest and most popular campground in the White Mountains. It has 176 sites interspersed through nearly a mile of forest on the west side of the Peabody River, 5 miles south of Gorham. From late May, when some campers may still be sporting skis, through the magic of the fall foliage in early October, the campground brims with visitors eager to explore the nearby mountain treasures.

The most popular waterfall attractions in the area are Glen Ellis Falls and Crystal Cascade, 6 miles south of the campground in Pinkham Notch (chapter 20). Even nearer, though, are seven less well known but interesting waterfalls on the north slopes of Mount Madison and Mount Adams. Three of these—Triple Falls, Coosauk Fall, and Hitchcock Fall—are located off Dolly Copp Road (Pinkham B Road), a short but rough route across Pine Mountain Notch from the campground. These three are the subject of the present chapter. Four more, reached easily from the Appalachia parking lot on US 2, are covered in the next chapter.

In character, the waterfalls off Dolly Copp Road are pretty woodland cataracts rather than grand mountain spectacles like their popular cousins in Pinkham Notch. By the same token, they are uncrowded, unspoiled, and undeveloped—just right for a quiet side trip when you're in the neighborhood and have half a day to spare.

The falls can also be included in the itinerary for a hike up Mount Madison. The Pine Link Trail, near Triple Falls, starts at the height-of-land on Dolly Copp Road. By virtue of its elevated trailhead, Pine Link cuts 400 vertical feet off the summit climb compared to any other trail in the northern Presidentials. Coosauk and Hitchcock Falls are also quite convenient for summiteers because they lie directly on the Howker Ridge Trail, a rough but rewarding route to Mount Madison.

All three of these waterfalls are fed by steep, narrow ravines that drain quickly after a rain. This means that the water flow can be quite low during dry weather. Also, all three falls have a northern exposure and heavy forest cover, diminishing the advantage of sunny skies. Consequently, these waterfalls can be fairly dull during periods of "good" weather. During or after "bad" weather, however, you can take advantage of the ideal conditions and head for the falls!

TRIPLE FALLS

Hiking Data
Distance: Parking area to falls, 0.2 mile
Altitude gain: 200 feet (altitude 1700 feet)
Difficulty: Easy

As the name suggests, Triple Falls is three for the price of one. A short walk up the Town Line Brook Trail takes you past Proteus Falls, Erebus Falls, and Evans Falls in quick succession. If you're tabulating waterfall visits, go ahead and count this as three falls; after all, they do have separate names.

Access
The path to Triple Falls starts next to the bridge where Dolly Copp Road crosses Town Line Brook, 1.5 miles from US 2 in Randolph and 2.5 miles from Dolly Copp Campground (0.8 mile north of the height-of-land). A small sign for Triple Falls on the upstream side of the road will confirm that you are at the right place. The only parking is on the narrow dirt shoulder of the road, which has room for just a few vehicles.

The Trail
The path simply climbs along the east bank of Town Line Brook as far as the top of Evans Falls. From start to finish the distance is only 0.2 mile. Some

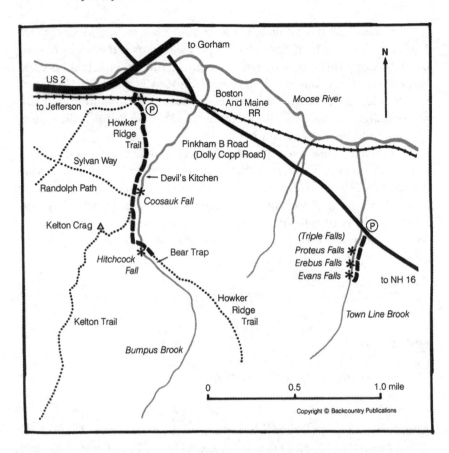

stretches, though, are a bit steep. Small signs are posted on trees along the way to identify each of the triplets. The route is heavily shaded by a canopy of tall hardwoods and riverine hemlocks, which conspire with the topography of the falls to make photography very difficult.

At Proteus Falls, about 100 yards up from the road, the brook emerges from a damp, narrow gorge and drops 25 feet in three steep steps. The name of the waterfall comes from a sea god in Homer's Odyssey who changed form at will. The derivative term "protean"—meaning exceedingly variable—aptly describes the way the falls change character in response to the rains. The gorge above the falls is impressive, but its steep, wet walls restrict access and limit the scope for exploring around the falls.

A short climb brings you to the most striking of the three falls, named Erebus after the mysterious darkness through which souls passed on their descent to Hades in Greek mythology. At Erebus Falls the brook slides across a huge bedrock foot (use your imagination) and plunges 30 feet over the "toes" to gneiss slabs below. Here, again, in dry weather the water flow may be meager. And as with Proteus Falls, there is little scope for exploring the slick, steep ledges around the falls.

Evans Falls is just above Erebus. Unlike its myth-conjuring neighbors downstream, Evans Falls is a minor cascade with small, clear pools above and below. Although the least interesting of the Triple Falls, this is the best place to stop for a snack or a picnic before heading back to the car. The name presumably honors the nonmythological Captain John Evans, who worked on the first road through Pinkham Notch in 1774 and later commanded troops in the Androscoggin valley following Indian raids in 1781.

The Town Line Brook Trail simply climbs past the falls and back down again, but in earlier years it formed a link to Mount Madison. Past Evans Falls the trail proceeded up the streambed for another mile, rising 1200 vertical feet before veering toward the west and climbing to the Howker Ridge Trail. Hikers also used to follow Town Line Brook downstream to its junction with the Moose River, from which point they walked the railroad bed to Mineral Spring Station. If you are in the mood for exploring, these old overgrown routes offer interesting options to spice up an otherwise simple hike.

COOSAUK AND HITCHCOCK FALLS

Hiking Data
Distance: Parking area to Coosauk Fall, 0.7 mile; to Hitchcock Fall,1.0 mile
Altitude gain: 300 feet to Coosauk Fall (altitude 1600 feet), and 300 feet more to Hitchcock Fall (altitude 1900 feet)
Difficulty: Moderate

Access
A large parking lot near the northern end of Dolly Copp Road, a few hundred yards south of US 2 in Randolph East, serves two trails: the Howker Ridge Trail and the Randolph Path.

The Trail
From the parking lot, don't be fooled by an orange arrow sign pointing into the woods a dozen yards up the railroad track. This sign is for snowmobiles, not hikers. Also, don't be fooled by the Forest Service sign indicating that

Coosauk Fall is only 0.2 mile away. You won't reach the brook in 0.2 mile, let alone the waterfall.

The two hiking trails head together across the railroad track and immediately diverge. Take the Howker Ridge Trail, which arcs southeast to approach Bumpus Brook. (These unusual names commemorate early Randolph farmers.) This first leg of the trail is very gentle. Though poorly blazed in spots, the path is generally well trodden and easy to follow, as long as you keep an eye out for occasional turns. The hardwood forest here is privately owned and bears evidence of recent logging. Not until Coosauk Falls does the trail enter the national forest.

At Bumpus Brook the trail rises steadily but not steeply along the west rim of a small gorge. Very soon a sign by the trail points to Stairs Falls. According to the *AMC White Mountain Guide,* there should be a cascade on the far wall of the gorge where a side stream spills into Bumpus Brook, but we have seen nothing other than the Bumpus tumbling through the gorge below. For this reason Stairs Falls is excluded from the list of attractions for this waterfall trip. If it's there when you visit, so much the better!

Not far beyond elusive Stairs Fall a second sign calls to your attention the Devil's Kitchen. This ominous name refers to a fascinating stretch of gorge where the brook slides past shattered, undercut walls of heavily jointed Bickford granite. The trail continues along the rim of the gorge, passing a large snag that has been carved to Swiss cheese by diligent woodpeckers. Coosauk Fall is at the head of the gorge, only 0.1 mile above the Devil's Kitchen.

Coosauk Fall is available in standard and deluxe versions, depending on the weather. Normally, the waterfall consists of a series of waterslides, cascades, and small pools formed by Bumpus Brook as it descends into the Devil's Kitchen gorge. From the trailside there is only a limited view, framed by hemlock boughs. A rough path drops into the gorge to provide close-up views of the cascades and the large slabs of sloping granite in the streambed. The damp, angular rocks and the narrow gorge greatly limit the scope for exploring this intriguing formation.

In wet weather a deluxe version of Coosauk Fall is on display. On the far side of the gorge, above the cascades, a lovely water veil appears draped over the terraced wall of a shallow, mossy alcove. A side stream skips across the crest of the alcove and drops 15 feet in a fine spray, before making a final dash to join the Bumpus.

Just past Coosauk Fall the Sylvan Way trail enters from the right, providing a 1.2-mile link to the Appalachia parking lot (see chapter 30).

Erebus Falls

Shortly beyond this junction the Kelton Trail forks off to the right and climbs steeply to Kelton Crag, Dome Rock, and Salmacis Fall (1.6 miles away). You should stay to the left on the Howker Ridge Trail, which ascends the side wall of Bumpus Basin for 0.2 mile to Hitchcock Fall.

Approaching Hitchcock Fall, the trail enters a new environment. The forest opens up as the hardwood canopy thins out and spruce trees gain a foothold. The appearance of the rock is also distinctly different from what you saw 0.2 mile downstream. You have climbed to the transition forest and crossed into a zone of banded gneiss bedrock, which geologists call the lower Littleton formation. Because the rock here is tougher, the currents have not carved out a gorge. Instead, the brook now passes through an open ravine bestrewn with huge, weathered boulders. From a break in the wall at the head of the ravine, falling waters zigzag in and out among the ledges and boulders, streaking the rock mosaic with gleaming white ribbons that range in height from 2 to 12 feet.

Unlike other waterfalls you encounter on this trip, Hitchcock Fall is a scrambler's delight. The field of large, angular boulders nearly begs you to explore its nooks and crannies. Be quite careful, though, since the footing is very uneven; this is not a playground for small children.

After crossing the brook, the trail climbs switchbacks up the east wall of the ravine to an interesting rock pit called the "Bear Trap," just above the falls. Nor far above is Blueberry Ledge, which speaks for itself. The trail then continues up the long Howker Ridge to Mount Madison. Back in Bumpus Basin, the Randolph Mountain Club guidebook, *Randolph Paths,* suggests three more waterfalls await bushwhackers farther upstream. One is called Muscanigra Fall (translation: blackfly!); the others are unnamed. There is no trail above Hitchcock Fall today, but until 1940 AMC trail maps showed a track up the west side of the brook to a small camp.

Historical Detour

It was around 1827 that Hayes Copp, of Stowe, Maine, bought a parcel of land in the wilderness south of Gorham on which to homestead. He lived at first in a crude shelter, hunting, trapping, and fishing to support himself while he readied the land for farming. In 1831, Hayes Copp took a bride. The lucky gal was Dolly Emery, a petite teenager from Bartlett. Dolly Copp returned with Hayes to his land, where they lived for fifty years. Though Hayes was there first, it was Dolly who became a White Mountain legend.

The Copps lived without neighbors for nineteen years, raising four children and living a life of virtual self-sufficiency. The family's backwoods mettle is illustrated by the story of how one son, Nathaniel, lost his way while hunting deer in a bitter January blizzard in 1855. With the temperature at 30 below zero and no chance to build a fire, Nathaniel continued walking until he found a ravine he could follow back to civilization. He ended up 40 miles away in Gilead, Maine. In the course of his wanderings he encountered and killed a deer, which his family recovered while searching for him the next day. So the drama ended with venison rather than tragedy.

In addition to raising her family and handling the household chores, Dolly began taking in travelers. Twenty-five cents a day covered bed and board and care for your horse. The Copp homestead became a haven for people passing through the notch and for tourists who were lured by excellent views of the Imp Cliffs across the Peabody valley. Dolly herself gained repute for her attractive woolwork, her gritty self-sufficiency, and her habit of smoking a clay pipe.

Her lasting fame, though, was earned in 1881 when she gathered the family together to announce: "Fifty years is long enough to live with any man!" So Dolly and Hayes split up, he returning to his birthplace, and she moving in with her daughter in Auburn, Maine.

As for the waterfalls, Coosauk was dubbed by William Peek, who helped build early trails in the Randolph area. The Hixsons, in their book *Place Names of the White Mountains,* claim that Peek thought the Abenaki Indian root *coos* meant "rough" and intended to have the falls called "rough place." Being a botanist rather than a linguist, however, he inadvertently chose an Abenaki word meaning "place of the pines"—of which there were none in the vicinity.

The Hixsons claim that Hitchcock Fall was named as a tribute to the renowned nineteenth-century White Mountain geologist, Professor Charles H. Hitchcock. Another possibility is that the falls were named after

Tiger Swallowtail and Orange Hawkweed

Hitchcock Falls

Colonel John R. Hitchcock, who had closer ties to the northern summit region. The colonel managed Gorham's premier hotel, the Alpine House, as well as the Tip Top House on the summit of Mount Washington and a summit lodge on Mount Moriah. He was also one of the founding directors of the Mount Washington Carriage Road Company.

Ironically, the two Hitchcocks were no strangers. Colonel Hitchcock, as proprietor, refused permission for Professor Hitchcock's research team to use the summit buildings on Mount Washington during the winter of

1869–70 to record meteorological observations. Instead, two of the professor's associates—led by J.H. Huntington, after whom a precipitous ravine on Mount Washington was later named—endured a tempestuous winter atop Mount Moosilauke. The following year, the Cog Railway company granted permission for the professor's team to lodge in the new telegraph building on the summit of Mount Washington. Thus the first systematic observations of the arctic winter conditions on New England's highest peak were obtained in 1870–71. Professor Hitchcock's 1871 book, *Mt. Washington in Winter* (coauthored with Huntington), is a White Mountain epic.

Considering that his hardy researchers braved temperatures as low as 59 degrees below zero on Mount Washington, and winds stronger than any ever before recorded (over one hundred miles per hour), one would hope that Hitchcock Fall indeed honors the professor.

CHAPTER 30

APPALACHIA WATERFALLS

◆

Gordon Fall
Salroc Falls
Tama Fall
Cold Brook Fall

Location: US 2 in Randolph
Maps: AMC #1 Presidential Range Map (E-9); DeLorme Trail Map (A-11)

Hiking Data
Distance: Parking area to Gordon Fall, 0.2 mile; to Salroc Falls, 0.5 mile; to
    Tama Fall, 0.7 mile; to Cold Brook Fall, 1.8 miles; round-trip, 2.6 miles
Altitude gain: 400 feet to high point at Tama Fall (altitude 1700 feet)
Difficulty: Easy to Gordon Fall and fairly easy for the rest of the 2.6-mile loop.
    (But optional round-trip grand tour: Strenuous.)

◆

When the Boston and Maine Railroad opened its rail link from Whitefield
to Berlin in 1892, the stop at Appalachia Station in Randolph was a gateway
to the Ravine House motel, a mecca for White Mountain climbers. Ravine
House served as a focal point for an expanding web of footpaths up the
daunting northern wall of the Presidentials. Tourists were already flooding
Mount Washington by carriage and cog railway coach, but the northern
peaks remained the exclusive domain of hardy mountaineers.

Accounts of early ascents up Mount Adams and Mount Madison described in detail the "exalted" summit views and the deplorable weather of
the summit ridge. Only in passing did they comment about the "many
pleasing cascades" encountered in the rugged ravines above Appalachia.
The nearby waterfalls were often visited, though, by genteel guests at
Randolph's mountain inns, as well as by tourists lodging in Gorham or
Jefferson. But for these visitors, too, the spectacular mountain scenery was

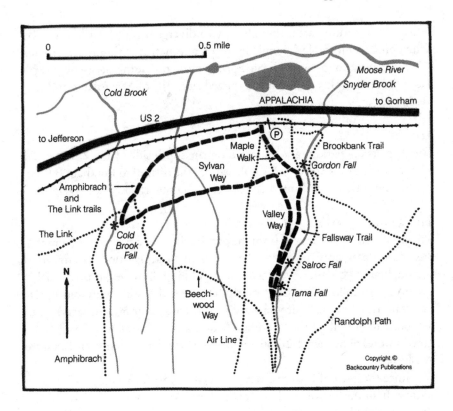

the foremost attraction.

Over the ensuing century Randolph has undergone many changes. The grand hotels all burned down or were demolished, even as the web of footpaths expanded into a rather bewildering maze of mountain trails. The railroad shut down, and the old trackbed traded its boxcar traffic for a clientele of moose. Appalachia Station, sharing the fate of many a New Hampshire cornfield, was transformed into a parking lot—for hikers.

In one respect, though, little has changed: The grand summits of the northern Presidentials still command the attention of most visitors to Randolph. In fact, the waterfalls may be nearly deserted even when the Appalachia parking lot is overflowing with hikers' cars. This is not entirely surprising because the summit ridge is truly dazzling, while the waterfalls are merely lovely. Yet nowhere else in the White Mountain does a single stop provide access to so many lovely, uncrowded falls!

This chapter describes an easy hike to four of these waterfalls—Gordon Fall, Salroc Falls, Tama Fall, and Cold Brook Fall—lying within a 1-mile radius of the parking area, though on two divergent trails. All four can be visited on a comfortable 2.6-mile loop. An alternative option is a strenuous 8.5-mile grand loop to Madison Spring Hut, providing access to over a *dozen* waterfalls, plus a shot at the rugged summits of Mt. Adams and Mt. Madison.

Access
The Appalachia parking lot is located on the south side of US 2, about 2.5 miles east of Lowe's Store, and 1 mile west of the turnoff to Pinkham B Road (Dolly Copp Road). It is marked by a conspicuous TRAILS PARKING sign.

The Trail
A maze of trails branches out from the parking lot. For a hike to the summits, this maze poses no problem: Take any path heading "up," or stick to a thoroughfare like Valley Way. The waterfall loop, however, is unavoidably circuitous, so follow directions carefully, watch the trail signs, and ignore irrelevant trail junctions. If you want to construct your own itinerary, your best bet is to buy either the Randolph Mountain Club trail map (available at Lowe's Store) or the new 1:20,000 map of the Presidential Range by Bradford Washburn.

Since there are at least five ways to begin the waterfall loop, it is best to start with an outline of the basic plan of attack: (1) mosey over to Snyder Brook, which descends from Madison Spring to join the Moose River just east of Appalachia; (2) follow the brook upstream for 0.5 mile; (3) double back and cut over to Cold Brook, 0.5 mile west; and (4) return to Appalachia. Only Leg 2 involves any significant uphill work, and even this is not at all steep. Now for details.

From the information board near the west end of the parking lot, take the Valley Way trail across the gravel bed of the former railroad tracks, through a power-line cut, and into the woods. After entering the woods you will come quickly to a fork where the Maple Walk trail branches to the left. Take it. This very easy trail contours over to Synder Brook, where you may descend 100 feet downstream to Gordon Fall, 0.3 mile from the parking lot. On the way, see if you can spot the "sugar shack" on the left. In late winter long tubes are strung through the woods to carry sap from the sugar maple trees to the sugar shack. There the sap simmers in large pans over a wood fire to become the world's best excuse for eating pancakes. At the river, Sylvan Way continues over the brook, connecting to Coosauk Falls from chapter 29.

ROBERT KOZLOW

Gordon Fall

From Gordon Fall, double back upstream along the Fallsway, climbing along the west bank of Snyder Brook, passing Salroc and Tama Falls. Gordon and Tama Falls have signs marking them, although Salroc does not. The only slight complication is that after Salroc Falls the trail merges briefly with Valley Way, before diverging again to swing past Tama Fall. You can also climb to Tama Fall on the Brookbank trail, a rougher route up the east bank of Snyder Brook. A third option, unless the water is high, is to forge straight up the streambed, barefoot, and detour to the formal trails when necessary.

The cascades and the old forests between Gordon and Tama Falls make up the Snyder Brook Scenic Area. You can thank the AMC for preserving this wonderful brookside scenery. The club purchased the 36-acre tract in 1895 and turned the land over to the White Mountain National Forest in 1937. Aside from this slender corridor along Snyder Brook, nearly all of the forest on the waterfall loop is still privately owned.

Fallsway and Brookbank converge immediately above Tama Fall and soon terminate at a junction with Valley Way. To continue the loop, double back down Valley Way for 0.4 mile to Sylvan Way. This path contours east-west across the lower slopes between Cold Brook Fall and Coosauk Fall (chapter 29), linking four major summit routes. Turn left (west) on Sylvan Way and follow this easy trail 0.7 mile to Cold Brook Fall.

280 Waterfalls of the White Mountains

Take note that Cold Brook feeds into the town drinking water, so swimming, wading, and all other polluting activities are strictly prohibited at the waterfall.

Sylvan Way ends 100 yards below Cold Brook Fall, where it meets the combined Link/Amphibrach Trails. A right (east) turn here takes you back to Appalachia, finishing the loop. On this last leg, old logging roads can lure you into wrong turns, so keep an eye out for trail blazes.

If the loop walk just described sounds tame, you might consider a grueling "grand loop" to the Madison Springs Hut, passing more than a dozen waterfalls and cascades. In outline form—it's a bit complicated, so please check more detailed trail maps—starting from Appalachia follow the Amphibrach Trail to the awesome King Ravine Trail. Climb to the Gulfside trail, which leads to the hut. Start back down via Valley Way, then after 1.0 mile, take the Lower Bruin Cutoff down steeply to the Brookside Trail, which returns to Valley Way 0.3 mile above Tama Fall. From Tama Fall descend along Snyder Brook back to Appalachia. Or the other way around. Note, though, that descending King Ravine can be treacherous.

This loop routes you directly past all four of lower falls, plus Mossy Fall, Coldspur Ledges, Duck Fall, and Salmacis Fall. In addition you can make short detours to: Spur Brook Fall (0.1 mile down Cliffway from Amphibrach); Canyon Fall (about 0.2 mile *down* King Ravine Trail from Amphibrach); a fine unnamed cascade on Randolph Path 50 yards above the junction with Ampibrach and King Ravine Trail; and Chandler Fall (0.3 mile up the steep Spur Trail from Amphibrach). For adventurous souls, the route passes several other cascades at points where the various trails parallel Cold Brook, Spur Brook, and Chandler Brook, respectively. Two off-trail features are named by the Randolph Mountain Club as Marian Fall and Thorndike Fall (see *Randolph Paths,* sixth edition). Both of these falls lie on Chandler Brook about 0.1 mile above Duck Fall, but they are difficult to reach due to steep walls of the ravine, with large boulders and heavy foliage blocking the way. As a bonus, the grand loop puts you in a good position to scamper up to the summit of Mount Adams (0.7 mile from the Gulfside Trail) or Mount Madison (0.5 mile above Madison Hut).

The Falls

Gordon Fall is a small, charming cascade, where Snyder Brook tumbles 20 feet through a corridor of tall hemlock trees into a shallow, rocky pool. The pitch is moderate enough that one can scramble up the weathered slabs of

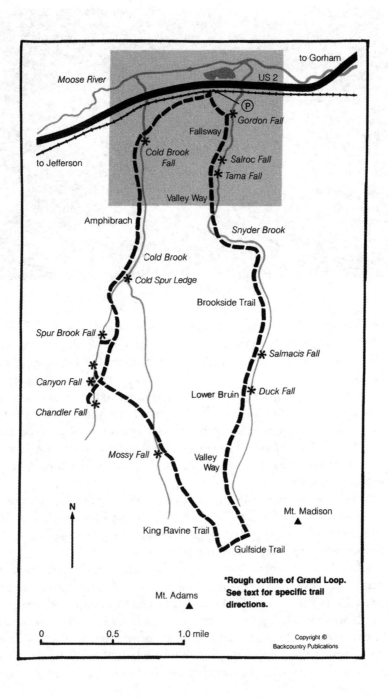

to Gorham

Moose River

US 2

(P)

Gordon Fall

Fallsway

Cold Brook
Fall

Salroc Fall

Tama Fall

to Jefferson

Valley Way

Amphibrach

Snyder Brook

Cold Brook

Cold Spur Ledge

Brookside Trail

Spur Brook Fall

Salmacis Fall

Canyon Fall

Lower Bruin

Duck Fall

Chandler Fall

Mossy Fall

Valley
Way

N

Mt. Madison

King Ravine Trail

Gulfside Trail

*Rough outline of Grand Loop.
See text for specific trail
directions.

Mt. Adams

0   0.5   1.0 mile

Copyright ©
Backcountry Publications

Salroc Falls

ROBERT KOZLOW

ancient volcanic bedrock to the line of minor cascades, waterslides, and shallow crystal pools above the falls. The character of the falls is captured by its old name, Ripple Falls, (which appeared in an 1888 *History of Coos County*).

Gordon Fall is a special place to bring young children. It was here that we took our son to wade and splash when he was not yet three years old, so he would learn to delight in the spirit of brook and forest. Some small pools above the falls are embedded in smooth terraces for easy wading. Even in midsummer, however, the water is quite cold because of the northern exposure and the tall trees.

Note: The Gordon Fall here on Snyder Brook should not be confused with Gordon Falls on Gordon Pond Brook in North Woodstock. The latter is an interesting formation, but not interesting enough to warrant the 7.4-mile round-trip hike required to reach it.

Salroc Falls lies about 500 yards farther up Snyder Brook. Here, the waters cascade over a short flight of mossy steps and then slip transparently down a 25-foot slide of pitched bedrock to a small, tranquil crescent pool. Directly above you will see a second fine waterslide and additional cascades. The two halves of the split composition are often referred to as Lower and Upper Salroc Falls. This distinction reflects a lack of harmony that makes Salroc less absorbing than its neighbors, despite its being higher and steeper than Gordon Fall. Nonetheless Salroc is an interesting formation, and the adjacent slides and cascades offer the best scrambling on the trip.

Tama Fall is the beauty queen of Snyder Brook. For the best view, climb down from the overlook to the edge of the shimmering pool at the bottom of the glen. Across the pool, the brook has beveled a broad channel into the bluff of heavily jointed granite. A fine curtain of whitewater drapes over the steep, recessed crest of the bluff. Below, this the brook makes a shallow turn and slides down a sloped ledge to the pool. The pattern is rather similar to that of Salroc Falls, but here the patient artist has perfected the design.

With some caution, you can manage to cross the ledge to reach the falls. The upper curtain of water makes an outstanding woodland shower for crazies who have a high tolerance for cold. If you like exploring, you should also investigate above the falls, where the brook has sculpted fascinating waterslides and pools in the granite.

Despite the temptation to fritter away hours exploring Snyder Brook, leave time for Cold Brook Fall. Though you can't play in the water—because Cold Brook feeds the town water supply—some observers consider this to be the "most spectacular" waterfall in Randolph (RMC, 1977). During the era of the grand hotels, this was a favorite tourist stop.

Cold Brook Fall forms a wide ribbon of lacy whitewater that sluices down a terraced wall into a rock-bound pool. The falls are about 30 feet high, with tree-topped cliffs to the left that rise half again as high above the lime-green pool. Midway up this wall a thick dark stripe can be seen, where a deep cave undercuts the uppermost bank of cliffs. The cave can be reached, with caution. Narrow fingers of carved rock at the base of the pool provide more accessible perches for admiring the picturesque glen. The immediate vicinity of the waterfall is protected today as a town reserve.

The granitic bedrock here, unlike that at the neighboring waterfalls, is formed from a dome of magma that invaded the region more than 400 million years ago. Not far above the falls Cold Brook exposes an even more ancient bedrock body of black Ammonoosuc volcanics, dating back half a billion years to an early period of intense volcanic activity.

As mentioned earlier, at least eight more waterfalls and cascades can be reached on the grand loop hike to Madison Hut. There is not space enough to describe each of these, but a few brief comments are in order. First, it's a hard slog up the steep ravines to the higher falls. Consider that Snyder Brook drops more than 3500 feet in 3-plus miles from Madison Hut. The lower loop described in this chapter may be easy going, but the rest of the grand tour is an exhausting, sustained climb. You have to be interested as much in the hike itself as in the waterfalls for the extra effort to be worthwhile.

Second, if you have the energy to tackle the grand loop, some of the higher falls are indeed worth a visit. Chandler Fall is especially elegant, while Duck Fall is lovely, and the ledges atop Salmacis Fall provide a wonderful, breezy spot for a picnic. Third, the narrow ravines grow wilder and more fascinating the higher you go, even as the water volume tapers off. Finally, the northern summits of the Presidential Range are spectacular; this is a trip you may want to do over and over again, combining waterfall ravines with other superb paths such as the Air Line Trail or the Spur Trail.

Historical Detour

Whether you are heading for the waterfalls or the summits, you will be surrounded by homages to the mountaineers of the late nineteenth century who devoted so much effort to building the trails. The most explicit tribute is at Memorial Bridge, a sturdy stone and wood structure spanning Cold Brook 100 yards below Cold Brook Fall. The bridge was built in 1924 for a reason that is explained by a plaque embedded in stone nearby.

> Memorial to J.R. Edmands and E.B. Cook and those other pioneer pathmakers: Gordon. Lowe. King. Hunt. Watson. Peek. Sargent. Nowell. Every man's work shall be made manifest.

Many of the place names hereabout also echo the spirit of the trail builders. Gordon Fall is named for James Gordon, a mountaineer from Gorham who guided Thomas Starr King on his excursions in Randolph. The three ridges drained by Snyder Brook and Cold Brook are likewise named for trail builders: Gordon, Durand, and Nowell. Even Snyder Brook is alleged to be named after a dog owned by Charles Lowe, who cut the first path up Mount Adams in 1876. Lowe was also one of the premier guides of the day, charging a then-princely fee of $3 per day.

Much of this early trail blazing was the work of public-spirited members of the Appalachian Mountain Club, which was founded in 1876. With Mount Washington already being served by the Cog Railway, the Carriage Road, and a handful of trails, energetic AMC members turned their attention initially to areas that were not yet easily accessible to the public. Their first projects included the completion of Lowe's path and the King Ravine Trail up Mount Adams in 1876. Two years later L.M. Watson blazed the first path up Snyder Brook. And in 1888, the AMC opened its first mountain hut at Madison Spring.

Not every Randolph place name commemorates a mountaineer. Indeed, the name of the town itself honors a Virginia congressman, and later senator, who was a descendant of Pocahontas. Nor have Randolph citizens always been avid mountaineers. Thomas Starr King, who popularized the northern summits in his 1868 book, *The White Hills,* wrote about one old Randolph farmer who held the mountains in low esteem: "Blast 'em, I wish they was flat." King did not ask for his opinion of the waterfalls.

Bemis Brook Falls

APPENDIXES

◆

APPENDIX A

Bedrock Geology at
Main Waterfalls and Cascades

CHAP.	WATERFALL	BEDROCK	MAP CODE*
1	Beaver Brook Cascades	Metagraywacke (Dlm)	WR
2	Bridal Veil Falls	Kinsman quartz monzonite (Dkqm) contact with Conway granite (Mzc)	FN
3	Silver Cascade	Littleton Formation, gray gneiss (Dllg)	CN
	Flume Cascade	Dllg	CN
	Gibbs Falls	Dllg	CN
	Beecher Cascade	Mzc	CN
	Pearl Cascade	Mzc	CN
4	Gem Pool	Littleton Formation, quartzite and schist (Dls)	MW
	the Gorge	Dls	MW
	the ledges	Dls	MW
	Upper Falls	Two-mica granite (Dgt, formerly Bickford granite)	MW
	Lower Falls	Mzc	MW
5	First Cascade	Littleton Formation, gneiss (Dlg)	MW
	Second Cascade	Dls	MW
6	Pond Brook Falls	Long Mountain granite (Lg)	P
7	Beaver Brook Falls	Waits River Formation (Dw)	DN
	Dixville Flume	Quartz monzonite (Qm)	DN
	Huntingdon's Cascade	Qm contact with Dixville Formation phyllite, schist, and quartzite (Od)	DN
8	Welton Falls	Dkqm	IGM
9	Cascade Brook	Norway quartz monzonite (Nqm)	MC
10	Georgiana Falls	Dkqm	FN

289

CHAP.	WATERFALL	BEDROCK	MAP CODE*
11	Avalanche Falls	Mzc	FN
	Liberty Gorge Cascade	Mzc	FN
	the Pool	Mzc	FN
12	the Basin	Mzc	WR
	Cascade Brook	Mzc	WR
	Kinsman Falls	Intrusive Dkqm breccia (Mzi)	WR
	Rocky Glen Falls	Dkqm	WR
13	Stairs Falls	Mzc	WR
	Swiftwater Falls	Mzc	WR
	Cloudland Falls	Kqm	WR
14	Franconia Falls	Mzc	WR
15	No. 13 Falls	Dkqm contact with Dlm	WR
16	Thoreau Falls	Mzc	CN
	Zealand Falls	Mzc	CN
17	Mad River Falls	Dlg	G
	Bickford Slides	Perry Mountain Formation, quartzite and schist (Spm) contact with Dtm	WR
18	Sabbaday Falls	Mzc, at diabase dike	MC
	Rocky Gorge	Dgt	WR
	Lower Falls	Porphyritic quartz syenite (Mzpqs)	WR
19	Jackson Falls	Mzpqs	WR
	Diana's Baths	Mzc	WR
20	Glen Ellis Falls	Rangeley Formation quartzite and schist (Sr)	R
	Crystal Cascade	Volcanic vent metadiabase (V), with Boott member schists at base	MW
	Thompson Falls	Dlg	GQ
21	Nancy Cascades	Dllg	CN
22	Arethusa Falls	Mount Osceola granite (Mog)	CN
	Bemis Brook Falls	Black-cap granite (Bcg)	CN
	Coliseum Falls	Bcg	CN
23	Dry River Falls	Dllg	CN

CHAP.	WATERFALL	BEDROCK	MAP CODE*
24	Ripley Falls	Mog	CN
	Sparkling Cascade	Mog	CN
25	Screw Auger Falls	Biotite and hornblende-biotite quartz diorite to grandiorite and Dgt (Dqgt)	WIM
	Step Falls	Dqgt	WIM
26	Moriah Brook	Dlg crossed by bands of lime-silicate rock and biotite	G
28	Weetamoo Falls	Dls	MW
29	Triple Falls	Dlg	MW
	Coosauk Fall	Dgt	WR
	Hitchcock Fall	Dlg	MW
30	Gordon Fall	Ammonoosuc volcanics (Oam)	MW
	Salroc Fall	Dgt	MW
	Tama Fall	Dgt	MW
	Cold Brook Fall	Contact between Oam and Dgt	MW

*Map Codes

WR   *Bedrock Geologic Map of the Wilderness and Roadless Areas of the White Mountain National Forest,* US Geological Survey (USGS), 1984.

FN   *Geologic Map of the Franconia Notch Quadrangle,* NH Department of Resources and Economic Development (NHDRED), 1935.

CN   *Geologic Map of the Crawford Notch Quadrangle,* NHDRED, 1977.

MW   *Geologic Map of the Mt. Washington Quadrangle,* NHDRED, 1979.

P   *Geologic Map of the Percy Quadrangle,* NHDRED, 1949.

DN   *Geologic Map of the Dixville Notch Quadrangle,* NHDRED, 1963.

IGM   *Interim Geologic Map of New Hampshire,* NHDRED, 1986.

MC   *Geologic Map of the Mt. Chocorua Quadrangle,* NHDRED, 1938.

G   *Geologic Map of the Gorham Quadrangle,* NHDRED, 1975.

WIM   *Geologic Map of Western Interior Maine,* USGS, 1988.

Note: Information in the table is based on the various bedrock geology maps identified above. Bedrock identifications are not definitive. Some waterfalls are difficult to locate precisely on the relevant map because of the scale used.

Other waterfalls occur in a well-defined bedrock zone, but have local irregularities that cannot be determined from the map. Also, some nomenclature changes from map to map, depending on the map's age. The table generally uses the nomenclature from the source map. Modifications have been made for consistency where confusion otherwise would arise from multiple labels for a single type of rock. We thank Professor Wallace A. Bothner of the Department of Earth Sciences, University of New Hampshire, for his assistance. Any inaccuracies, though, are fully our own responsibility.

APPENDIX B

Public Campgrounds and Mountain Huts

FACILITY	CAPACITY	NEARBY WATERFALL TRIPS (BY CHAPTER NUMBER)
White Mountain National Forest Campgrounds		
Campgrounds off Kancamagus Highway		
Big Rock—6 miles E of Lincoln	28 sites*	10, 11, 12, 13, 14, 18
Blackberry Crossing—6 miles W of Conway	20 sites*	18
Covered Bridge—6 miles W of Conway	49 sites	18
Hancock—4 miles E of Lincoln	56 sites*	10, 11, 12, 13, 14
Jigger Johnson—13 miles W of Conway	75 sites	14, 18
Passaconaway—15 miles W of Conway	33 sites	14, 18
White Ledge—NH 16, 5 miles S of Conway	28 sites	18, 19
Campgrounds between Franconia Notch and Crawford Notch		
Sugarloaf I—2 miles E of Twin Mountain	29 sites	3, 4, 16, 22, 23, 24
Sugarloaf II—Same as Sugarloaf I	33 sites*	3, 4, 16, 22, 23, 24
Zealand—Same as Sugarloaf campgrounds	11 sites*	3, 4, 16, 22, 23, 24
Campgrounds off I-93		
Campton—Exit 28, 2 miles on NH 49	58 sites	9
Campton Group Area—across from Campton Campground	16 sites* (3 for groups)	9

FACILITY	CAPACITY	NEARBY WATERFALL TRIPS (BY CHAPTER NUMBER)
Russell Pond—Exit 31, 3 miles off Tripoli Road	87 sites	1, 9, 10, 11, 12, 13, 14
Waterville—Exit 28, 8 miles on NH 49	27 sites*	9
Wildwood—Exit 32, 7 miles W on NH 112	26 sites*	1, 2

Campgrounds in or near Maine portion of National Forest

Basin—Route 113, 15 miles N of Fryeburg, ME	21 sites	17
Cold River—same as Basin	14 sites*	17
Crocker Pond—ME 5, S of Bethel	7 sites*	25
Hastings—Route 113, 3 miles S of US 2	24 sites*	25, 26, 27
Wild River—Wild River Road, 5 miles SW of Hastings, ME	11 sites*	26

Campgrounds near Pinkham Notch

Dolly Copp—6 miles S of Gorham on NH 16	176 sites	5, 19, 20, 27, 28, 29, 30
Barnes Field—Near Dolly Copp	11 group sites*	5, 19, 20, 27, 28, 29, 30

New Hampshire State Parks with Campgrounds

Coleman—N of NH 26, 6 miles E of Colbrook	30 sites	7
Crawford Notch—US 302	30 sites	3, 4, 16, 21, 22, 23, 24
Franconia Notch—I-93	98 sites	2, 10, 11, 12, 13, 14
Moose Brook—N of US 2, just W of Gorham	42 sites	5, 20, 27, 28, 29, 30

Appalachian Mountain Club Huts (reservations required)

Carter Notch Hut—between Carter Dome and Wildcat Mountain	40 guests*	20
Galehead Hut—W of South Twin Mountain	36 guests	15

FACILITY	CAPACITY	NEARBY WATERFALL TRIPS (BY CHAPTER NUMBER)
Greenleaf Hut—Mount Lafayette	40 guests	12, 13
Lakes of the Clouds Hut—Mount Washington	90 guests	4, 23
Lonesome Lake Hut—Cannon Mountain	44 guests	12, 13
Madison Spring Hut—Mount Madison	50 guests	29, 30
Mizpah Hut—above Crawford Notch	60 guests	3, 23
Pinkham Notch Camp—NH 16, Pinkham Notch	100+ guests	19, 20, 28
Zealand Falls Hut—Zealand Notch	36 guests*	16

Notes:

* Open year-round without services; other campgrounds are open from before Memorial Day until after Labor Day, exact dates varying by site.

For additional information:

- On White Mountain National Forest campgrounds and recreation sites:
  White Mountain National Forest, P.O. Box 638, Laconia, NH 03247
  Phone 1-603-528-8721.

- On New Hampshire State Park facilities:
  New Hampshire Division of Economic Development, P.O. Box 856, Concord, NH 03301. Phone 1-603-271-2666.

- On privately operated campgrounds:
  Office of Vacation Travel, P.O. Box 856, Concord, NH 03301.

- On AMC mountain huts:
  Hut Reservations, AMC Pinkham Notch Camp, P.O. Box 298, Gorham, NH 03581. Phone 1-603-466-2727 for reservations or 1-603-466-2725 for information and weather.

BIBLIOGRAPHY

1. Trail Guides and Histories

American Guide Series, *New Hampshire: A Guide to the Granite State.* Boston: Houghton Mifflin, 1938.

Anderson, John and Stearns Morse, *The Book of the White Mountains.* New York: Balch & Co., 1930.

Appalachian Mountain Club, *AMC White Mountain Guide,* 26th ed. Boston, 1998. Other editions used: 1922, 1931, 1940, 1952, 1976, 1987, 1992.

Appalachian Mountain Club, *Appalachia,* various issues.

Appalachian Mountain Club, *AMC Field Guide to Mountain Wildflowers of New England.* Boston, 1977.

Beals, Charles Edward, Jr., *Passaconaway in the White Mountains.* Boston: Richard G. Badger, 1916.

Belcher, C. Francis, *Logging Railroads of the White Mountains.* Boston: AMC, 1980.

Bisbee, Ernest, *The White Mountain Scrap Book: Early Stories and Legends of the "Crystal Hills."* Lancaster, NH: Bisbee Press, 1939.

Brown, William Robinson, *Our Forest Heritage,* Concord, NH: New Hampshire Historical Society, 1951.

Colby, Solon B., *Colby's Indian History.* Conway, NH: Walker's Pond Press, 1975.

DeLorme Mapping Company, *The New Hampshire Atlas and Gazetteer,* 11th ed. Freeport, ME: DeLorme, 1998.

Doan, Daniel and Ruth Doan MacDougall, *Fifty Hikes in the White Mountains,* 5th ed. Woodstock, VT: The Countryman Press, 1997.

Doan, Daniel and Ruth Doan MacDougall, *Fifty More Hikes in New Hampshire,* 4th ed. Woodstock, VT: The Countryman Press, 1998.

Drake, Samuel Adams, *The History of the White Mountains.* New York: Harper & Brothers, 1881.

Feller-Roth, Barbara (ed.), *Western Region.* Vol. 2 of *Hiking.* Maine Geographic series. Freeport, ME: DeLorme, 1987.

Fobes, Charles B., *Grafton, Maine—A Human and Geographical Study*, Bulletin No. 42, Technology Experiment Station, Orono, ME: University of Maine, 1951.

Gabler, Ray, *New England White Water River Guide*. Boston: AMC, 1981.

Gibson, John, *Fifty Hikes in Southern and Coastal Maine*, 2nd ed. Woodstock, VT: The Countryman Press, 1996.

Gifford, William H., "Colebrook." *Colebrook, News and Sentinel*, 1970.

Harrington, Karl P., *Walks and Climbs in the White Mountains*. New Haven, CT: Yale University Press, 1926.

Hawthorne, Nathaniel, "The Great Carbuncle," "The Ambitious Guest," "The Great Stone Face," from *The Complete Short Stories of Nathaniel Hawthorne*. Garden City, NY: Hanover House, 1959.

History of Coos Country. Syracuse, NY: W.A. Fergusson, 1888.

Hixson, Robert and Mary, *The Place Names of the White Mountains*. Camden, ME: Down East, 1980. [Note: the correct spelling of authors' surname is used here (at their request), but the book is listed in catalogues and indexes under "Hixon."]

Hodge, Frederick W. (ed.), *Handbook of American Indians*. New York: Rowman and Littlefield, 1971.

Holbrook, Stewart H., *Yankee Loggers*. New York: International Paper Company, 1961.

Hunt, Elmer, *New Hampshire Town Names*. Peterborough, NH: Noone House, 1970.

King, Thomas Starr, *The White Hills: Their Legends, Landscape, and Poetry*. Boston: Crosby and Ainsworth, 1859.

Kostecke, Diane M. (ed.), *Franconia Notch: An In-Depth Guide*. Concord, NH: Society for the Protection of New Hampshire Forests, 1975.

Lapham, Donald A., *Former White Mountain Hotels*. New York: Carlton Press, 1975.

Lehr, Frederic B., *Carroll, New Hampshire: The First Two Hundred Years*. Littleton, NH: Courier, 1972.

McNight, Kent H. and Vera B., *A Field Guide to Mushrooms of North America*. Boston: Houghton Mifflin, 1987.

Morse, Stearns (ed.), *Lucy Crawford's History of the White Mountains*. Boston: AMC, 1978.

Monegain, Bernie, *Natural Sites: A Guide to Maine's Natural Phenomena.* Maine Geographic series. Freeport, ME: DeLorme, 1988.

Nutting, Wallace, *New Hampshire Beautiful.* Framingham, NH: Old American, 1923.

Oakes, William, *Scenery of the White Mountains.* Boston, 1848. Reprinted by New Hampshire Publishing Company, Somersworth, 1970.

Pike, Robert E., *Tall Trees, Tough Men.* New York: W.W. Norton, 1967.

Pike, Robert E., *Spiked Boots.* St. Johnsbury, VT: The Cowles Press, 1961.

Pinette, Richard E., *North Woods Echoes.* Colebrook, NH: Liedl, 1986.

Poole, Ernest, *The Great White Hills of New Hampshire.* Garden City, NY: Doubleday, 1946.

Randolph Mountain Club, *Randolph Paths.* Randolph, NH: Randolph Mountain Club, 1977.

Reifsnyder, William E., *High Huts of the White Mountains.* Boston: AMC, 1979.

Spaulding, John Hubbard, *Historical Relics of the White Mountains.* Boston: Spaulding, 1855.

Speare, Mrs. Guy E., *New Hampshire Folk Tales.* Plymouth, NH, 1945 (revised edition).

Sweetser, M. F. (ed.), *Ticknor's The White Mountains: Handbook for Travellers.* Boston: Ticknor & Co., 1887.

Sweetser, M. F., *Chisholm's White-Mountain Guide-Book.* Portland, ME: Chisholm Brothers, 1917.

Trail Map & Guide to the White Mountain National Forest, Freeport, ME: DeLorme, 1986.

Trigger, Bruce G. (ed.), *Handbook of North American Indians.* Washington, DC: Smithsonian, 1978.

Vose, Arthur W., *The White Mountains: Heroes and Hamlets.* Barre, VT: Barre Publishers, 1968.

Ward, Julius H., *The White Mountains.* New York: D. Appleton, 1890.

Waterman, Laura and Guy, *Backwoods Ethics,* 2nd ed. Woodstock, VT: The Countryman Press, 1993.

Waterman, Laura and Guy, *Forest and Crag.* Boston: AMC, 1990.

Welch, Sarah N., *A History of Franconia.* Littleton, NH: Courier, 1973.

Weygandt, Cornelius, *The White Hills.* New York: Henry Holt and Co., 1934.

Wight, D. B., *Wild River Wilderness.* Littleton, NH: Courier, 1971.

Wikoff, Jerold, *The Upper Valley.* Chelsea, VT: Chelsea Green Publishing Co., 1985.

Willey, Benjamin G., *Incidents in White Mountain History.* Boston: Nathaniel Noys, 1856.

2. Nature Guides

Billings, Marland P., et al., *The Geology of the Mt. Washington Quadrangle.* Concord, NH: State of New Hampshire, 1979.

Chapman, Donald H., "New Hampshire's Landscape: How It Was Formed," *New Hampshire Profiles,* January 1974, pp. 41–56.

Cobb, Boughton, *A Field Guide to the Ferns.* Boston: Houghton Mifflin, 1963.

Foley, Ernest, *Gold: How to Find and Pan Gold in New England.* Woodsville, NH, 1980.

Hall, Donald, *Seasons at Eagle Pond.* New York: Ticknor & Fields, 1987.

Henderson, Donald M., et al., *Geology of the Crawford Notch Quadrangle.* Concord, NH: State of New Hampshire, 1977.

Jorgenson, Neil, *New England's Landscape.* Chester, CT: Globe Pequot Press, 1977.

Lawrence, Gale, *The Beginning Naturalist.* Shelburne, VT: The New England Press, 1979.

Marchand, Peter J., *North Woods.* Boston: AMC, 1987.

Morisawa, Marie, *Streams: Their Dynamics and Morphology.* New York: McGraw Hill, 1968.

Nyiri, Alan, *The White Mountains of New Hampshire.* Camden, ME: Down East Books, 1987.

Petrides, George A., *A Field Guide to Trees and Shrubs.* Boston: Houghton Mifflin, 1988.

Press, Frank and Raymond Siever, *Earth.* San Francisco: W.H. Freeman, 1974.

Robbins, Chandler S., et al., *Birds of North America.* New York: Golden Press, 1983.

Sorrel, Charles A., *Rocks and Minerals.* New York: Golden Press, 1973.

Steele, Frederic L., *A Beginner's Guide: Trees and Shrubs of Northern New England.* Concord, NH: Society for the Protection of New Hampshire Forests, 1971.

Steele, Frederic L., *At Timberline: A Nature Guide to the Mountains of the Northeast.* Boston: AMC, 1982.

Stokes, Donald and Lillian, *A Guide to Animal Tracking and Behavior.* Boston: Little, Brown, 1986.

Sutton, Ann and Myron, *Eastern Forests.* New York: Alfred A. Knopf, 1986.

Thompson, Betty Flanders, *The Changing Face of New England.* New York: Macmillan, 1958.

Van Diver, Bradford, B., *Roadside Geology of Vermont and New Hampshire.* Missoula, MT: Mountain Press, 1987.

INDEX AND MASTER LIST OF
WHITE MOUNTAIN WATERFALLS

Notes:

- Waterfalls covered in book are indicated by appropriate page number.
- Details are provided only for waterfalls not covered in book.
- Hiking distances are one way.
- Altitude gain shows approximate net vertical change from start of hike to destination, excluding intermediate ups and downs.
- (U) = uncertain.

Basin Trail Cascades
Location: Blue Brook, from Wild River Campground.
Hiking Distance: 1.3 miles.
Altitude Gain: 1200 feet to 1500 feet = 300 feet.
Comment: Small but attractive cascades above brook crossing.

Beaver Brook Cascades, 43– 48

Beaver Brook Falls, 89– 96

Beecher Cascade, 56– 64

Beede Falls (also called Bearcamp Falls)
Location: Bearcamp River, Sandwich.
Hiking Distance: 0.1 mile.
Altitude Gain: zero.
Comment: In Sandwich town recreation area, posted for "exclusive use of town residents and their guests."

Bell's Cascade
Location: Gordon Pond Brook, North Woodstock.
Hiking Distance: 1.8 miles.
Altitude Gain: 0.
Comment: Below reservoir, along with Balanced Rock. Public access via Gordon Pond Trail.

Bemis Brook Falls, 207– 214

Bickford Slides, 165–173

Black Cascade
Location: Slide Brook, Waterville.
Hiking Distance: 3.3 miles
Altitude Gain: 1600 feet to 2200 feet = 600 feet.
Comment: Below South Slide on Mount Tripyramid.

Boulder Falls, 258– 265

Bowl and Pitcher Falls
Location: Austin Brook, Shelburne.
Hiking Distance: 1.0 mile.
Altitude Gain: 800 feet to 1200 feet = 400 feet
Comment: Hike may be shortened if logging road gate is open; if so, be sure not to block road when you park.

Brickett Falls, 173

Bridal Veil Falls, 49– 55

Campton Falls
Location: Beebe River, Campton Hollow.
Hiking Distance: roadside.

Crystal Falls
    Location: Phillips Brook, Stark.
    Hiking Distance: roadside.
    Altitude Gain: zero.
    Comment: In Crystal village.
Davis Falls
    Location: Davis Brook, Crawford Notch.
    Hiking Distance: >1 mile.
    Altitude Gain: 1100 feet.
Eagle Cascade
    Location: branch of Charles Brook, North Chatham.
    Hiking Distance: 2.4 miles.
    Altitude Gain: 500 feet to 2000 feet = 1500 feet.
    Comment: "Eagle" refers to nearby Crag, not to the falls!
Eliza Brook Cascades
    Location: Kinsman Ridge Trail on Eliza Brook just past Eliza Brook
        Shelter.
    Hiking Distance: 7.8 miles.
    Altitude Gain: 1900 feet to 2800 feet = 900 feet.
Ellens Falls
    Location: Hobbs Brook, Albany.
    Hiking Distance: 1.0 mile(U)
    Altitude Gain: 800 feet to 1100 feet = 300 feet(U)
    Comment: Off Kancamagus Highway; no trail.
Ellingwood Falls
    Location: Swift Diamond River, College Grant.
    Hiking Distance: (U)
    Altitude Gain: (U)
    Comment: Set of rapids on private timberland, with public access dis-
        couraged.

Altitude Gain: 1200 feet to 1300 feet = 100 feet.

Comment: Above Joses' Bridge; private property; no trail.

Hawthorne Fall

Location: Gale River.

Hiking Distance: (U)

Altitude gain: (U)

Hellgate Falls

Location: Dead Diamond River, Academy Grant.

Hiking Distance: (U)

Altitude Gain: (U)

Comment: Gorge on private timber property north of Wentworth Location; public access discouraged.

Hermit Falls

Location: Basin Brook, North Chatham.

Hiking Distance: 1.3 miles.

Altitude Gain: 700 feet to 800 feet = 100 feet.

Comment: Not big, but worth the easy walk if you're camped at the Basin.

Kees Falls

Location: Morrison Brook, Evans Notch.

Hiking Distance: 1.6 miles.

Altitude Gain: 900 feet to 1600 feet = 700 feet.

Comment: 25-foot cataract on Caribou Trail. Other unnamed cascades above.

Livermore Falls

Location: Pemigewasset River, near Plymouth.

Hiking Distance: roadside.

Altitude Gain: 600 feet to 500 feet = –100 feet.

Comment: Old dam; popular swimming hole.

Altitude Gain: 2400 feet to 4000 feet(U) = 1600 feet(U)

Comment: Bushwhack high in Jobildunk Ravine. Featured in *Atlantic Monthly,* November 1880.

The Pool, 120–126

Pond Brook Falls, 81–88

Profile Falls

Location: Smith River, Bristol.

Hiking Distance: 0.1 mile.

Altitude Gain: zero.

Comment: Actually too far south to be in White Mountains, but en route to Welton Falls.

Falls of Proserpine, 43–48

Proteus Falls, 266–275

Rainbow Falls (see Mill Brook Cascades)

Rattlesnake Brook, 165–173

Raymond Cataract

Location: shoulder between Tuckerman and Huntington Ravines, in high water this is clearly visible from Route 16 in Pinkham Notch.

Distance: (U)

Altitude Gain: 2000 feet to 4500 feet = 2500 feet.

Ripley Falls, 223–230

Rocky Glen Falls, 127–133

Rocky Gorge, 174–182

Rollo Fall

Location: Moose River, Mount Adams (U)

Hiking Distance: (U)

Altitude Gain: (U)

Sabbaday Falls, 174–182

Salmacis Fall, 276–285

Salroc Falls, 276–285

Sawhegenet Falls

Location: Pemigewasset River, Bridgewater.

Hiking Distance: 0.1 mile.

Altitude Gain: –100 feet.

Comment: Swimming spot on the Pemi, below Plymouth.

Screw Auger Falls, 233–241

Sculptured Rock

Location: Cockermouth River, Groton.

Hiking Distance: roadside.

Hiking Distance: (U).
Altitude Gain: (U).

Weetamoo Falls, 258–265
Welton Falls, 99–105
Winneweta Falls
Location: Miles Brook, Jackson.
Hiking Distance: 1.0 mile.
Altitude Gain: 1000 feet to 1200 feet = 200 feet.
Comment: Off NH 16 north of Jackson village.
Zealand Falls, 155–162

Let Backcountry Guides Take You There

Our experienced backcountry authors will lead you to the finest trails, parks, and back roads in the following areas:

50 Hikes Series

50 Hikes in the Adirondacks
50 Hikes in Connecticut
50 Hikes in the Maine Mountains
50 Hikes in Coastal and Southern Maine
50 Hikes in Maryland
50 Hikes in Massachusetts
50 Hikes in Michigan
50 Hikes in the White Mountains
50 More Hikes in New Hampshire
50 Hikes in New Jersey
50 Hikes in the Hudson Valley
50 Hikes in Central New York
50 Hikes in Western New York
50 Hikes in the Mountains of North Carolina
50 Hikes in Ohio
50 Hikes in Eastern Pennsylvania
50 Hikes in Central Pennsylvania
50 Hikes in Western Pennsylvania
50 Hikes in the Tennessee Mountains
50 Hikes in Vermont
50 Hikes in Northern Virginia

Walks and Rambles Series

Walks and Rambles on Cape Cod and the Islands
Walks and Rambles on the Delmarva Peninsula
Walks and Rambles in the Western Hudson
    Valley
Walks and Rambles on Long Island
Walks and Rambles in Ohio's Western Reserve
Walks and Rambles in Rhode Island
Walks and Rambles in and around St. Louis

25 Bicycle Tours Series

25 Bicycle Tours in the Adirondacks
25 Bicycle Tours on Delmarva
25 Bicycle Tours in Coastal Georgia and the
    Carolina Low Country
25 Bicycle Tours in Maine
25 Bicycle Tours in Maryland
25 Bicycle Tours in the Twin Cities and Southeast-
    ern Minnesota
30 Bicycle Tours in New Jersey
30 Bicycle Tours in the Finger Lakes Region
25 Bicycle Tours in the Hudson Valley
25 Bicycle Tours in Ohio's Western Reserve
25 Bicycle Tours in the Texas Hill Country and
    West Texas
25 Bicycle Tours in Vermont
25 Bicycle Tours in and around Washington, D.C.
30 Bicycle Tours in Wisconsin
25 Mountain Bike Tours in the Adirondacks
25 Mountain Bike Tours in the Hudson Valley
25 Mountain Bike Tours in Massachusetts
25 Mountain Bike Tours in New Jersey
Backroad Bicycling on Cape Cod, Martha's
    Vineyard, and Nantucket
Backroad Bicycling in Eastern Pennsylvania
Backroad Bicycling in Connecticut

Bicycling America's National Parks Series

Bicycling America's National Parks: Arizona &
    New Mexico
Bicycling America's National Parks: California
Bicycling America's National Parks: Oregon &
    Washington
Bicycling America's National Parks: Utah &
    Colorado

We offer many more books on hiking, fly-fishing, travel, nature, and other subjects. Our books are available at bookstores and outdoor stores everywhere. For more information or a free catalog, please call 1-800-245-4151 or write to us at The Countryman Press, P.O. Box 748, Woodstock, Vermont 05091. You can find us on the Internet at www.countrymanpress.com.